iOS 9 Swift Programming
Cookbook

Vandad Nahavandipoor

Beijing · Boston · Farnham · Sebastopol · Tokyo

iOS 9 Swift Programming Cookbook

by Vandad Nahavandipoor

Printed in the United States of America.

Published by O'Reilly Media, Inc., 1005 Gravenstein Highway North, Sebastopol, CA 95472.

O'Reilly books may be purchased for educational, business, or sales promotional use. Online editions are also available for most titles (*http://safaribooksonline.com*). For more information, contact our corporate/institutional sales department: 800-998-9938 or corporate@oreilly.com.

Editors: Rachel Roumeliotis and Andy Oram	**Indexer:** Judy McConville
Production Editor: Nicole Shelby	**Interior Designer:** David Futato
Copyeditor: Kim Cofer	**Cover Designer:** Ellie Volckhausen
Proofreader: James Fraleigh	**Illustrator:** Rebecca Demarest

December 2015:   First Edition

Revision History for the First Edition
2015-12-08:   First Release

See *http://oreilly.com/catalog/errata.csp?isbn=9781491936696* for release details.

978-1-491-93669-6

[LSI]

Preface

When I started writing this edition of this book (which has been in the field and regularly updated since iOS version 4), I thought to myself: what I should do to really overhaul it and make it even more exciting than the previous editions? The answer was to rewrite the whole book—every single word from scratch. Up to and including the *iOS 8 Swift Programming Cookbook* (where I made the big switch from Objective-C to Swift) was to base every edition on the previous edition. I would go through all the examples from the previous edition to remove the ones that were irrelevant for the new edition or just expendable because they were very simple and basic. I'd then update the remaining examples to make sure they work great with the new iOS version. Then I would also write new content for the new version of iOS. However, after 5 editions, I noticed that many recipes were not really useful anymore and had stayed almost the same since the beginning. So how could I solve this issue? The solution was to not do this any longer. I had to write all new content, and that's what I did for this book.

The amount of work that went into writing this book was tremendous, on my side and on O'Reilly's side. I have had to think long and hard about every new recipe, writing all the example code anew and ensuring it works with the latest production tools from Apple. You will learn a lot about Swift 2 and iOS 9 SDK in this book.

And yes, there is a great deal of watchOS material in this book. The chapter dedicated to watchOS has more content in it than any other chapter. The reason behind that decision was that watchOS was the main focus for this year's WWDC and that Apple has paid more attention to watchOS in iOS 9 SDK than to other frameworks or tools that they have published this year. I hope you'll enjoy writing watchOS apps as much as I do.

One last thing. Since Swift changes a lot and is constantly updated, please always check the GitHub repo for this book to get the most up-to-date code. I have ensured that all code compiles and works fine with Xcode 7 and the iOS 9 SDK, but if for some reason you are on a beta Xcode that is newer than the production version of

Xcode 7 that Apple has released, do ensure that you have the latest code by checking out this book's GitHub repo.

Have fun and I hope you'll enjoy reading this book.

Audience

I assume that you are comfortable writing iOS apps, at least know your way around Xcode, and can work with the simulator. This book is *not* for beginners. If you have never programmed in Xcode before for iOS, it will be tough to learn iOS programming only from this book. So I suggest that you complement your skills with other online resources. The best market for this book is intermediate and advanced users.

I also assume that you have written a little bit of Swift code. In this book, I use Swift 2 and will teach you some of the concepts, but if you don't know Swift, this is not the right place to start. Please pick up Apple's book on Swift programming first; try with that and once you are a bit comfortable with Swift, come back to this book and I'm sure you'll learn a lot of new things, even about Swift 2.

Organization of This Book

Here I'll explain what each chapter is about so that you'll get a feeling for what this book is going to teach you:

Chapter 1, Swift 2.0, Xcode 7, and Interface Builder
> In this chapter, we go through a lot of new stuff in Swift, Xcode, and Interface Builder (IB), such as the addition of the guard keyword to Swift and conditionally extending types with Swift's new runtime features. Swift has really matured with Swift 2, and I want to share some of the most important additions with you.

Chapter 2, Apple Watch
> This year's WWDC star, without a doubt, is watchOS 2 with all its additions. Now apps can run natively on the watchOS without having to talk to the iOS counterpart app, and this is great for us. More work, more things to do, more fun. We will talk about complications, transferring files between iOS and watchOS 2 apps, downloading files right on the watch, recording audio, and playing multimedia on your watch.

Chapter 3, The User Interface
> Even though additions to UIKit were not talked about as extensively as watchOS 2 at this year's WWDC, there are still tons of new features that we can discuss, including anchored constraints, stack views, and the new Safari view controller.

Chapter 4, Contacts
> The all-new contacts APIs will be discussed in this chapter. The frameworks on which this chapter is based are both completely new to iOS 9. With the APIs in these frameworks, you'll learn how to add new contacts to the user's device, remove con-

tacts, edit them, or even allow the user to pick a contact from the list so that you can perform your tasks on it.

Chapter 5, Extensions

Safari Content Blockers shocked a lot of developers during this year's WWDC. This allows us developers to create apps that get installed as extensions on the user's Safari browser, and allows us to block various elements of web pages that the user views. For instance, you can now block pictures or various unwanted elements in the websites that you specify in your app, and you can share these content blockers with those who use your app. This chapter is all about new extension points that you can add to your apps.

Chapter 6, Web and Search

Apps can now provide content to iOS. iOS will then index these contents and allow the user to search for these contents right within Spotlight on their devices. Your contents can also be indexed globally on Apple's servers so even those who don't have your app can see your content on their devices. Intrigued? Read this chapter, then!

Chapter 7, Multitasking

We now have Picture in Picture (PiP) in iOS. Your app can provide a video player to iOS and allow the user to minimize your whole app into that video player while she works with other apps. It's really cool, in my opinion.

Chapter 8, Maps and Location

With the additions to Core Location and MapKit frameworks, you can now, for example, display an ETA for transit between two locations or display your custom view inside the annotation of a pin on the map.

Chapter 9, UI Testing

One of the stars of this year's WWDC is Apple's new UI Testing framework. We can now write native Swift code to do our UI testing, and in this chapter I'm going to show you how.

Chapter 10, Core Motion

Core Motion is now also available on watchOS 2 and in this chapter you'll learn some of the new things that you can do with this framework, including reading cadence information from sensors on the device.

Chapter 11, Security

ATS is a welcome addition in iOS that forces all requests to go through HTTPS. If you build your project with Xcode 7 and iOS 9 SDK, all your network requests will go through HTTPS by default, protecting your content and possibly breaking a few things if you don't support HTTPS in your web services. Read this chapter to learn more.

Chapter 12, Multimedia

We have some new additions to how apps can interact with Siri and you can read about them in this chapter.

Last but not least, there are some amazing effects that you can achieve in your user interface with the new additions to UI Dynamics, including the ability to create turbulence or magnetic fields. In this chapter, I'll show you these additions with examples.

Additional Resources

This book is not for beginners, so I assume you have already gotten a grip on Swift and can do basic things with it. Please read Apple's documentation on Swift by doing a quick web search. You can either read it on your browser, as a PDF, or you can read it in iBooks.

Also please check this book's GitHub repository in order to get the most up-to-date code, as I update the code to ensure it works with the latest Swift and Xcode versions.

Using Code Examples

Supplemental material (code examples, exercises, etc.) is available for download at *https://github.com/vandadnp/iOS-9-Swift-Programming-Cookbook*.

This book is here to help you get your job done. In general, if example code is offered with this book, you may use it in your programs and documentation. You do not need to contact us for permission unless you're reproducing a significant portion of the code. For example, writing a program that uses several chunks of code from this book does not require permission. Selling or distributing a CD-ROM of examples from O'Reilly books does require permission. Answering a question by citing this book and quoting example code does not require permission. Incorporating a significant amount of example code from this book into your product's documentation does require permission.

We appreciate, but do not require, attribution. An attribution usually includes the title, author, publisher, and ISBN. For example: "*iOS 9 Swift Programming Cookbook* by Vandad Nahavandipoor (O'Reilly). Copyright 2016 Vandad Nahavandippor, 978-1-491-93669-6."

If you feel your use of code examples falls outside fair use or the permission given above, feel free to contact us at *permissions@oreilly.com*.

Acknowledgments

Thank you to:

Sara, Julian, and Molly
For continuously supporting and encouraging me.

Rachel Roumeliotis

For always having trust in me and knowing that I stick to my words when I promise to write a whole new book in a short period of time with quality material. Your trust means a lot to me and I hope this book will make you proud, as much as it made me.

Andy Oram

The editor that anybody would dream about, Andy has been by my side editing this book nonstop since I started. His relentless efforts have allowed me to relax while he craftfully works his way through the book, making it even more understandable for the readers. I would not have been able to write this book without Andy's help.

Niklas Saers

For his detailed technical review of this book.

Nicole Shelby

For all her work in getting this book ready for production. It's been a pleasure working with you, Nicole.

Table of Contents

CHAPTER 1

Swift 2.0, Xcode 7, and Interface Builder

In this chapter, we are going to have a look at some of the updates to Swift (Swift 2.0), Xcode, and Interface Builder. We will start with Swift and some of the really exciting features that have been added to it since you read the *iOS 8 Swift Programming Cookbook*.

1.1 Handling Errors in Swift

Problem

You want to know how to throw and handle exceptions in Swift.

 I'll be using *errors* and *exceptions* interchangeably in this book. When an error occurrs in our app, we usually *catch* it, as you will soon see, and handle it in a way that is pleasant and understandable to the user.

Solution

To throw an exception, use the `throw` syntax. To catch exceptions, use the `do, try, catch` syntax.

Discussion

Let's say that you want to create a method that takes in a first name and last name as two arguments and returns a full name. The first name and the last name have to each at least be one character long for this method to work. If one or both have 0 lengths, we are going to want to throw an exception.

The first thing that we have to do is to define our errors of type ErrorType:

```swift
enum Errors : ErrorType{
  case EmptyFirstName
  case EmptyLastName
}
```

And then we are going to define our method to take in a first and last name and join them together with a space in between:

```swift
func fullNameFromFirstName(firstName: String,
  lastName: String) throws -> String{

  if firstName.characters.count == 0{
    throw Errors.EmptyFirstName
  }

  if lastName.characters.count == 0{
    throw Errors.EmptyLastName
  }

  return firstName + " " + lastName

}
```

The interesting part is really how to call this method. We use the do statement like so:

```swift
do{
  let fullName = try fullNameFromFirstName("Foo", lastName: "Bar")
  print(fullName)
} catch {
  print("An error occurred")
}
```

The catch clause of the do statement allows us to trap errors in a fine-grained manner. Let's say that you want to trap errors in the Errors enum differently from instances of NSException. Separate your catch clauses like this:

```swift
do{
  let fullName = try fullNameFromFirstName("Foo", lastName: "Bar")
  print(fullName)
}
catch let err as Errors{
  //handle this specific type of error here
  print(err)
}
catch let ex as NSException{
  //handle exceptions here
  print(ex)
}
catch {
  //otherwise, do this
}
```

Recipe 1.3

1.2 Specifying Preconditions for Methods

Problem

You want to make sure a set of conditions are met before continuing with the flow of your method.

Solution

Use the guard syntax.

Discussion

The guard syntax allows you to:

1. Specify a set of conditions for your methods.
2. Bind variables to optionals and use those variables in the rest of your method's body.

Let's have a look at a method that takes an optional piece of data as the NSData type and turns it into a String only if the string has some characters in it and is not empty:

```
func stringFromData(data: NSData?) -> String?{

  guard let data = data,
    let str = NSString(data: data, encoding: NSUTF8StringEncoding)
    where data.length > 0 else{
    return nil
  }

  return String(str)

}
```

And then we are going to use it like so:

```
if let _ = stringFromData(nil){
  print("Got the string")
} else {
  print("No string came back")
}
```

We pass nil to this method for now and trigger the failure block ("No string came back"). What if we passed valid data? And to have more fun with this, let's create our

NSData instance this time with a guard. Because the NSString constructor we are about to use returns an optional value, we put a guard statement before it to ensure that the value that goes into the data variable is in fact a value, and not nil:

```
guard let data = NSString(string: "Foo")
  .dataUsingEncoding(NSUTF8StringEncoding) where data.length > 0 else{
    return
}

if let str = stringFromData(data){
  print("Got the string \(str)")
} else {
  print("No string came back")
}
```

So we can mix guard and where in the same statement. How about multiple let statements inside a guard? Can we do that? You betcha:

```
func example3(firstName firstName: String?, lastName: String?, age: UInt8?){

  guard let firstName = firstName, let lastName = lastName , _ = age where
    firstName.characters.count > 0 && lastName.characters.count > 0 else{
      return
  }

  print(firstName, " ", lastName)

}
```

See Also

Recipe 1.1

1.3 Ensuring the Execution of Code Blocks Before Exiting Methods

Problem

You have various conditions in your method that can exit the method early. But before you do that, you want to ensure that some code always gets executed, for instance to do some cleanup.

Solution

Use the defer syntax.

Discussion

Anything that you put inside a defer block inside a method is guaranteed to get executed before your method returns to the caller. However, this block of code will get executed *after* the return call in your method. The code is also called when your method throws an exception.

Let's say that you want to define a method that takes in a string and renders it inside a new image context with a given size. Now if the string is empty, you want to throw an exception. However, before you do that, we want to make sure that we have ended our image context. Let's define our error first:

```
enum Errors : ErrorType{
  case EmptyString
}
```

Then we move onto our actual method that uses the defer syntax:

```
func imageForString(str: String, size: CGSize) throws -> UIImage{

  defer{
    UIGraphicsEndImageContext()
  }

  UIGraphicsBeginImageContextWithOptions(size, true, 0)

  if str.characters.count == 0{
    throw Errors.EmptyString
  }

  //draw the string here...

  return UIGraphicsGetImageFromCurrentImageContext()

}
```

I don't want to put print() statements everywhere in the code because it makes the code really ugly. So to see whether this really works, I suggest that you paste this code into your Xcode—or even better, grab the source code for this book's example code from GitHub, where I have already placed breakpoints in the defer and the return statements so that you can see that they are working properly.

You can of course then call this method like so:

```
do{
  let i = try imageForString("Foo", size: CGSize(width: 100, height: 50))
  print(i)
} catch let excep{
  print(excep)
}
```

See Also

Recipe 1.2

1.4 Checking for API Availability

Problem

You want to check whether a specific API is available on the host device running your code.

Solution

Use the #available syntax.

Discussion

We've all been waiting for this for a very long time. The days of having to call the respondsToSelector: method are over (hopefully). Now we can just use the #available syntax to make sure a specific iOS version is available before making a call to a method.

Let's say that we want to write a method that can read an array of bytes from an NSData object. NSData offers a handy getBytes: method to do this, but Apple decided to deprecate it in iOS 8.1 and replace it with the better getBytes:length: version that minimizes the risk of buffer overflows. So assuming that one of our deployment targets is iOS 8 or older, we want to ensure that we call this new method if we are on iOS 8.1 or higher and the older method if we are on iOS 8.0 or older:

```
enum Errors : ErrorType{
  case EmptyData
}

func bytesFromData(data: NSData) throws -> [UInt8]{

  if (data.length == 0){
    throw Errors.EmptyData
  }

  var buffer = [UInt8](count: data.length, repeatedValue: 0)

  if #available(iOS 8.1, *){
    data.getBytes(&buffer, length: data.length)
  } else {
    data.getBytes(&buffer)
  }

  return buffer
```

```
    }
```

And then we go ahead and call this method:

```swift
func example1(){

  guard let data = "Foo".dataUsingEncoding(NSUTF8StringEncoding) else {
    return
  }

  do{
    let bytes = try bytesFromData(data)
    print("Data = \(bytes)")
  } catch {
    print("Failed to get bytes")
  }


}
```

See Also

Recipe 1.1

1.5 Categorizing and Downloading Assets to Get Smaller Binaries

Problem

You have many assets in your app for various circumstances, and want to save storage space and network usage on each user's device by shipping the app without the optional assets. Instead, you would want to dynamically download them and use them whenever needed.

Solution

Use Xcode to tag your assets and then use the `NSBundleResourceRequest` class to download them.

Discussion

For this recipe, I will create three packs of assets, each with three images in them. One pack may run for x3 screen scales, another for iPhone 6, and the last for iPhone 6+, for instance. I am taking very tiny clips of screenshots of my desktop to create these images—nothing special. The first pack will be called "level1," the second "level2," and the third "level3."

Use the GitHub repo of this book for a quick download of the said resources. Also, for the sake of simplicity, I am assuming that we are going to run this only on x3 scale screens such as iPhone 6+.

Place all nine images (three packs of three images) inside your *Assets.xcassets* file and name them as shown in Figure 1-1. Then select all the images in your first asset pack and open the Attributes inspector. In the "On Demand Resource Tags" section of the inspector, enter **level1** and do the same thing for other levels—but of course bump the number up for each pack.

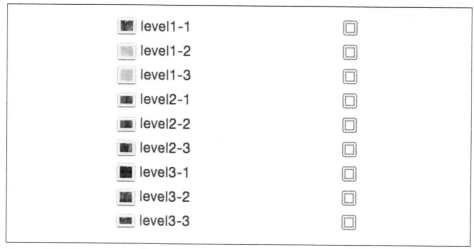

Figure 1-1. Name your assets as shown

Now, in your UI, place three buttons and three image views, hook the buttons' actions to the code, and hook the image view references to the code:

```
@IBOutlet var img1: UIImageView!
@IBOutlet var img2: UIImageView!
@IBOutlet var img3: UIImageView!

var imageViews: [UIImageView]{
  return [self.img1, self.img2, self.img3]
}
```

To find out whether the resource pack that you need has already been downloaded, call the conditionallyBeginAccessingResourcesWithCompletionHandler function on your resource request. Don't blame me! I didn't name this function. This will return a Boolean of true or false to tell you whether you have or don't have access to the resource. If you don't have access, you can simply download the resources with a

call to the `beginAccessingResourcesWithCompletionHandler` function. This will
return an error if one happens, or nil if everything goes well.

 We keep a reference to the request that we send for our asset pack
so that the next time our buttons are tapped, we don't have to check
their availability again, but release the previously downloaded
resources using the `endAccessingResources` function.

```swift
var currentResourcePack: NSBundleResourceRequest?

func displayImagesForResourceTag(tag: String){
  NSOperationQueue.mainQueue().addOperationWithBlock{
    for n in 0..<self.imageViews.count{
      self.imageViews[n].image = UIImage(named: tag + "-\(n+1)")
    }
  }
}

func useLevel(lvl: UInt32){

  let imageViews = [img1, img2, img3]

  for img in imageViews{
    img.image = nil
  }

  let tag = "level\(lvl)"

  if let req = currentResourcePack{
    req.endAccessingResources()
  }

  currentResourcePack = NSBundleResourceRequest(tags: [tag])

  guard let req = currentResourcePack else {
    return
  }

  req.conditionallyBeginAccessingResourcesWithCompletionHandler{available in
    if available{
      self.displayImagesForResourceTag(tag)
    } else {
      req.beginAccessingResourcesWithCompletionHandler{error in
        guard error == nil else{
          //TODO: you can handle the error here
          return
        }
        self.displayImagesForResourceTag(tag)
      }
    }
  }
```

```
        }

    }

    @IBAction func useLevel3(sender: AnyObject) {
        useLevel(3)
    }

    @IBAction func useLevel2(sender: AnyObject) {
        useLevel(2)
    }

    @IBAction func useLevel1(sender: AnyObject) {
        useLevel(1)
    }
```

Run the code now in your simulator. When Xcode opens, go to the Debug Navigator (Command-6 key) and then click the Disk section. You will see something like that shown in Figure 1-2.

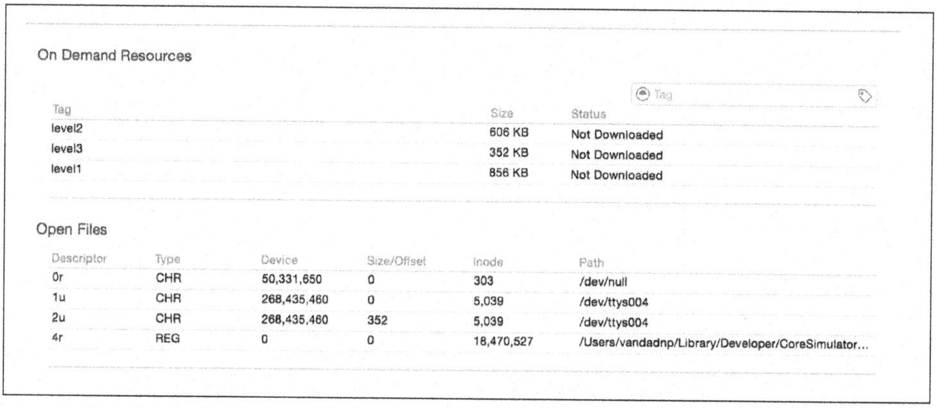

Figure 1-2. Xcode displaying all our On Demand Resources and status of whether or not they are downloaded locally

Note how none of the asset packs are in use. Now in your UI, click the first button to get the first asset pack and watch how the first asset pack's status will change to "In Use." Once you switch from that pack to another, the previously chosen pack will be set to "Downloaded" and be ready to be purged.

See Also

Recipe 1.6

1.6 Exporting Device-Specific Binaries

Problem

You want to extract your app's binary for a specific device architecture to find out how big your binary will be on that device when the user downloads your app.

Solution

Follow these steps:

1. Archive your app in Xcode.
2. In the Archives screen, click the Export button.
3. Choose the "Save for Ad Hoc Deployment" option in the new screen and click Next.
4. In the new window, choose "Export for specific device" and then choose your device from the list.
5. Once you are done, click the Next button and save your file to disk.

Discussion

With iOS 9, Apple introduced bitcode. This is Apple's way of specifying how the binary that you submit to the App Store will be downloaded on target devices. For instance, if you have an asset catalogue with some images for the iPad and iPhone and a second set of images for the iPhone 6 and 6+ specifically, users on iPhone 5 should not get the second set of assets. You don't have to do anything really to enable this functionality in Xcode 7. It is enabled by default. If you are working on an old project, you can enable bitcode from Build Settings in Xcode.

If you are writing an app that has a lot of images and assets for various devices, I suggest that you use this method, before submitting your app to the store, to ensure that the required images and assets are indeed included in your final build. Remember, if bitcode is enabled in your project, Apple will detect the host device that is downloading your app from the store and will serve the right binary to that device. You don't have to separate your binaries when submitting to Apple. You submit a big fat juicy binary and Apple will take care of the rest.

See Also

Recipe 1.5

1.7 Linking Separate Storyboards Together

Problem

You have a messy storyboard, so you would like to place some view controllers in their own storyboard and still be able to cross-reference them in your other storyboards.

Solution

Use IB's new "Refactor to Storyboard" feature under the Editor menu.

Discussion

I remember working on a project where we had a really messy storyboard and we had to separate the view controllers. What we ended up doing was putting the controllers on separate storyboards manually, after which we had to write code to link our buttons and other actions to the view controllers, instantiate them manually, and then show them. Well, none of that anymore. Apple has taken care of that for us!

As an exercise, create a single-view controller project in Xcode and then open your main storyboard. Then choose the Editor menu, then Embed In, and then Navigation Controller. Now your view controller has a navigation controller. Place a button on your view controller and then place another view controller on your storyboard. Select the button on the first view controller, hold down the Control button on your keyboard, drag the line over to the second view controller, and then choose the Show option. This will ensure that when the user taps your button, the system will push the second view controller onto the screen, as Figure 1-3 shows.

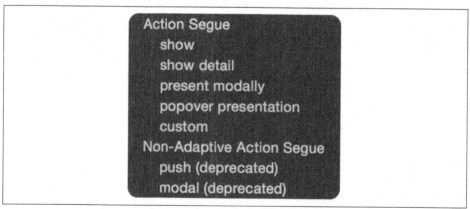

Figure 1-3. We need to create a show segue ensuring that pressing our button will show the second view controller

Now select your second view controller and then, from the Editor menu, choose the "Refactor to Storyboard" item. In the dialog, enter **Second.storyboard** as the file name and save. That's really it. Now run your app and see the results if you want.

If you prefer to do some of this stuff manually instead of embedding things like this, you can always drag the new item called Storyboard Reference from the Object Library onto your storyboard and set up the name of the storyboard manually. Xcode will give you a drop-down box so that you don't have to write the name of the storyboard all by yourself. You will also be able to specify an identifier for your storyboard. This identifier will then be useful when working with the segue. You of course have to set up this ID for your view controller in advance.

See Also

Recipe 3.5

1.8 Adding Multiple Buttons to the Navigation Bar

Problem

You want to add multiple instances of `UIBarButtonItem` to your navigation bar.

Solution

In Xcode 7, you can now add multiple bar button items to your navigation bar. Simply open the Object Library and search for "bar button." Once you find the buttons, drag and drop them onto your navigation bar and then simply reference them in your code if you have to. For instance, Figure 1-4 shows two bar buttons on the right-hand side of the navigation bar. In previous versions of Xcode, we could add only one button to each side. If we wanted more buttons, we had to write code to add them.

Figure 1-4. Two buttons on the same side of the navigation bar

Discussion

Prior to Xcode 7 you could not place multiple bar button items next to each other on your navigation bar. Well, now you can. You can also access these buttons just as you would expect, by creating a reference to them in your code. And you can always find them using the barButtonItems property of your navigation bar.

See Also

Recipe 1.7

1.9 Optimizing Your Swift Code

Problem

You want to adopt some simple practices that can make your Swift code run much faster than before.

Solution

Use the following techniques:

1. Enable whole module optimization on your code.
2. Use value types (such as structs) instead of reference types where possible.
3. Consider using final for classes, methods, and variables that aren't going to be overridden.
4. Use the CFAbsoluteTimeGetCurrent function to profile your app inside your code.

5. Always use Instruments to profile your code and find bottlenecks.

Discussion

Let's have a look at an example. Let's say that we have a `Person` class like so:

```
class Person{
  let name: String
  let age: Int
  init(name: String, age: Int){
    self.name = name
    self.age = age
  }
}
```

Now we will write a method that will generate 100,000 instances of this class, place them inside a mutable array, and then enumerate the array. We will time this operation using the `CFAbsoluteTimeGetCurrent` function. We'll then be able to tell how many milliseconds this took:

```
func example1(){

  var x = CFAbsoluteTimeGetCurrent()

  var array = [Person]()

  for _ in 0..<100000{
    array.append(Person(name: "Foo", age: 30))
  }

  //go through the items as well
  for n in 0..<array.count{
    let _ = array[n]
  }

  x = (CFAbsoluteTimeGetCurrent() - x) * 1000.0

  print("Took \(x) milliseconds")

}
```

When I ran this code, it took 41.28 milliseconds to complete; it will probably be different in your computer. Now let's create a struct similar to the class we created before but without an initializer, because we get that for free. Then do the same that we did before and time it:

```
struct PersonStruct{
  let name: String
  let age: Int
}
```

```
func example2(){

  var x = CFAbsoluteTimeGetCurrent()

  var array = [PersonStruct]()

  for _ in 0..<100000{
    array.append(PersonStruct(name: "Foo", age: 30))
  }

  //go through the items as well
  for n in 0..<array.count{
    let _ = array[n]
  }

  x = (CFAbsoluteTimeGetCurrent() - x) * 1000.0

  print("Took \(x) milliseconds")

}
```

 Don't suffix your struct names with "Struct" like I did. This is for demo purposes only, to differentiate between the class and the struct.

When I run this code, it takes only 35.53 milliseconds. A simple optimization brought some good savings. Also notice that in the release version these times will be massively improved, because your binary will have no debug information. I have tested the same code without the debugging, and the times are more around 4 milliseconds. Also note that I am testing these on the simulator, not on a real device. The profiling will definitely report different times on a device, but the ratio *should* be quite the same.

Another thing that you will want to do is think about which parts of your code are final and mark them with the `final` keyword. This will tell the compiler that you are not intending to override those properties, classes, or methods and will help Swift optimize the dispatch process. For instance, let's say we have this class hierarchy:

```
class Animal{
  func move(){
    if "Foo".characters.count > 0{
      //some code
    }
  }
}

class Dog : Animal{
```

```
  }
```

And we create instances of the Dog class and then call the move function on them:

```
func example3(){
  var x = CFAbsoluteTimeGetCurrent()
  var array = [Dog]()
  for n in 0..<100000{
    array.append(Dog())
    array[n].move()
  }
  x = (CFAbsoluteTimeGetCurrent() - x) * 1000.0
  print("Took \(x) milliseconds")
}
```

When we run this, the runtime will first have to detect whether the move function is on the super class or the subclass and then call the appropriate class based on this decision. This checking takes time. For instance, if you know that the move function won't be overridden in the subclasses, mark it as final:

```
class AnimalOptimized{
  final func move(){
    if "Foo".characters.count > 0{
      //some code
    }
  }
}

class DogOptimized : AnimalOptimized{

}

func example4(){
  var x = CFAbsoluteTimeGetCurrent()
  var array = [DogOptimized]()
  for n in 0..<100000{
    array.append(DogOptimized())
    array[n].move()
  }
  x = (CFAbsoluteTimeGetCurrent() - x) * 1000.0
  print("Took \(x) milliseconds")
}
```

When I run these on the simulator, I get 90.26 milliseconds for the non-optimized version and 88.95 milliseconds for the optimized version. Not that bad.

I also recommend that you turn on whole module optimization for your release code. Just go to your Build Settings and under the optimization for your release builds (App Store scheme), simply choose "Fast" with Whole Module Optimization, and you are good to go.

See Also

Recipe 1.1 and Recipe 1.2

1.10 Showing the Header View of Your Swift Classes

Problem

You want to get an overview of what your Swift class's interface looks like.

Solution

Use Xcode's new Generated Interface Assistant Editor. This is how you do it. Open your Swift file first and then, in Xcode, use Show Assistant Editor, which you can find in the Help menu if you just type that name. After you open the assistant, you will get a split screen of your current view. Then in the second editor that opened, on top, instead of Counterparts (which is the default selection), choose Generated Interface. You'll see your code as shown in Figure 1-5.

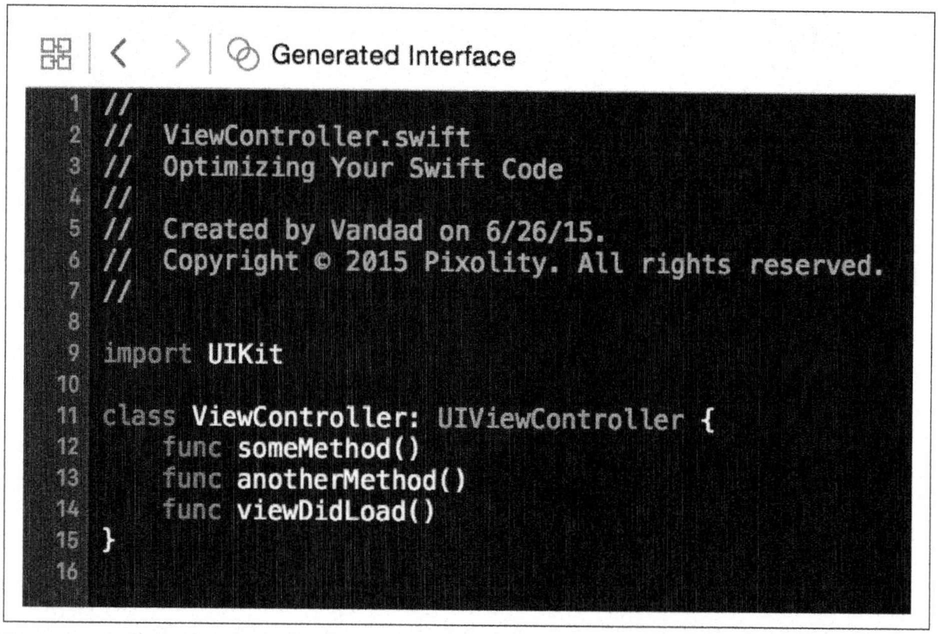

```
//
//  ViewController.swift
//  Optimizing Your Swift Code
//
//  Created by Vandad on 6/26/15.
//  Copyright © 2015 Pixolity. All rights reserved.
//

import UIKit

class ViewController: UIViewController {
    func someMethod()
    func anotherMethod()
    func viewDidLoad()
}
```

Figure 1-5. Code shown in Xcode assistant

Discussion

I find the Generated Interface functionality of the assistant editor quite handy if you want to get an overview of how clean your code is. It probably won't be day-to-day functionality that you use all the time, but I cannot be sure. Maybe you will love it so much that you will dedicate a whole new monitor just to see your generated interface all the time. By the way, there is a shortcut to the assistant editor in Xcode 7: Command-Alt-Enter. To get rid of the editor, press Command-Enter.

See Also

Recipe 1.7

1.11 Creating Your Own Set Types

Problem

You want to create a type in Swift that can allow all operators that normal sets allow, such as the contain function.

Solution

Conform to the OptionSetType protocol. As a bonus, you can also conform to the CustomDebugStringConvertible protocol, as I will do in this recipe, in order to set custom debug descriptions that the print function can use during debugging of your sets.

Discussion

Let's say that I have a structure that keeps track of iPhone models. I want to be able to create a set of this structure's values so that I can say that I have an iPhone 6, iPhone 6+, and iPhone 5s (fancy me!). Here is the way I would do that:

```
struct IphoneModels : OptionSetType, CustomDebugStringConvertible{

  let rawValue: Int
  init(rawValue: Int){
    self.rawValue = rawValue
  }

  static let Six = IphoneModels(rawValue: 0)
  static let SixPlus = IphoneModels(rawValue: 1)
  static let Five = IphoneModels(rawValue: 2)
  static let FiveS = IphoneModels(rawValue: 3)

  var debugDescription: String{
    switch self{
    case IphoneModels.Six:
      return "iPhone 6"
    case IphoneModels.SixPlus:
      return "iPhone 6+"
```

```
        case IphoneModels.Five:
          return "iPhone 5"
        case IphoneModels.FiveS:
          return "iPhone 5s"
        default:
          return "Unknown iPhone"
        }
      }


    }
```

And then I can use it like so:

```
func example1(){

  let myIphones: [IphoneModels] = [.Six, .SixPlus]

  if myIphones.contains(.FiveS){
    print("You own an iPhone 5s")
  } else {
    print("You don't seem to have an iPhone 5s but you have these:")
    for i in myIphones{
      print(i)
    }
  }

}
```

Note how I could create a set of my new type and then use the contains function on it just as I would on a normal set. Use your imagination—this is some really cool stuff.

See Also

Recipe 1.1, Recipe 1.2, and Recipe 1.3

1.12 Conditionally Extending a Type

Problem

You want to be able to extend existing data types that pass a certain test.

Solution

Use protocol extensions. Swift 2.0 allows protocol extensions to contain code.

Discussion

Let's say that you want to add a method on any array in Swift where the items are integers. In your extension, you want to provide a method called canFind that can find a specific item in the array and return yes if it could be found. I know that we can do this with other system methods. I am offering this simple example to demonstrate how protocol extensions work:

```
extension SequenceType where
  Generator.Element : IntegerArithmeticType{
  public func canFind(value: Generator.Element) -> Bool{
    for (_, v) in self.enumerate(){
      if v == value{
        return true
      }
    }
    return false
  }
}
```

Then you can go ahead and use this method like so:

```
func example1(){

  if [1, 3, 5, 7].canFind(5){
    print("Found it")
  } else {
    print("Could not find it")
  }

}
```

As another example, let's imagine that you want to extend all array types in Swift (SequenceType) that have items that are either double or floating point. It doesn't matter which method you add to this extension. I am going to add an empty method for now:

```
extension SequenceType where Generator.Element : FloatingPointType{
  //write your code here
  func doSomething(){
    //TODO: code this
  }
}
```

And you can, of course, use it like so:

```
func example2(){

  [1.1, 2.2, 3.3].doSomething()

}
```

However, if you try to call this method on an array that contains non–floating-point data, you will get a compilation error.

Let me show you another example. Let's say that you want to extend all arrays that contain only strings, and you want to add a method to this array that can find the longest string. This is how you would do that:

```
extension SequenceType where Generator.Element : StringLiteralConvertible{
  func longestString() -> String{
    var s = ""
    for (_, v) in self.enumerate(){
      if let temp = v as? String
        where temp.characters.count > s.characters.count{
          s = temp
      }
    }
    return s
  }
}
```

Calling it is as simple as:

```
func example3(){

    print(["Foo", "Bar", "Vandad"].longestString())

}
```

See Also

Recipe 1.6

1.13 Building Equality Functionality into Your Own Types

Problem

You have your own structs and classes and you want to build equality-checking functionality into them.

Solution

Build your equality functionality into the protocols to which your types conform. This is the way to go!

Discussion

Let me give you an example. Let's say that we have a protocol called Named:

```
protocol Named{
  var name: String {get}
}
```

We can build the equality functionality into this protocol. We can check the name property and if the name is the same on both sides, then we are equal:

```
func ==(lhs : Named, rhs: Named) -> Bool{
  return lhs.name == rhs.name
}
```

Now let's define two types, a car and a motorcycle, and make them conform to this protocol:

```
struct Car{}
struct Motorcycle{}

extension Car : Named{
  var name: String{
    return "Car"
  }
}

extension Motorcycle : Named{
  var name: String{
    return "Motorcycle"
  }
}
```

That was it, really. You can see that I didn't have to build the equality functionality into Car and into Motorcycle separately. I built it into the protocol to which both types conform. And then we can use it like so:

```
func example1(){

  let v1: Named = Car()
  let v2: Named = Motorcycle()

  if v1 == v2{
    print("They are equal")
  } else {
    print("They are not equal")
  }

}
```

This example will say that the two constants are not equal because one is a car and the other one is a motorcycle, but what if we compared two cars?

```
func example2(){

  let v1: Named = Car()
  let v2: Named = Car()
```

```
    if v1 == v2{
      print("They are equal")
    } else {
      print("They are not equal")
    }

  }
```

Bingo. Now they are equal. So instead of building the equality functionality into your types, build them into the protocols that your types conform to and you are good to go.

See Also

Recipe 1.12

1.14 Looping Conditionally Through a Collection

Problem

You want to go through the objects inside a collection conditionally and state your conditions right inside the loop's statement.

Solution

Use the new for x in y where syntax, specifying a where clause right in your for loop. For instance, here I will go through all the keys and values inside a dictionary and only get the values that are integers:

```
let dic = [
  "name" : "Foo",
  "lastName" : "Bar",
  "age" : 30,
  "sex" : 1,
]

for (k, v) in dic where v is Int{
  print("The key \(k) contains an integer value of \(v)")
}
```

Discussion

Prior to Swift 2.0, you'd have to create your conditions *before* you got to the loop statement—or even worse, if that wasn't possible and your conditions depended on the items inside the array, you'd have to write the conditions *inside* the loop. Well, no more.

Here is another example. Let's say that you want to find all the numbers that are divisible by 8, inside the range of 0 to 1000, inclusively:

```
let nums = 0..<1000
let divisibleBy8 = {$0 % 8 == 0}
for n in nums where divisibleBy8(n){
  print("\(n) is divisible by 8")
}
```

And of course you can have multiple conditions for a single loop:

```
let dic = [
  "name" : "Foo",
  "lastName" : "Bar",
  "age" : 30,
  "sex" : 1,
]

for (k, v) in dic where v is Int && v as! Int > 10{
  print("The key \(k) contains the value of \(v) that is larger than 10")
}
```

See Also

Recipe 1.11

1.15 Designing Interactive Interface Objects in Playgrounds

Problem

You want to design a view the way you want, but don't want to compile your app every time you make a change.

Solution

Use storyboards while designing your UI, and after you are done, put your code inside an actual class. In IB, you can detach a view so that it is always visible in your playground while you are working on it, and any changes you make will immediately be shown.

Discussion

Create a single-view app and add a new playground to your project, as shown in Figure 1-6.

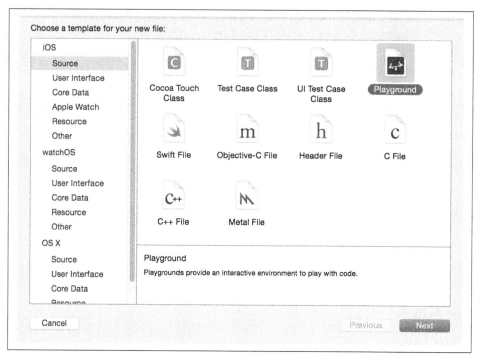

Figure 1-6. Add a new playground to your project

Write code similar to this to create your view:

```
import UIKit

var view = UIView(frame: CGRect(x: 0, y: 0, width: 300, height: 300))
view.backgroundColor = UIColor.greenColor()
```

Now on the right hand side of the last line of code that you wrote, you should see a + button. Click that (see Figure 1-7).

```
88  <  >  📄 Designing I...laygrounds › 📁 Designing Interactive Interface Objects in Playgrounds › 📘 MyPlayground.playground
1  //: Playground — noun: a place where people can play
2
3  import UIKit
4
5  var view = UIView(frame: CGRect(x: 0, y: 0, width: 300, height: 300))    UIView
6  view.backgroundColor = UIColor.greenColor()                             UIView
7
```

Figure 1-7. Click the little + button to get your view right onto your playground

By clicking that button, you will get a live preview of your view inside your playground. Now you can continue changing your view's properties and once you are done, add a new preview of your view, so that you can compare the previous and the new states (see Figure 1-8). The first view shown has only the properties you assigned to it up to the point that view was drawn. The second view has more properties, such as the border width and color, even though it is the same view instance in memory. However, because it is drawn at a different time inside IB, it shows different results. This helps you compare how your views look before and after modifications.

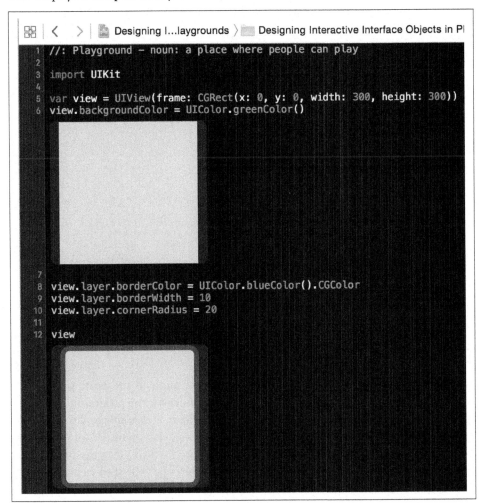

Figure 1-8. Two versions of a view

See Also

Recipe 1.7

1.16 Grouping Switch Statement Cases Together

Problem

You want to design your cases in a `switch` statement so that some of them fall through to the others.

Solution

Use the `fallthrough` syntax. Here is an example:

```
let age = 30

switch age{
case 1...10:
  fallthrough
case 20...30:
  print("Either 1 to 10 or 20 to 30")
default:
  print(age)
}
```

 This is just an example. There are better ways of writing this code than to use `fallthrough`. You can indeed batch these two cases together into one `case` statement.

Discussion

In Swift, if you want one `case` statement to fall through to the next, you have to explicitly state the `fallthrough` command. This is more for the programmers to look at than the compiler, because in many languages the compiler is able to fall through to the next `case` statement if you just leave out the `break` statement. However, this is a bit tricky because the developer might have just forgotten to place the `break` statement at the end of the `case` and all of a sudden her app will start behaving really strangely. Swift now makes you request fall-through explicity, which is safer.

1.17 Bundling and Reading Data in Your Apps

Problem

You want to bundle device-specific data into your app. At runtime, you want to easily load the relevant device's data and use it without having to manually distinguish between devices at runtime.

Solution

Follow these steps:

1. In your asset catalogue, tap the + button and create a new Data Set (see Figure 1-9).

Figure 1-9. Data sets contain our raw device-specific data

2. In the Attributes inspector of your data set, specify for which devices you want to provide data (see Figure 1-10).

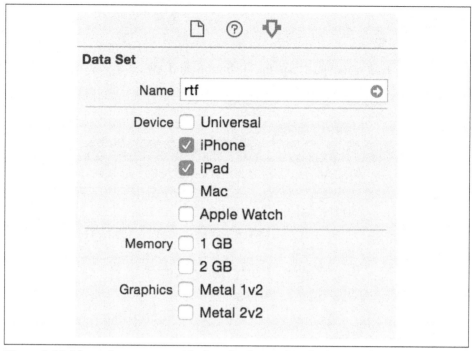

Figure 1-10. I have chosen to provide data for the iPad and iPhone in this example

3. Drag and drop your actual raw data file into place in IB
4. In your asset list, rename your asset to something that you wish to refer it to by later (see Figure 1-11).

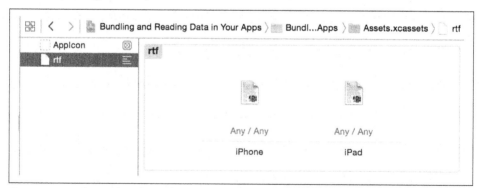

Figure 1-11. I have placed two RTF files into this data asset: one for iPhone and another for iPad

In the iPhone RTF I've written "iPhone Says Hello," and the iPad one says "iPad Says Hello"; the words iPhone and iPad are bold (attributed texts). I am then going to load these as attributed strings and show them on the user interface (see Figure 1-13).

5. In your code, load the asset with the `NSDataAsset` class's initializer.
6. Once done, use the `data` property of your asset to access the data.

Discussion

Place a label on your UI and hook it up to your code under the name `lbl` (see Figure 1-12).

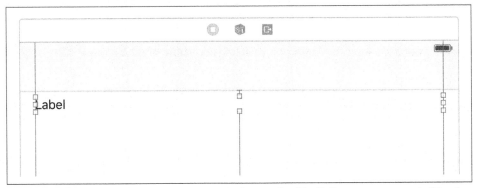

Figure 1-12. Place a label on your user interface and add all the constraints to it (Xcode can do this for you). Hook it up to your code as well.

Then create an intermediate property that can set your label's text for you:

```
import UIKit

class ViewController: UIViewController {

  @IBOutlet var lbl: UILabel!

  var status = ""{
    didSet{lbl.text = status}
  }

  ...
```

When the view is loaded, attempt to load the custom data set:

```
guard let asset = NSDataAsset(name: "rtf") else {
  status = "Could not find the data"
  return
}
```

The name of the data asset is specified in the asset catalogue (see Figure 1-11).

Because data assets can be of any type (raw data, game levels, etc.), when loading an attributed string, we need to specify what type of data we are loading in. We do that using an *options* dictionary that we pass to NSAttributedString's constructor. The important key in this dictionary is NSDocumentTypeDocumentAttribute, whose value in this case should be NSRTFTextDocumentType. We can also specify the encoding of our data with the NSCharacterEncodingDocumentAttribute key:

```
let options = [
  NSDocumentTypeDocumentAttribute : NSRTFTextDocumentType,
  NSCharacterEncodingDocumentAttribute : NSUTF8StringEncoding
  ] as [String : AnyObject]
```

Last but not least, load the data into our string and show it (see Figure 1-13):

```
do{
  let str = try NSAttributedString(data: asset.data, options: options,
    documentAttributes: nil)
  lbl.attributedText = str
} catch let err{
  status = "Error = \(err)"
}
```

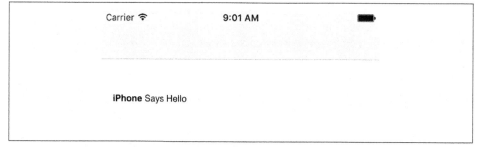

Figure 1-13. This is how my string looked when I saved it in RTF format and now it is loaded into the user interface of my app

See Also

Recipe 1.6

CHAPTER 2

Apple Watch

Version 2 of watchOS gives us developers a lot more control and brings cool features to the users as well. Now that we can download files directly and get access to sensors directly on the watch, the users will benefit.

In this chapter, I am going to assume that you have a simple iOS application in Xcode already created and you want to add a watchOS 2 target to your app. So go to Xcode and create a new Target. On the new window, on the left-hand side, under the watchOS category, choose WatchKit App (see Figure 2-1) and proceed to the next stage.

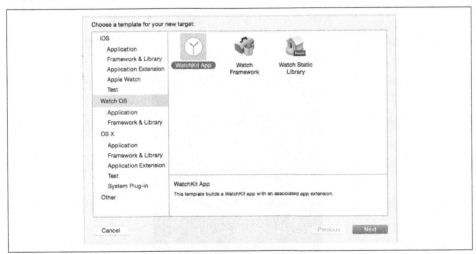

Figure 2-1. Adding a WatchKit App target to your main application

In the next stage, make sure that you have enabled complications (we'll talk about it later) and the glance scene (see Figure 2-2).

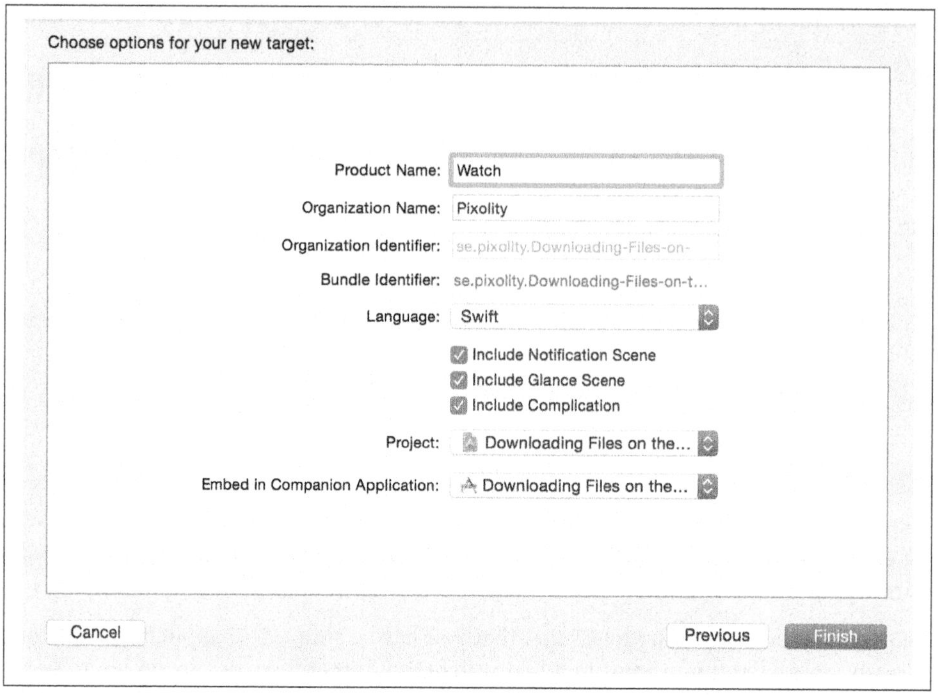

Figure 2-2. *Add a complication and a glance scene to your watch app*

After you have created your watch extension, you want to be able to run it on the simulator. To do this, simply choose your app from the targets in Xcode and click the run button (see Figure 2-3).

Figure 2-3. *A simple watch interface*

2.1 Downloading Files onto the Apple Watch

Problem

You want to be able to download files from your watch app directly without needing to communicate your intentions to the paired iOS device.

Solution

Use `NSURLSession` as you would on a phone, but with more consideration toward resources and the size of the file you are downloading.

Always consider whether or not you need the file immediately. If you need the file and the size is quite manageable, download it on the watch itself. If the file is big, try to download it on the companion app on the iOS device first and then send the file over to the watch, which itself takes some time.

Discussion

Let's create an interface similar to Figure 2-4 in our watch extension.

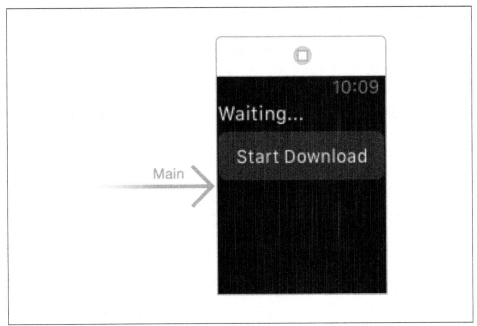

Figure 2-4. Place a label and a button on your interface

Make sure the label can contain at least four lines of text (see Figure 2-5).

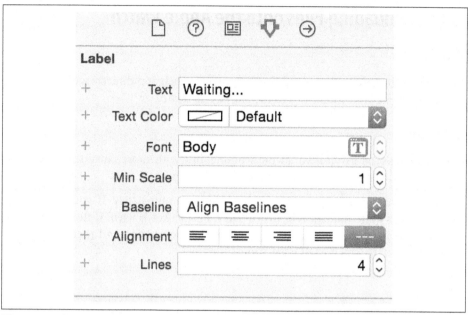

Figure 2-5. Lines property must be set to at least 4

Hook up your button's action to a method in your code named download. Also hook up your label to code under the name statusLbl.

```
import WatchKit
import Foundation

class InterfaceController: WKInterfaceController, NSURLSessionDelegate,
NSURLSessionDownloadDelegate {

  @IBOutlet var statusLbl: WKInterfaceLabel!

  var status: String = ""{
    didSet{
      dispatch_async(dispatch_get_main_queue()){[unowned self] in
        self.statusLbl.setText(self.status)
      }
    }
  }
}

...
```

 Because NSURLSession delegate methods get called on private queues (not the main thread), I've coded a property on our class called status. This is a string property that functions on the private thread can set to indicate what they're doing, and that is displayed as the text on our label by the main thread.

The most important method of the NSURLSessionDownloadDelegate protocol that we are going to have to implement is the URLSession(_:downloadTask:didFinishDown loadingToURL:) method. It gets called when our file has been downloaded into a URL onto the disk, accessible to the watch. The file there is temporary: when this method returns, the file will be deleted by watchOS. In this method, you can do two things:

- Read the file directly from the given URL. If you do so, you have to do the reading on a separate thread so that you won't block NSURLSession's private queue.
- Move the file using NSFileManager to another location that is accessible to your extension and then read it later.

We are going to move this file to a location that will later be accessible to our app.

```
func URLSession(session: NSURLSession,
    downloadTask: NSURLSessionDownloadTask,
    didFinishDownloadingToURL location: NSURL) {

    let fm = NSFileManager()
    let url = try! fm.URLForDirectory(.DownloadsDirectory,
      inDomain: .UserDomainMask,
      appropriateForURL: location, create: true)
      .URLByAppendingPathComponent("file.txt")

    do{
      try fm.removeItemAtURL(url)
      try fm.moveItemAtURL(location, toURL: url)
      self.status = "Download finished"
    } catch let err{
      self.status = "Error = \(err)"
    }

    session.invalidateAndCancel()

}
```

The task that we are going to start in order to download the file (you'll see that soon) will have an identifier. This identifier is quite important for controlling the task after we have started it.

You can see that we also have to call the invalidateAndCancel() method on our task so that we can reuse the same task identifier later. If you don't do this, the next time you tap the button to redownload the item you won't be able to.

We are then going to implement a few more useful methods from NSURLSessionDele gate and NSURLSessionDownloadDelegate just so we can show relevant status messages to the user as we are downloading the file:

```
func URLSession(session: NSURLSession,
    downloadTask: NSURLSessionDownloadTask, didWriteData bytesWritten: Int64,
```

```
      totalBytesWritten: Int64, totalBytesExpectedToWrite: Int64) {
      status = "Downloaded \(bytesWritten) bytes"
  }

  func URLSession(session: NSURLSession,
    downloadTask: NSURLSessionDownloadTask,
    didResumeAtOffset fileOffset: Int64, expectedTotalBytes: Int64) {
      status = "Resuming the download"
  }

  func URLSession(session: NSURLSession, task: NSURLSessionTask,
    didCompleteWithError error: NSError?) {
      if let e = error{
        status = "Completed with error = \(e)"
      } else {
        status = "Finished"
      }
  }

  func URLSession(session: NSURLSession,
    didBecomeInvalidWithError error: NSError?) {
      if let e = error{
        status = "Invalidated \(e)"
      } else {
        //no errors occurred, so that's alright
      }
  }
```

When the user taps the download button, we first define our URL:

```
let url = NSURL(string: "http://localhost:8888/file.txt")!
```

 I am running MAMP and hosting my own file called *file.txt*. This URL won't get downloaded successfully on your machine if you are not hosting the exact same file with the same name on your local machine on the same port! So I suggest that you change this URL to something that makes more sense for your app.

Then use the `backgroundSessionConfigurationWithIdentifier(_:)` class method of `NSURLSessionConfiguration` to create a background URL configuration that you can use with `NSURLSession`:

```
let id = "se.pixolity.app.backgroundtask"
let conf = NSURLSessionConfiguration
  .backgroundSessionConfigurationWithIdentifier(id)
```

Once all of that is done, you can go ahead and create a download task and start it (see Figure 2-6):

```
let session = NSURLSession(configuration: conf, delegate: self,
  delegateQueue: NSOperationQueue())
```

```
let request = NSURLRequest(URL: url)

session.downloadTaskWithRequest(request).resume()
```

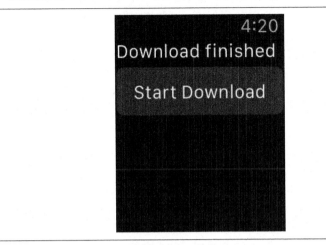

Figure 2-6. Our file is successfully downloaded

See Also

Recipe 1.6

2.2 Noticing Changes in Pairing State Between the iOS and Watch Apps

Problem

You want to know, both on the watch and in your companion iOS app, whether there is connectivity between them and whether you can send messages between them. Specifically, you want to find out whether one device can receive a signal sent from the other.

Solution

Import the WatchConnectivity framework on both projects. Then use the WCSession's delegate of type WCSessionDelegate to implement the sessionWatchStateDid Change(_:) method on your iOS side and the sessionReachabilityDidChange(_:) method on the watch side. These methods get called by WatchConnectivity whenever the state of the companion app is changed (whether that is on the iOS side or on the watchOS side).

Discussion

Both devices contain a flag called *reachability* that indicates whether the device can connect to the other. This is represented by a property on WCSession called reacha ble, of type Bool. On the iOS side, if you check this flag, it tells you whether your companion *watch app* is reachable, and if you check it on the watchOS side, it tells you whether your companion *iOS app* is reachable.

The idea here is to use the WCSession object to listen for state changes. Before doing that, we need to find out whether the session is actually supported. We do that using the isSupported() class function of WCWCSession. Once you know that sessions are supported, you have to do the following *on the iOS app* side:

1. Obtain your session with WCSession.defaultSession().
2. Set the delegate property of your session.
3. Become the delegate of your session, of type WCSessionDelegate.
4. Implement the sessionWatchStateDidChange(_:) function of your session dele- gate and in there, check the reachable flag of the session.
5. Call the activateSession() method of your session.

Make sure that you do this in a function that can be called even if your app is launched in the background.

On the *watch side*, do the exact same things as you did on the iOS side, but instead of implementing the sessionWatchStateDidChange(_:) method, implement the ses sionReachabilityDidChange(_:) method.

 The sessionWatchStateDidChange(_:) delegate method is called on the iOS side when at least one of the properties of the session changes. These properties include paired, watchAppInstalled, complicationEnabled, and watchDirectoryURL, all of type Bool. In contrast, the sessionReachabilityDidChange(_:) method is called on the watch only when the reachable flag of the compan- ion iOS app is changed, as the name of the delegate method suggests.

So on the iOS side, let's implement an extension on WCSession that can print all its relevant states, so that when the sessionWatchStateDidChange(_:) method is called, we can print the session's information:

```
import UIKit
import WatchConnectivity

extension WCSession{
  public func printInfo(){
```

```
      //paired
      print("Paired: ", terminator: "")
      print(self.paired ? "Yes" : "No")

      //watch app installed
      print("Watch app installed: ", terminator: "")
      print(self.watchAppInstalled ? "Yes" : "No")

      //complication enabled
      print("Complication enabled: ", terminator: "")
      print(self.complicationEnabled ? "Yes" : "No")

      //watch directory
      print("Watch directory url", terminator: "")
      print(self.watchDirectoryURL)

  }
}
```

Make your app delegate the delegate of the session as well:

```
@UIApplicationMain
class AppDelegate: UIResponder, UIApplicationDelegate, WCSessionDelegate {

  var window: UIWindow?

  ...
```

Now start listening for state and reachablity changes:

```
func sessionReachabilityDidChange(session: WCSession) {
  print("Reachable: ",  terminator: "")
  print(session.reachable ? "Yes" : "No")
}

func sessionWatchStateDidChange(session: WCSession) {
  print("Watch state is changed")
  session.printInfo()
}
```

Last but not least, on the iOS side, set up the session and start listening to its events:

```
guard WCSession.isSupported() else {
  print("Session is not supported")
  return
}

let session = WCSession.defaultSession()
session.delegate = self
session.activateSession()
```

Now on the watch side, in the ExtensionDelegate class, import WatchConnectivity and become the session delegate as well:

```
import WatchKit
import WatchConnectivity

class ExtensionDelegate: NSObject, WKExtensionDelegate, WCSessionDelegate {

  ...
```

And listen for reachablity changes:

```
func sessionReachabilityDidChange(session: WCSession) {
  print("Reachablity changed. Reachable?", terminator: "")
  print(session.reachable ? "Yes" : "No")
}
```

Then in the `applicationDidFinishLaunching()` function of our extension delegate, set up the session:

```
guard WCSession.isSupported() else {
  print("Session is not supported")
  return
}

let session = WCSession.defaultSession()
session.delegate = self
session.activateSession()
```

See Also

Recipe 2.1

2.3 Transferring Small Pieces of Data to and from the Watch

Problem

You want to transfer some plist-serializable content between your apps (iOS and watchOS). This content can be anything: for instance, information about where a user is inside a game on an iOS device, or more random information that you can serialize into a plist (strings, integers, booleans, dictionaries, and arrays). Information can be sent in either direction.

Solution

Follow these steps:

1. Use what you learned in Recipe 2.2 to find out whether both devices are reachable.

2. On the sending app, use the `updateApplicationContext(_:)` method of your session to send the content over to the other app.
3. On the receiving app, wait for the `session(_:didReceiveApplicationContext:)` delegate method of `WCSessionDelegate`, where you will be given access to the transmitted content.

 The content that you transmit must be of type `[String : AnyObject]`.

Discussion

Various types of content can be sent between iOS and watchOS. One is plist-serializable content, also called an *application context*. Let's say that you are playing a game on watchOS and you want to send the user's game status to iOS. You can use the application context for this.

Let's begin by creating a sample application. Create a single-view iOS app and add a watchOS target to it as well (see Figure 2-1). Design your main interface like Figure 2-7. We'll use the top label to show the download status. The buttons are self-explanatory. The bottom label will show the pairing status between our watchOS and iOS apps.

Figure 2-7. Labels and button for sample app

Hook up the top label to your view controller as statusLbl, the first button as sendBtn, the second button as downloadBtn, and the bottom label as reachabilityStatusLbl. Hook up the action of the download button to a method called download() and the send button to a method called send().

Download and install MAMP (*https://www.mamp.info/en/*) (it's free) and host the following contents as a file called *people.json* on your local web server's root folder:

```
{
  "people" : [
    {
      "name" : "Foo",
      "age" : 30
    },
    {
      "name" : "Bar",
      "age" : 50
    }
  ]
}
```

Now the top part of your iOS app's view controller should look like this:

```
import UIKit
import WatchConnectivity

class ViewController: UIViewController, WCSessionDelegate,
NSURLSessionDownloadDelegate {

  @IBOutlet var statusLbl: UILabel!
  @IBOutlet var sendBtn: UIButton!
  @IBOutlet var downloadBtn: UIButton!
  @IBOutlet var reachabilityStatusLbl: UILabel!


  ...
```

When you download that JSON file, it will become a dictionary of type [String : AnyObject], so let's define that as a variable in our vc:

```
var people: [String : AnyObject]?{
  didSet{
    dispatch_async(dispatch_get_main_queue()){
      self.updateSendButton()
    }
  }
}

func updateSendButton(){
  sendBtn.enabled = isReachable && isDownloadFinished && people != nil
}
```

Setting the value of the people variable will call the updateSendButton() function, which in turn enables the send button only if all the following conditions are met:

1. The watch app is reachable.

2. The file is downloaded.

3. The file was correctly parsed into the people variable.

Also define a variable that can write into your status label whenever the reachability flag is changed:

```
var isReachable = false{
  didSet{
    dispatch_async(dispatch_get_main_queue()){
      self.updateSendButton()
      if self.isReachable{
        self.reachabilityStatusLbl.text = "Watch is reachable"
      } else {
        self.reachabilityStatusLbl.text = "Watch is not reachable"
      }
    }
  }
}
```

We need two more properties: one that sets the status label and another that keeps track of when our file is downloaded successfully:

```
var isDownloadFinished = false{
  didSet{
    dispatch_async(dispatch_get_main_queue()){
      self.updateSendButton()
    }
  }
}

var status: String?{
  get{return self.statusLbl.text}
  set{
    dispatch_async(dispatch_get_main_queue()){
      self.statusLbl.text = newValue
    }
  }
}
```

All three variables (people, isReachable, and isDownloadFinished) that we defined call the updateSendButton() function so that our send button will be disabled if conditions are not met, and enabled otherwise.

Now when the download button is pressed, start a download task:

```
@IBAction func download() {

  //if loading HTTP content, make sure you have disabled ATS
  //for that domain
  let url = NSURL(string: "http://localhost:8888/people.json")!
  let req = NSURLRequest(URL: url)
  let id = "se.pixolity.app.backgroundtask"

  let conf = NSURLSessionConfiguration
    .backgroundSessionConfigurationWithIdentifier(id)

  let sess = NSURLSession(configuration: conf, delegate: self,
    delegateQueue: NSOperationQueue())

  sess.downloadTaskWithRequest(req).resume()
}
```

After that, check if you got any errors while trying to download the file:

```
func URLSession(session: NSURLSession, task: NSURLSessionTask,
  didCompleteWithError error: NSError?) {

  if error != nil{
    status = "Error happened"
    isDownloadFinished = false
  }

  session.finishTasksAndInvalidate()

}
```

Now implement the URLSession(_:downloadTask:didFinishDownloadingToURL:)
method of NSURLSessionDownloadDelegate. Inside there, tell your view controller
that you have downloaded the file by setting isDownloadFinished to true. Then construct a more permanent URL for the temporary URL to which our JSON file was
downloaded by iOS:

```
func URLSession(session: NSURLSession,
  downloadTask: NSURLSessionDownloadTask,
  didFinishDownloadingToURL location: NSURL){

  isDownloadFinished = true

  //got the data, parse as JSON
  let fm = NSFileManager()
  let url = try! fm.URLForDirectory(.DownloadsDirectory,
    inDomain: .UserDomainMask,
    appropriateForURL: location,
    create: true).URLByAppendingPathComponent("file.json")

  ...
```

Then move the file over:

```
do {try fm.removeItemAtURL(url)} catch {}

do{
  try fm.moveItemAtURL(location, toURL: url)
} catch {
  status = "Could not save the file"
  return
}
```

After that, simply read the file as a JSON file with NSJSONSerialization:

```
//now read the file from url
guard let data = NSData(contentsOfURL: url) else{
  status = "Could not read the file"
  return
}

do{
  let json = try NSJSONSerialization.JSONObjectWithData(data,
  options: .AllowFragments) as! [String : AnyObject]
  self.people = json
  status = "Successfully downloaded and parsed the file"
} catch{
  status = "Could not read the file as json"
}
```

Great—now go to your watch interface, place a label there, and hook it up to your code under the name statusLabel (see Figure 2-8).

In the interface controller file, place a variable that can set the status:

```
import WatchKit
import Foundation

class InterfaceController: WKInterfaceController {

  @IBOutlet var statusLabel: WKInterfaceLabel!

  var status = "Waiting"{
    didSet{
      statusLabel.setText(status)
    }
  }

}
```

Figure 2-8. Our watch interface has a simple label only

Go to your *ExtensionDelegate* file on the watch side and do these things:

1. Define a structure that can hold instances of a person you will get in your application context.
2. Define a property called `status` that when set, will set the `status` property of the interface controller:

```
import WatchKit
import WatchConnectivity

struct Person{
  let name: String
  let age: Int
}

class ExtensionDelegate: NSObject, WKExtensionDelegate, WCSessionDelegate{

  var status = ""{
    didSet{
      dispatch_async(dispatch_get_main_queue()){
        guard let interface =
          WKExtension.sharedExtension().rootInterfaceController as?
          InterfaceController else{
          return
        }
        interface.status = self.status
      }
```

```
    }
}
```

. . .

Now activate the session using what you learned in Recipe 2.2. I won't write the code for that in this recipe again. Then the session will wait for the `session(_:didRecei veApplicationContext:)` method of the `WCSessionDelegate` protocol to come in. When that happens, just read the application context and convert it into `Person` instances:

```
func session(session: WCSession,
  didReceiveApplicationContext applicationContext: [String : AnyObject]) {

  guard let people = applicationContext["people"] as?
    Array<[String : AnyObject]> where people.count > 0 else{
      status = "Did not find the people array"
      return
  }

  var persons = [Person]()
  for p in people where p["name"] is String && p["age"] is Int{
    let person = Person(name: p["name"] as! String, age: p["age"] as! Int)
    persons.append(person)
  }

  status = "Received \(persons.count) people from the iOS app"

}
```

Now run both your watch app and your iOS app. At first glance, your watch app will look like Figure 2-9.

Figure 2-9. Your watch app is waiting for the context to come through from the iOS app

Your iOS app in its initial state will look like Figure 2-10.

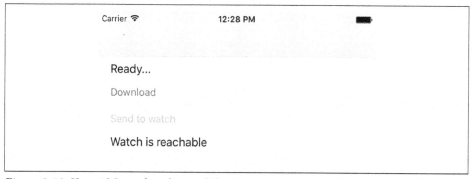

Figure 2-10. Your iOS app has detected that its companion watch app is reachable

When I press the download button, my iOS app's interface will change to Figure 2-11.

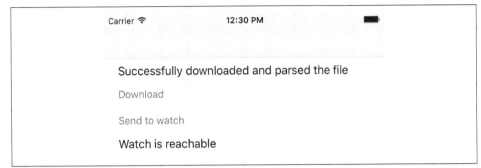

Carrier 🛜   12:30 PM

Successfully downloaded and parsed the file

Download

Send to watch

Watch is reachable

Figure 2-11. The iOS app is now ready to send the data over to the watch app

After pressing the send button, the watch app's interface will change to something like Figure 2-12.

12:31

Received 2 people from the iOS app

Figure 2-12. The watch app received the data

See Also

Recipe 2.1

2.4 Transferring Dictionaries in Queues to and from the Watch

Problem

You want to send dictionaries of information to and from the watch in a queuing (FIFO) fashion.

Solution

Call the transferUserInfo(_:) method on your WCSession on the sending part. On the receiving part, implement the session(_:didReceiveUserInfo:) method of the WCSessionDelegate protocol.

 A lot of the things that I'll refer to in this recipe have been discussed already in Recipe 2.3, so have a look if you feel a bit confused.

Discussion

Create a single-view app in iOS and put your root view controller in a nav controller. Then add a watch target to your app (see this chapter's introduction for an explanation). Make sure that your root view controller in IB looks like Figure 2-13.

Figure 2-13. Place a label and a button on your UI

Hook up the label to a variable in your code named statusLbl and hook up the button to a variable named sendBtn. Hook up your button's action to a method in your code called send(). The top of your vc should now look like:

```
import UIKit
import WatchConnectivity
```

```
class ViewController: UIViewController, WCSessionDelegate {

  @IBOutlet var statusLbl: UILabel!
  @IBOutlet var sendBtn: UIButton!


  ...
```

You also need a property that can set the status for you on your label. The property must be on the main thread, because WCSession methods (where we may want to set our status property) usually are *not* called on the main thread:

```
var status: String?{
  get{return self.statusLbl.text}
  set{
    dispatch_async(dispatch_get_main_queue()){
      self.statusLbl.text = newValue
    }
  }
}
```

When the user presses the send button, we will use the WCSession.defaultSession().transferUserInfo(_:) method to send a simple dictionary whose only key is kCFBundleIdentifierKey and a value that will be our *Info.plist*'s bundle identifier:

```
@IBAction func send() {

  guard let infoPlist = NSBundle.mainBundle().infoDictionary else{
    status = "Could not get the Info.plist"
    return
  }

  let key = kCFBundleIdentifierKey as String

  let plist = [
    key : infoPlist[key] as! String
  ]

  let transfer = WCSession.defaultSession().transferUserInfo(plist)
  status = transfer.transferring ? "Sent" : "Could not send yet"


}
```

The transferUserInfo(_:) method returns an object of type WCSessionUserInfo Transfer that has properties such as userInfo and transferring and a method called cancel(). You can always use the cancel() method of an instance of WCSessio nUserInfoTransfer to cancel the transfer of this item if it is not already transfer ring. You can also find all the user info transfers that are ongoing by using the out standingUserInfoTransfers property of your session object.

The app also contains code to disable the button if the watch app is not reachable, but I won't discuss that code here because we have already discussed it in Recipe 2.2 and Recipe 2.3.

On the watch side, in `InterfaceController`, write the exact same code that you wrote in Recipe 2.3. In the `ExtensionDelegate` class, however, our code will be a bit different. Its `status` property is exactly how we wrote it in Recipe 2.3.

When the `applicationDidFinishLaunching()` method of our delegate is called, we set up the session just as we did in Recipe 2.2. We will wait for the `session(_:didReceiveUserInfo:)` method of the `WCSessionDelegate` protocol to be called. There, we will simply read the bundle identifier from the user info and display it in our view controller:

```
func session(session: WCSession,
  didReceiveUserInfo userInfo: [String : AnyObject]) {

    guard let bundleVersion = userInfo[kCFBundleIdentifierKey as String]
      as? String else{
      status = "Could not read the bundle version"
      return
    }

    status = bundleVersion

}
```

If you run the iOS app, your UI should look like Figure 2-14.

Figure 2-14. The app has detected that the watch app is reachable so the button is enabled

And your watch app should look like Figure 2-15.

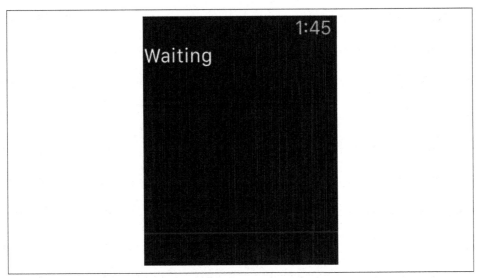

Figure 2-15. The watch app is waiting for incoming user info data

When you press the send button, the user interface will change to Figure 2-16.

Figure 2-16. The data is sent to the watch

And the watch app will look like Figure 2-17.

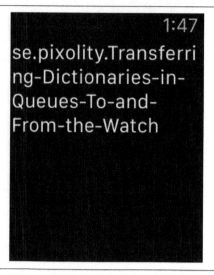

Figure 2-17. The watch app successfully received our user info

See Also

Recipe 2.1 and Recipe 2.3

2.5 Transferring Files to and from the Watch

Problem

You want to transfer a file between your iOS app and the watch app. The technique works in both directions.

Solution

Follow these steps:

1. Use the `transferFile(_:metadata:)` method of your `WCSession` object on the sending device.
2. Implement the `WCSessionDelegate` protocol on the sender and wait for the `session(_:didFinishFileTransfer:error:)` delegate method to be called. If the optional `error` parameter is `nil`, it indicates that the file is transferred successfully.
3. On the receiving part, become the delegate of `WCSession` and wait for the `session(_:didReceiveFile:)` delegate method to be called.
4. The incoming file on the receiving side is of type `WCSessionFile` and has properties such as `fileURL` and `metadata`. The metadata is the same metadata of type

[String : AnyObject] that the sender sent with the `transferFile(_:meta data:)` method.

Discussion

Let's have a look at a simple UI on the sending device (the iOS side in this example). It contains a label that shows our status and a button that sends our file. When the button is pressed, we create a file in the iOS app's *caches* folder and then send that file through to the watch app if it is reachable (see Recipe 2.2).

Make your UI on the iOS (sender) side look like Figure 2-18. The button will be disabled if the watch app is not reachable (see Recipe 2.2).

Figure 2-18. Status label and button on sender

Hook up your button's action code to a method in your view controller called `send()` and make sure your view controller conforms to `WCSessionDelegate`:

```swift
import UIKit
import WatchConnectivity

class ViewController: UIViewController, WCSessionDelegate {

  @IBOutlet var statusLbl: UILabel!
  @IBOutlet var sendBtn: UIButton!

  var status: String?{
    get{return self.statusLbl.text}
    set{
      dispatch_async(dispatch_get_main_queue()){
        self.statusLbl.text = newValue
      }
    }
  }

  ...
```

We implemented and talked about the status property of our view controller in Recipe 2.3, so I won't explain it here.

Then, when the send button is pressed, construct a URL that will point to your file. It doesn't exist yet, but you will write it to disk soon:

```
let fileName = "file.txt"

let fm = NSFileManager()

let url = try! fm.URLForDirectory(.CachesDirectory,
  inDomain: .UserDomainMask, appropriateForURL: nil,
  create: true).URLByAppendingPathComponent(fileName)
```

Now write some text to disk, reachable through the URL:

```
let text = "Foo Bar"

do{
  try text.writeToURL(url, atomically: true,
    encoding: NSUTF8StringEncoding)
} catch {
  status = "Could not write the file"
  return
}
```

Once that is done, send the file over:

```
let metadata = ["fileName" : fileName]
WCSession.defaultSession().transferFile(url, metadata: metadata)
```

Also, when your session's reachability state changes, enable or disable your button:

```
func updateUiForSession(session: WCSession){
  status = session.reachable ? "Ready to send" : "Not reachable"
  sendBtn.enabled = session.reachable
}

func sessionReachabilityDidChange(session: WCSession) {
  updateUiForSession(session)
}
```

On the watch side, make your UI look like Figure 2-8. Then, in your `ExtensionDele` `gate` class, implement the exact same status property that we implemented in Recipe 2.3.

Now implement the `session(_:didReceiveFile:)` method of `WCSessionDelegate`. Start by double-checking that the metadata is as you expected it:

```
guard let metadata = file.metadata where metadata["fileName"]
  is String else{
```

```
    status = "No metadata came through"
    return
}
```

If it is, read the file and show it in the user interface:

```
do{
  let str = try String(NSString(contentsOfURL: file.fileURL,
    encoding: NSUTF8StringEncoding))
  guard str.characters.count > 0 else{
    status = "No file came through"
    return
  }
  status = str
} catch {
  status = "Could not read the file"
  return
}
```

When you run the watch app, it will look like Figure 2-15. When you run the iOS app, it will look like Figure 2-19.

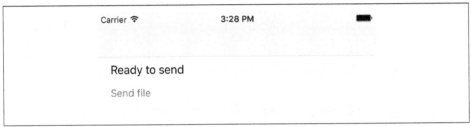

Figure 2-19. The file is ready to be sent from iOS to watchOS

When the file is sent, your user interface on iOS will look like Figure 2-20.

Figure 2-20. iOS sent our file to watchOS

And the UI on your receiver (watchOS) will look like Figure 2-21.

Figure 2-21. watchOS successfully received our file, read its content, and is displaying it in our label

See Also

Recipe 2.1, Recipe 2.2, and Recipe 2.3

2.6 Communicating Interactively Between iOS and watchOS

Problem

You want to interactively send messages from iOS to watchOS (or vice versa) and receive a reply immediately.

Solution

On the sender side, use the `sendMessage(_:replyHandler:errorHandler:)` method of `WCSession`. On the receiving side, implement the `session(_:didReceiveMes sage:replyHandler:)` method to handle the incoming message if your sender expected a reply, or implement `session(_:didReceiveMessage:)` if no reply was expected from you. Messages and replies are of type `[String : AnyObject]`.

Discussion

Let's implement a chat program where the iOS app and the watch app can send messages to each other. On the iOS app, we will allow the user to type text and then send it over to the watch. On the watch, since we cannot type anything, we will have four predefined messages that the user can send us. In order to decrease the amount of data the watch sends us, we define these messages as `Int` and send the integers instead. The iOS app will read the integers and then print the correct message onto the screen. So let's first define these messages. Create a file called *PredefinedMessages* and write the following Swift code there:

```swift
import Foundation

enum PredefinedMessage : Int{
    case Hello
    case ThankYou
    case HowAreYou
    case IHearYou
}
```

Add this file to both your watch extension and your iOS app so that they both can use it (see Figure 2-22).

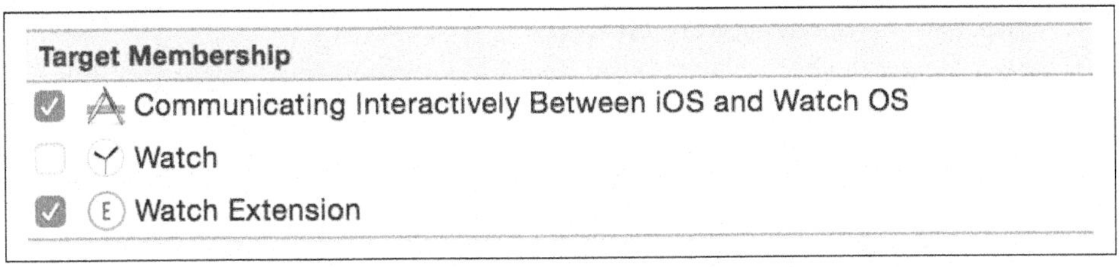

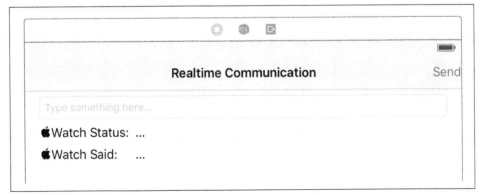

Figure 2-22. We will include the file on our iOS app and watch extension

Now move to your main iOS app's storyboard and design a UI that looks like Figure 2-23. There are two labels that say "..." at the moment. They will be populated dynamically in our code.

Figure 2-23. Initial iOS app UI

Hook up your UI to your code as follows:

- Hook up your send button to an outlet called `sendBtn`. Hook up its action method to a function called `send(_:)` in your vc.
- Hook up the text field to your code under the name `textField`.
- Hook up the label that says "..." in front of "Watch Status:" to an outlet called `watchStatusLbl`.
- Hook up the label that says "..." in front of "Watch Said:" to an outlet called `watch ReplyLbl`.

So now the top part of your vc on the iOS side should look like this:

```
import UIKit
import WatchConnectivity

class ViewController: UIViewController, WCSessionDelegate {

    @IBOutlet var sendBtn: UIBarButtonItem!
    @IBOutlet var textField: UITextField!
    @IBOutlet var watchStatusLbl: UILabel!
    @IBOutlet var watchReplyLbl: UILabel!


    ...
```

As we have done before, we need two variables that can populate the text inside the `watchStatusLbl` and `watchReplyLbl` labels, always on the main thread:

```
var watchStatus: String{
  get{return self.watchStatusLbl.text ?? ""}
  set{onMainThread{self.watchStatusLbl.text = newValue}}
}

var watchReply: String{
  get{return self.watchReplyLbl.text ?? ""}
  set{onMainThread{self.watchReplyLbl.text = newValue}}
}
```

 The definition of `onMainThread` is very simple. It's a custom function I've written in a library to make life easier:

```
import Foundation

public func onMainThread(f: () -> Void){
  dispatch_async(dispatch_get_main_queue(), f)
}
```

When the send button is pressed, we first have to make sure that the user has entered some text into the text field:

```
guard let txt = textField.text where txt.characters.count > 0 else{
  textField.placeholder = "Enter some text here first"
```

```
    return
  }
```

Then we will use the sendMessage(_:replyHandler:errorHandler:) method of our session to send our text over:

```
WCSession.defaultSession().sendMessage(["msg" : txt],
  replyHandler: {dict in

    guard dict["msg"] is String &&
      dict["msg"] as! String == "delivered" else{
      self.watchReply = "Could not deliver the message"
      return
    }

    self.watchReply = dict["msg"] as! String

}){err in
  self.watchReply = "An error happened in sending the message"
}
```

Later, when we implement our watch side, we will also be sending messages from the watch over to the iOS app. Those messages will be inside a dictionary whose only key is "msg" and the value of this key will be an integer. The integers are already defined in the PredefinedMessage enum that we saw earlier. So in our iOS app, we will wait for messages from the watch app, translate the integer we get to its string counterpart, and show it on our iOS UI. Remember, we send integers (instead of strings) from the watch to make the transfer snappier. So let's implement the session(_:didReceive Message:) delegate method in our iOS app:

```
func session(session: WCSession,
  didReceiveMessage message: [String : AnyObject]) {

    guard let msg = message["msg"] as? Int,
      let value = PredefinedMessage(rawValue: msg) else{
        watchReply = "Received invalid message"
      return
    }

    switch value{
    case .Hello:
      watchReply = "Hello"
    case .HowAreYou:
      watchReply = "How are you?"
    case .IHearYou:
      watchReply = "I hear you"
    case .ThankYou:
      watchReply = "Thank you"
    }

}
```

Let's use what we learned in Recipe 2.2 to enable or disable our send button when the watch's reachability changes:

```
func updateUiForSession(session: WCSession){
    watchStatus = session.reachable ? "Reachable" : "Not reachable"
    sendBtn.enabled = session.reachable
}

func sessionReachabilityDidChange(session: WCSession) {
    updateUiForSession(session)
}
```

On the watch side, design your UI like Figure 2-24. On the watch, the user cannot type, but she can press a predefined message in order to send it (remember `Predefi nedMessage`?). That little line between "Waiting..." and "Send a reply" is a separator.

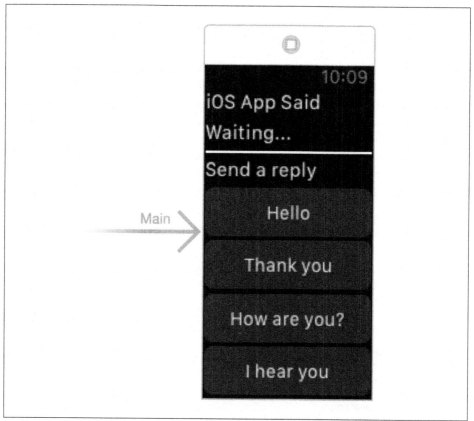

Figure 2-24. Strings that a user can send from a watch

Hook up your watch UI to your code by following these steps:

- Hook up the "Waiting..." label to an outlet named `iosAppReplyLbl`. We will show the text that our iOS app has sent to us in this label.
- Place all the buttons at the bottom of the page inside a group and hook that group up to an outlet called `repliesGroup`. We will hide this whole group if the iOS app is not reachable to our watch app.
- Hook the action of the "Hello" button to a method in your code called `send Hello()`.
- Hook the action of the "Thank you" button to a method in your code called `send ThankYou()`.
- Hook the action of the "How are you?" button to a method in your code called `sendHowAreYou()`.
- Hook the action of the "I hear you" button to a method in your code called `sendI HearYou()`.

In our `InterfaceController` on the watch side, we need a generic method that takes in an `Int` (our predefined message) and sends it over to the iOS side with the `sendMes sage(_:replyHandler:errorHandler:)` method of the session:

```
import WatchKit
import Foundation
import WatchConnectivity

class InterfaceController: WKInterfaceController {

  @IBOutlet var iosAppReplyLbl: WKInterfaceLabel!
  @IBOutlet var repliesGroup: WKInterfaceGroup!

  func send(int: Int){

    WCSession.defaultSession().sendMessage(["msg" : int],
      replyHandler: nil, errorHandler: nil)

  }

  ...
```

And whenever any of the buttons is pressed, we call the `send(_:)` method with the right predefined message:

```
@IBAction func sendHello() {
  send(PredefinedMessage.Hello.hashValue)
}

@IBAction func sendThankYou() {
  send(PredefinedMessage.ThankYou.hashValue)
}

@IBAction func sendHowAreYou() {
  send(PredefinedMessage.HowAreYou.hashValue)
```

```
      }
      @IBAction func sendIHearYou() {
        send(PredefinedMessage.IHearYou.hashValue)
      }
```

In the `ExtensionDelegate` class on the watch side, we want to hide all the reply buttons if the iOS app is not reachable. To do that, write a property called `isReachable`
of type `Bool`. Whenever this property is set, the code sets the `hidden` property of our
replies group:

```
import WatchKit
import WatchConnectivity

class ExtensionDelegate: NSObject, WKExtensionDelegate, WCSessionDelegate{

  var isReachable = false{
    willSet{
      self.rootController?.repliesGroup.setHidden(!newValue)
    }
  }

  var rootController: InterfaceController?{
    get{
      guard let interface =
        WKExtension.sharedExtension().rootInterfaceController as?
        InterfaceController else{
          return nil
      }
      return interface
    }
  }

  ...
```

You also are going to need a `String` property that will be your iOS app's reply. Whenever you get a reply from the iOS app, place it inside this property. As soon as this
property is set, the watch extension will write this text on our UI:

```
  var iosAppReply = ""{
    didSet{
      dispatch_async(dispatch_get_main_queue()){
        self.rootController?.iosAppReplyLbl.setText(self.iosAppReply)
      }
    }
  }
```

Now let's wait for messages from the iOS app and display those messages on our UI:

```
func session(session: WCSession,
  didReceiveMessage message: [String : AnyObject],
  replyHandler: ([String : AnyObject]) -> Void) {
```

```
    guard message["msg"] is String else{
      replyHandler(["msg" : "failed"])
      return
    }

    iosAppReply = message["msg"] as! String
    replyHandler(["msg" : "delivered"])

  }
```

Also when our iOS app's reachability changes, we want to update our UI and disable the reply buttons:

```
func sessionReachabilityDidChange(session: WCSession) {
  isReachable = session.reachable
}

func applicationDidFinishLaunching() {

  guard WCSession.isSupported() else{
    iosAppReply = "Sessions are not supported"
    return
  }

  let session = WCSession.defaultSession()
  session.delegate = self
  session.activateSession()
  isReachable = session.reachable

}
```

Running our app on the watch first, we will see an interface similar to Figure 2-25. The user can scroll to see the rest of the buttons.

Figure 2-25. Available messages on watch

And when we run our app on iOS while the watch app is reachable, the UI will look like Figure 2-26.

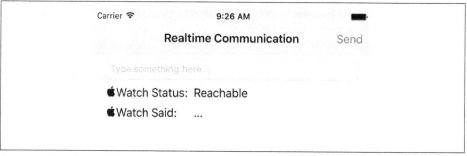

Figure 2-26. The send button on our app is enabled and we can send messages

Type "Hello from iOS" in the iOS UI and press the send button. The watch app will receive the message (see Figure 2-27).

Figure 2-27. The watch app received the message sent from the iOS app

Now press the How are you? button on the watch UI and see the results in the iOS app (Figure 2-28).

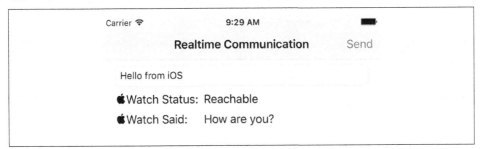

Figure 2-28. The iOS app received the message from the watch app

See Also

Recipe 2.1, Recipe 2.2, Recipe 2.3, Recipe 2.4, and Recipe 2.5

2.7 Setting Up Apple Watch for Custom Complications

Problem

You want to create a barebones watch project with support for complications and you want to see a complication on the screen.

Solution

Follow these steps:

1. Add a watch target to your project (see Figure 2-1). Make sure that it includes complications upon setting it up.
2. In Xcode, in your targets, select your watch extension. Under the General tab, ensure that the Modular Small complication is the only complication that is enabled. Disable all the others (see Figure 2-29).
3. Write your complication code in your `ComplicationController` class. We'll discuss this code soon.
4. Run your app on the watch simulator.
5. Once your app is opened in the simulator, press Command-Shift-H to go to the clock face (see Figure 2-3).
6. Press Command-Shift-2 to simulate Deep Press on the watch simulator and then tap and hold on the watch face (see Figure 2-30).

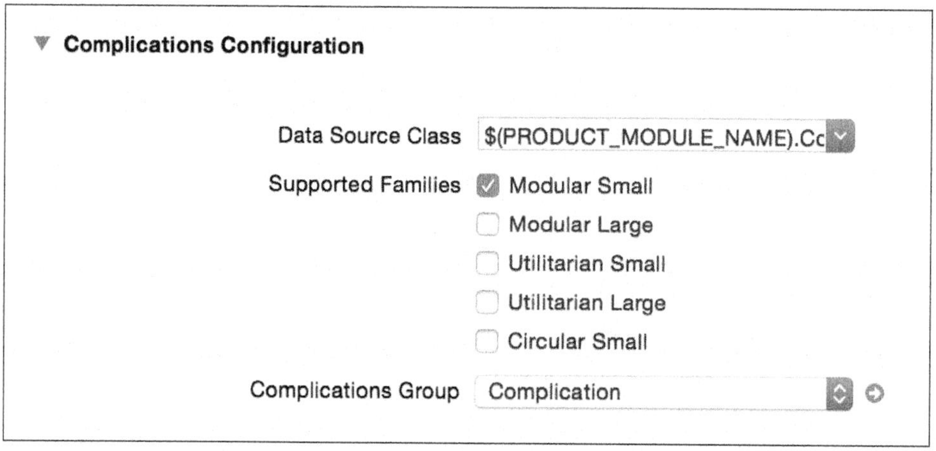

Figure 2-29. We are going to support only small-modular complications

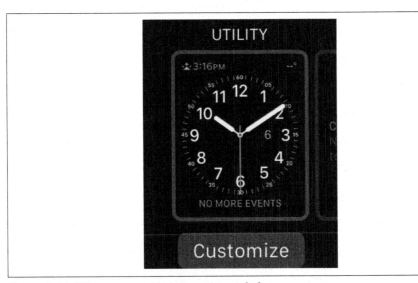

Figure 2-30. We can now customize our watch face

7. Press Command-Shift-1 to simulate Shallow Press and then scroll to the modular watch face (see Figure 2-31).

Figure 2-31. Select the modular watch face

8. Press the Customize button (see Figure 2-32).

Figure 2-32. Now you can customize your modular watch face

9. Scroll to the next page to the right, and then tap the small-modular complication at the bottom left of the screen until it becomes selected (see Figure 2-33). You will replace this with your own complication.

Figure 2-33. Select the small modular complication at the bottom left

10. Now use the up and down arrows on your keyboard (or if on the device, use the digital crown) to select your complication (see Figure 2-34). What you see on the

screen is the preview template that you have provided to the system. We will implement this template soon, but in the figure I have already done that, hence the number 22.

Figure 2-34. Your own small-modular complication is shown

11. Press Cmd-Shift-2 to simulate Deep Press and then tap the screen (see Figure 2-35).

Figure 2-35. We have now configured our complication on the selected watch face

12. Press Command-Shift-H to go to the clock app on the screen (see Figure 2-36). Notice that your complication is gone and shows no data. That is because what we displayed on the screen while configuring our watch face was just a preview template. What the clock app displays is real data and we are not providing any of it.

Figure 2-36. Our complication is on the bottom left but is empty

Discussion

Complications are pieces of information that apps can display on a watch face. They are divided into a few main categories:

Modular small
>   A very small amount of space with minimal text and/or a very small image (see Figure 2-37; the date on the top left is a modular small complication).

Modular large
>   An image, title, and up to two lines of text (see Figure 2-37; the calendar event in the center of the screen is a modular large complication).

Utilitarian small
>   Mainly a small image with optional text (see Figure 2-37; the activity icon in the bottom center is of this type).

Utilitarian large
>   A date/text mixed with an image, rendered on one line. This is similar to modular large but on just one line.

Circular small

A circular image with optional text (see Figure 2-37; the sunrise/sunset complication on the bottom right is an example of a circular-small complication).

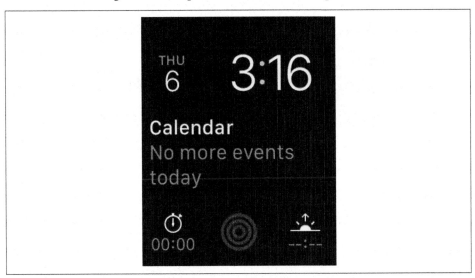

Figure 2-37. Everything except the time is a complication

Assuming that you have already created a watch target with a complication attached to it, go into your `ComplicationController` class and find the `getPlaceholderTem` `plateForComplication(_:withHandler:)` method. This method gets called by iOS when your complication is being added to a watch face. This gives you the chance to provide a placeholder for what the user has to see while adjusting her watch face. It won't usually be real data.

After this method is called, you need to create a complication template of type `CLKCom` `plicationTemplate` (or one of its many subclasses) and return that into the `replyHan` `dler` block that you are given. For now, implement the template like this:

```
func getPlaceholderTemplateForComplication(complication: CLKComplication,
  withHandler handler: (CLKComplicationTemplate?) -> Void) {
  let temp = CLKComplicationTemplateModularSmallSimpleText()
  temp.textProvider = CLKSimpleTextProvider(text: "22")
  handler(temp)
}
```

I am not going to discuss the details of this code right now. You'll learn them in other recipes in this chapter.

One more thing that you have to know is that once you have provided watchOS with your placeholder template, you won't be asked to do it again unless the user uninstalls your watchOS app and installs it again from her iPhone (see Figure 2-38).

Figure 2-38. If the user uninstalls and reinstalls your app, it can provide a new place-holder template

If you are working on the `getPlaceholderTemplateForComplication(_:withHan dler:)` method and want to test out different templates, you can simply reset the watch simulator and then run your app again. This will retrigger the `getPlaceholder TemplateForComplication(_:withHandler:)` method on your complication controller.

See Also

Recipe 2.8 and Recipe 2.9

2.8 Constructing Small Complications with Text and Images

Problem

You want to construct a small-modular complication and provide the user with past, present, and future data. In this example, a small modular complication (Figure 2-39, bottom left) shows the current hour with a ring swallowing it. The ring is divided into 24 sections and increments for every 1 hour in the day. At the end of the day, the ring will be completely filled and the number inside the ring will show 24.

Figure 2-39. Small-modular complication (bottom left) showing the current hour surrounded by a ring

Solution

Follow these steps:

1. Create your main iOS project with a watch target and make sure your watch target has a complication.

2. In your complication, implement the `getSupportedTimeTravelDirectionsFor Complication(_:withHandler:)` method of the `CLKComplicationDataSource` protocol. In this method, return your supported time travel directions (more on this later). The directions are of type `CLKComplicationTimeTravelDirections`.

3. Implement the `getTimelineStartDateForComplication(_:withHandler:)` method inside your complication class and call the given handler with an `NSDate` that indicates the start date of your available data.

4. Implement the `getTimelineEndDateForComplication(_:withHandler:)` method of your complication and call the handler with the last date for which your data is valid.

5. Implement the `getTimelineEntriesForComplication(_:before Date:limit:withHandler:)` method of your complication, create an array of type `CLKComplicationTimelineEntry`, and send that array into the given handler object. These will be the timeline entries before the given date that you would want to return to the watch (more on this later).

6. Implement the `getTimelineEntriesForComplication(_:after Date:limit:withHandler:)` method of your complication and return all the events that your complication supports, after the given date.
7. Implement the `getNextRequestedUpdateDateWithHandler(_:)` method of your complication and let watchOS know when it has to ask you next for more content.

Discussion

When providing complications, you are expected to provide data to the watchOS as the time changes. In our example, for every hour in the day, we want to change our complication. So each day we'll return 24 events to the runtime.

With the digital crown on the watch, the user can scroll up and down while on the watch face to engage in a feature called "time travel." This allows the user to change the time known to the watch just so she can see how various components on screen change with the new time. For instance, if you provide a complication to the user that shows all football match results of the day, the user can then go back in time a few hours to see the results of a match she has just missed. Similarly, in the context of a complication that shows the next fast train time to the city where the user lives, she can scroll forward, with the digital crown on the watch face, to see the future times that the train leaves from the current station.

The time is an absolute value on any watch, so let's say that you want to provide the time of the next football match in your complication. Let's say it's 14:00 right now and the football match starts at 15:00. If you give 15:00 as the start of that event to your complication, watchOS will show the football match (or the data that you provide for that match to your user through your complication) to the user at 15:00, not before. That is a bit useless, if you ask me. You want to provide that information to the user *before* the match starts so she knows what to look forward to, and *when*. So keep that in mind when providing a starting date for your events.

watchOS complications conform to the `CLKComplicationDataSource` protocol. They get a lot of delegate messages from this protocol calling methods that you have to implement even if you don't want to return any data. For instance, in the `getNextRe questedUpdateDateWithHandler(_:)` method, you get a handler as a parameter that you must call with an `NSDate` object, specifying when you want to be asked for more data next time. If you don't want to be asked for any more data, you still have to call this handler object but with a `nil` date. You'll find out soon that most of these handlers ask for optional values, so you can call them with `nil` if you want to.

While working with complications, you can tell watchOS which directions of time travel you support, or if you support time travel at all. If you don't support it, your complication returns only data for the current time. And if the user scrolls the watch face with the digital crown, your complication won't update its information. I don't suggest you opt out of time travel unless your complication really cannot provide relevant data to the user. Certainly, if your complication shows match results, it cannot show results for matches that have not happened. But even then, you can still support forward and backward time travel. If the user chooses forward time travel, just hide the scores, show a question mark, or do something similar.

As you work with complications, it's important to construct a data model to return to the watch. What you usually return to the watch for your complication is either of type `CLKComplicationTemplate` or of type `CLKComplicationTimelineEntry`. The template defines how your data is viewed on screen. The timeline entry only binds your template (your visible data) to a date of type `NSDate` that dictates to the watch when it has to show your data. As simple as that. In the case of small-modular complications, you can provide the following templates to the watch:

`CLKComplicationTemplateModularSmallSimpleText`
   Has just text.

`CLKComplicationTemplateModularSmallSimpleImage`
   Has just an image.

`CLKComplicationTemplateModularSmallRingText`
   Has text inside a ring that you can fill from 0 to 100%.

`CLKComplicationTemplateModularSmallRingImage`
   Has an image inside a ring that you can fill.

`CLKComplicationTemplateModularSmallStackText`
   Has two lines of code, the second of which can be highlighted.

`CLKComplicationTemplateModularSmallStackImage`
   Has an image and a text, with the text able to be highlighted.

`CLKComplicationTemplateModularSmallColumnsText`
   Has a 2 × 2 text display where you can provide four pieces of textual data. The second column can be highlighted and have its text alignment adjusted.

As you saw in Figure 2-33, this example bases our small-modular template on `CLKCom plicationTemplateModularSmallRingText`. So we provide only a text (the current hour) and a value between 0 and 1 that will tell watchOS how much of the ring around our number it has to fill (0...100%).

Let's now begin defining our data for this example. For every hour, we want our template to show the current hour. Just before midnight, we provide another 24 new complication data points for that day to the watch. So let's define a data structure that can contain a date, the hour value, and the fraction (between 0...1) to set for our complication. Start off by creating a file called *DataProvider.swift* and write all this code in that:

```
protocol WithDate{
  var hour: Int {get}
  var date: NSDate {get}
  var fraction: Float {get}
}
```

Now we can define our actual structure that conforms to this protocol:

```
struct Data : WithDate{
  let hour: Int
  let date: NSDate
  let fraction: Float
  var hourAsStr: String{
    return "\(hour)"
  }
}
```

Later, when we work on our complication, we will be asked to provide, inside the getCurrentTimelineEntryForComplication(_:withHandler:) method of CLKCom plicationDataSource, a template to show to the user for the current time. We are also going to create an array of 24 Data structures. So it would be great if we could always, inside this array, easily find the Data object for the current date:

```
extension NSDate{
  func hour() -> Int{
    let cal = NSCalendar.currentCalendar()
    return cal.components(NSCalendarUnit.Hour, fromDate: self).hour
  }
}

extension CollectionType where Generator.Element : WithDate {

  func dataForNow() -> Generator.Element?{
    let thisHour = NSDate().hour()
    for d in self{
      if d.hour == thisHour{
        return d
      }
    }
    return nil
  }

}
```

 The dataForNow() function goes through any collection that has objects that conform to the WithDate protocol that we specified earlier, and finds the object whose current hour is the same as that returned for the current moment by NSDate().

Let's now create our array of 24 `Data` objects. We do this by iterating from 1 to 24, creating `NSDate` objects using `NSDateComponents` and `NSCalendar`. Then, using those objects, we construct instances of the `Data` structure that we just wrote:

```
struct DataProvider{

  func allDataForToday() -> [Data]{

    var all = [Data]()

    let now = NSDate()
    let cal = NSCalendar.currentCalendar()
    let units = NSCalendarUnit.Year.union(.Month).union(.Day)
    let comps = cal.components(units, fromDate: now)
    comps.minute = 0
    comps.second = 0
    for i in 1...24{
      comps.hour = i
      let date = cal.dateFromComponents(comps)!
      let fraction = Float(comps.hour) / 24.0
      let data = Data(hour: comps.hour, date: date, fraction: fraction)
      all.append(data)
    }

    return all

  }

}
```

That was our entire data model. Now let's move onto the complication class of our watch app. In the `getNextRequestedUpdateDateWithHandler(_:)` method of the `CLKComplicationDataSource` protocol to which our complication conforms, we are going to be asked when watchOS should next call our complication and ask for new data. Because we are going to provide data for the whole day, *today*, we would want to be asked for new data for tomorrow. So we need to ask to be updated a few seconds before the start of the next day. For that, we need an `NSDate` object that tells watchOS when the next day is. So let's extend `NSDate`:

```
extension NSDate{

  class func endOfToday() -> NSDate{
    let cal = NSCalendar.currentCalendar()
    let units = NSCalendarUnit.Year.union(NSCalendarUnit.Month)
      .union(NSCalendarUnit.Day)
    let comps = cal.components(units, fromDate: NSDate())
    comps.hour = 23
    comps.minute = 59
    comps.second = 59
    return cal.dateFromComponents(comps)!
  }
```

```
    }
```

Moving to our complication, let's define our data provider first:

```
class ComplicationController: NSObject, CLKComplicationDataSource {

  let dataProvider = DataProvider()

  ...
```

We know that our data provider can give us an array of `Data` objects, so we need a way of turning those objects into our templates so they that can be displayed on the screen:

```
func templateForData(data: Data) -> CLKComplicationTemplate{
  let template = CLKComplicationTemplateModularSmallRingText()
  template.textProvider = CLKSimpleTextProvider(text: data.hourAsStr)
  template.fillFraction = data.fraction
  template.ringStyle = .Closed
  return template
}
```

Our template of type `CLKComplicationTemplateModularSmallRingText` has a few important properties:

`textProvider` *of type* `CLKTextProvider`

> Tells watchOS how our text has to appear. We never instantiate `CLKTextProvider` directly, though. We use one of its subclasses, such as the `CLKSimpleTextProvider` class. There are other text providers that we will talk about later.

`fillFraction` *of type* `Float`

> A number between 0.0 and 1.0 that tells watchOS how much of the ring around our template it has to fill.

`ringStyle` *of type* `CLKComplicationRingStyle`

> The style of the ring we want around our text. It can be `Open` or `Closed`.

Later we are also going to be asked for timeline entries of type `CLKComplicationTimelineEntry` for the data that we provide to watchOS. So for every `Data` object, we need to be able to create a timeline entry:

```
func timelineEntryForData(data: Data) -> CLKComplicationTimelineEntry{
  let template = templateForData(data)
  return CLKComplicationTimelineEntry(date: data.date,
    complicationTemplate: template)
}
```

In this example, we support forward and backward time travel (of type `CLKComplicationTimeTravelDirections`) so let's tell watchOS that:

```
func getSupportedTimeTravelDirectionsForComplication(
  complication: CLKComplication,
  withHandler handler: (CLKComplicationTimeTravelDirections) -> Void) {
    handler([.Forward, .Backward])
}
```

 If you don't want to support time travel, call the handler argument
with the value of CLKComplicationTimeTravelDirections.None.

The next thing we have to do is implement the getTimelineStartDateForComplica
tion(_:withHandler:) method of CLKComplicationDataSource. This method gets
called on our delegate whenever watchOS wants to find out the beginning of the date/
time range of our time travel. For our example, since we want to provide 24 templates, one for each hour in the day, we tell watchOS the date of the first template:

```
func getTimelineStartDateForComplication(complication: CLKComplication,
  withHandler handler: (NSDate?) -> Void) {
    handler(dataProvider.allDataForToday().first!.date)
}
```

Similarly, for the getTimelineEndDateForComplication(_:withHandler:) method,
we provide the date of the last event:

```
func getTimelineEndDateForComplication(complication: CLKComplication,
  withHandler handler: (NSDate?) -> Void) {
    handler(dataProvider.allDataForToday().last!.date)
}
```

Complications can be displayed on the watch's lock screen. Some complications might
contain sensitive data, so they might want to opt out of appearing on the lock screen.
For this, we have to implement the getPrivacyBehaviorForComplication(_:with
Handler:) method as well. We call the handler with an object of type CLKComplica
tionPrivacyBehavior, such as ShowOnLockScreen or HideOnLockScreen. Because we
don't have any sensitive data, we show our complication on the lock screen:

```
func getPrivacyBehaviorForComplication(complication: CLKComplication,
  withHandler handler: (CLKComplicationPrivacyBehavior) -> Void) {
    handler(.ShowOnLockScreen)
}
```

Now to the stuff that I like. The getCurrentTimelineEntryForComplication(_:with
Handler:) method will get called on our delegate whenever the runtime needs to get
the complication timeline (the template plus the date to display) for the complication
to display no. Do you remember the dataForNow() method that we wrote a while ago
as an extension on CollectionType? Well, we are going to use that now:

```
func getCurrentTimelineEntryForComplication(complication: CLKComplication,
  withHandler handler: ((CLKComplicationTimelineEntry?) -> Void)) {

    if let data = dataProvider.allDataForToday().dataForNow(){
      handler(timelineEntryForData(data))
    } else {
      handler(nil)
    }

}
```

Always implement the handlers that the class gives you. If they accept optional values and you don't have any data to pass, just pass `nil`.

Now we have to implement the `getTimelineEntriesForComplication(_:before Date:limit:beforeDate:)` method of our complication delegate. This method gets called whenever watchOS needs timeline entries for data before a certain date, with a maximum of *limit* entries. So let's say that you have 1,000 templates to return but the limit is 100. Do not return more than 100 in that case. In our example, I will go through all the data items that we have, filter them by their dates, find the ones coming before the given date (the `beforeDate` parameter), and create a timeline entry for all of those with the `timelineEntryForData(_:)` method that we wrote:

```
func getTimelineEntriesForComplication(complication: CLKComplication,
  beforeDate date: NSDate, limit: Int,
  withHandler handler: (([CLKComplicationTimelineEntry]?) -> Void)) {

    let entries = dataProvider.allDataForToday().filter{
      date.compare($0.date) == .OrderedDescending
    }.map{
      self.timelineEntryForData($0)
    }

    handler(entries)
}
```

Similarly, we have to implement the `getTimelineEntriesForComplication(_:after Date:limit:withHandler:)` method to return the timeline entries *after* a certain date (`afterDate` parameter):

```
func getTimelineEntriesForComplication(complication: CLKComplication,
  afterDate date: NSDate, limit: Int,
  withHandler handler: (([CLKComplicationTimelineEntry]?) -> Void)) {

    let entries = dataProvider.allDataForToday().filter{
      date.compare($0.date) == .OrderedAscending
    }.map{
```

```
        self.timelineEntryForData($0)
    }

    handler(entries)

}
```

The `getNextRequestedUpdateDateWithHandler(_:)` method is the next method we need to implement. This method gets called to ask us when we would like to be asked for more data later. For our app we specify the next day, because we have already provided all the data for today:

```
func getNextRequestedUpdateDateWithHandler(handler: (NSDate?) -> Void) {
  handler(NSDate.endOfToday());
}
```

Last but not least, we have to implement the `getPlaceholderTemplateForComplication(_:withHandler:)` method that we talked about before. This is where we provide our placeholder template:

```
func getPlaceholderTemplateForComplication(complication: CLKComplication,
  withHandler handler: (CLKComplicationTemplate?) -> Void) {
    if let data = dataProvider.allDataForToday().dataForNow(){
      handler(templateForData(data))
    } else {
      handler(nil)
    }
}
```

Now when I run my app on my watch, because the time is 10:24 and the hour is 10, our complication will show 10 and fill the circle around it to show how much of the day has passed by 10:00 (see Figure 2-40).

Figure 2-40. Our complication on the bottom left is showing the hour

And if I engage time travel and move forward to 18:23, our complication updates itself as well, showing 18 as the hour (see Figure 2-41).

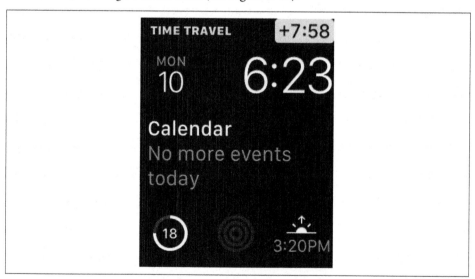

Figure 2-41. The user moves the time to the future and our complication updates itself as well

See Also

Recipe 2.7

2.9 Displaying Time Offsets in Complications

Problem

The data that you want to present has to be shown as an offset to a specific time. For instance, you want to show the remaining minutes until the next train that the user can take to get home.

Solution

Use the CLKRelativeDateTextProvider to provide your information inside a template. In this example, we are going to use CLKComplicationTemplateModularLargeS tandardBody, which is a large and modular template.

Discussion

In this recipe, let's create a watch app that shows the next available train that the user can take to get home. Trains can have different properties:

- Date and time of departure
- Train operator
- Type of train (high speed, commuter train, etc.)
- Service name (as shown on the time table)

In our example, I want the complication to look like Figure 2-42. The complication shows the next train (a Coastal service) and how many minutes away that train departs.

Figure 2-42. Complication shows that the next train leaves in 25 minutes

When you create your watchOS project, enable only the modular large complication in the target settings (see Figure 2-43).

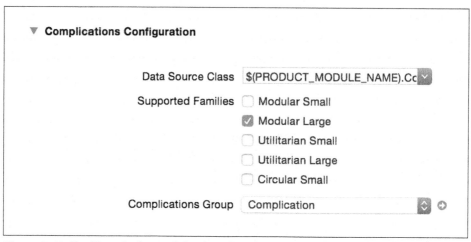

Figure 2-43. Enable only the modular large complication for this example

Now create your data model. It will be similar to what we did in Recipe 2.8, but this time we want to provide train times. For the train type and the train company, create enumerations:

```
enum TrainType : String{
  case HighSpeed = "High Speed"
  case Commuter = "Commuter"
  case Coastal = "Coastal"
}

enum TrainCompany : String{
  case SJ = "SJ"
  case Southern = "Souther"
  case OldRail = "Old Rail"
}
```

 These enumerations are of type `String`, so you can display them on your UI easily without having to write a `switch` statement.

Then define a protocol to which your train object will conform. Protocol-oriented programming offers many possibilities (see Recipe 1.12), so let's do that now:

```
protocol OnRailable{
  var type: TrainType {get}
  var company: TrainCompany {get}
```

```
  var service: String {get}
  var departureTime: NSDate {get}
}

struct Train : OnRailable{
  let type: TrainType
  let company: TrainCompany
  let service: String
  let departureTime: NSDate
}
```

As we did in Recipe 2.8, we are going to define a data provider. In this example, we create a few trains that depart at specific times with different types of services and from different operators:

```
struct DataProvider{

  func allTrainsForToday() -> [Train]{

    var all = [Train]()

    let now = NSDate()
    let cal = NSCalendar.currentCalendar()
    let units = NSCalendarUnit.Year.union(.Month).union(.Day)
    let comps = cal.components(units, fromDate: now)

    //first train
    comps.hour = 6
    comps.minute = 30
    comps.second = 0
    let date1 = cal.dateFromComponents(comps)!
    all.append(Train(type: .Commuter, company: .SJ,
      service: "3296", departureTime: date1))

    //second train
    comps.hour = 9
    comps.minute = 57
    let date2 = cal.dateFromComponents(comps)!
    all.append(Train(type: .HighSpeed, company: .Southern,
      service: "2307", departureTime: date2))

    //third train
    comps.hour = 12
    comps.minute = 22
    let date3 = cal.dateFromComponents(comps)!
    all.append(Train(type: .Coastal, company: .OldRail,
      service: "3206", departureTime: date3))

    //fourth train
    comps.hour = 15
    comps.minute = 45
    let date4 = cal.dateFromComponents(comps)!
```

```
all.append(Train(type: .HighSpeed, company: .SJ,
  service: "3703", departureTime: date4))

//fifth train
comps.hour = 18
comps.minute = 19
let date5 = cal.dateFromComponents(comps)!
all.append(Train(type: .Coastal, company: .Southern,
  service: "8307", departureTime: date5))

//sixth train
comps.hour = 22
comps.minute = 11
let date6 = cal.dateFromComponents(comps)!
all.append(Train(type: .Commuter, company: .OldRail,
  service: "6802", departureTime: date6))

  return all

  }

}
```

Move now to the `ComplicationController` class of your watch extension. Here, you will provide watchOS with the data it needs to display your complication. The first task is to extend `CollectionType` so that you can find the next train in the array that the `allTrainsForToday()` function of `DataProvider` returns:

```
extension CollectionType where Generator.Element : OnRailable {

  func nextTrain() -> Generator.Element?{
    let now = NSDate()
    for d in self{
      if now.compare(d.departureTime) == .OrderedAscending{
        return d
      }
    }
    return nil
  }

}
```

And you need a data provider in your complication:

```
class ComplicationController: NSObject, CLKComplicationDataSource {

  let dataProvider = DataProvider()

  ...
```

For every train, you need to create a template that watchOS can display on the screen. All templates are of type `CLKComplicationTemplate`, but don't initialize that class directly. Instead, create a template of type `CLKComplicationTemplateModularLargeS tandardBody` that has a header, two lines of text with the second line being optional, and an optional image. The header will show a constant text (see Figure 2-42), so instantiate it of type `CLKSimpleTextProvider`. For the first line of text, you want to show how many minutes away the next train is, so that would require a text provider of type `CLKRelativeDateTextProvider` as we talked about it before.

The initializer for `CLKRelativeDateTextProvider` takes in a parameter of type `CLKRe lativeDateStyle` that defines the way the given date has to be shown. In our example, we use `CLKRelativeDateStyle.Offset`:

```
func templateForTrain(train: Train) -> CLKComplicationTemplate{
    let template = CLKComplicationTemplateModularLargeStandardBody()
    template.headerTextProvider = CLKSimpleTextProvider(text: "Next train")

    template.body1TextProvider =
      CLKRelativeDateTextProvider(date: train.departureTime,
        style: .Offset,
        units: NSCalendarUnit.Hour.union(.Minute))

    let secondLine = "\(train.service) - \(train.type)"

    template.body2TextProvider = CLKSimpleTextProvider(text: secondLine,
      shortText: train.type.rawValue)

    return template
}
```

 The second line of text we are providing has a `shortText` alternative. If the watch UI has no space to show our `secondLine` text, it will show the `shortText` alternative.

We are going to need to provide timeline entries (date plus template) for every train as well, so let's create a helper method for that:

```
func timelineEntryForTrain(train: Train) -> CLKComplicationTimelineEntry{
    let template = templateForTrain(train)
    return CLKComplicationTimelineEntry(date: train.departureTime,
      complicationTemplate: template)
}
```

When we are asked for the first and the last date of the data we provide, we read our data provider's array of trains and return the first and the last train's dates, respectively:

```
func getTimelineStartDateForComplication(complication: CLKComplication,
  withHandler handler: (NSDate?) -> Void) {
    handler(dataProvider.allTrainsForToday().first!.departureTime)
```

```
}

func getTimelineEndDateForComplication(complication: CLKComplication,
  withHandler handler: (NSDate?) -> Void) {
    handler(dataProvider.allTrainsForToday().last!.departureTime)
}
```

I want to allow the user to be able to time travel so that she can see the next train as she changes the time with the digital crown. I also believe our data is not sensitive, so I'll allow viewing this data on the lock screen:

```
func getSupportedTimeTravelDirectionsForComplication(
  complication: CLKComplication,
  withHandler handler: (CLKComplicationTimeTravelDirections) -> Void) {
    handler([.Forward, .Backward])
}

func getPrivacyBehaviorForComplication(complication: CLKComplication,
  withHandler handler: (CLKComplicationPrivacyBehavior) -> Void) {
    handler(.ShowOnLockScreen)
}
```

Regarding time travel, when asked for trains after and before a certain time, your code should go through all the trains and filter out the times you don't want displayed, as we did in Recipe 2.8:

```
            UU
func getTimelineEntriesForComplication(complication: CLKComplication,
  beforeDate date: NSDate, limit: Int,
  withHandler handler: (([CLKComplicationTimelineEntry]?) -> Void)) {

    let entries = dataProvider.allTrainsForToday().filter{
      date.compare($0.departureTime) == .OrderedDescending
    }.map{
      self.timelineEntryForTrain($0)
    }

    handler(entries)
}

func getTimelineEntriesForComplication(complication: CLKComplication,
  afterDate date: NSDate, limit: Int,
  withHandler handler: (([CLKComplicationTimelineEntry]?) -> Void)) {

    let entries = dataProvider.allTrainsForToday().filter{
      date.compare($0.departureTime) == .OrderedAscending
    }.map{
      self.timelineEntryForTrain($0)
    }

    handler(entries)

}
```

When the `getCurrentTimelineEntryForComplication(_:withHandler:)` method is called on our delegate, we get the next train's timeline entry and return it:

```
func getCurrentTimelineEntryForComplication(complication: CLKComplication,
  withHandler handler: ((CLKComplicationTimelineEntry?) -> Void)) {

    if let train = dataProvider.allTrainsForToday().nextTrain(){
      handler(timelineEntryForTrain(train))
    } else {
      handler(nil)
    }

}
```

Because we provide data until the end of today, we ask watchOS to ask us for new data tomorrow:

```
func getNextRequestedUpdateDateWithHandler(handler: (NSDate?) -> Void) {
  handler(NSDate.endOfToday());
}
```

Last but not least, we provide our placeholder template:

```
func getPlaceholderTemplateForComplication(complication: CLKComplication,
  withHandler handler: (CLKComplicationTemplate?) -> Void) {
    if let data = dataProvider.allTrainsForToday().nextTrain(){
      handler(templateForTrain(data))
    } else {
      handler(nil)
    }
}
```

We saw an example of our app showing the next train (see Figure 2-42), but our app can also participate in time travel (see Figure 2-44). The user can use the digital crown on the watch to move forward or backward and see the next available train at the new time.

Figure 2-44. Moving our complication backward in time

See Also

Recipe 2.7

2.10 Displaying Dates in Complications

Problem

You want to display NSDate instances on your complications.

Solution

Use an instance of the CLKDateTextProvider class, which is a subclass of CLKTextProvider, as your text provider.

> I am going to use CLKComplicationTemplateModularLargeColumns (a modular large template) for this recipe. So configure your watch target to provide only large-modular templates (see Figure 2-43).

Discussion

Let's develop a modular large complication that provides us with the name and the date of the next three public holidays (see Figure 2-45). We are not formatting the date ourselves. We leave it to watchOS to decide how to display the date by using an instance of CLKDateTextProvider.

Figure 2-45. The next three public holidays, with their names and dates

Just as in Recipe 2.8 and Recipe 2.9, we are going to add a new class to our watch app called `DataProvider`. In there, we are going to program all the holidays this year. Let's start off by defining what a holiday object looks like:

```
protocol Holidayable{
  var date: NSDate {get}
  var name: String {get}
}

struct Holiday : Holidayable{
  let date: NSDate
  let name: String
}
```

In our data provider class, we start off by defining some holiday names:

```
struct DataProvider{

  private let holidayNames = [
    "Father's Day",
    "Mother's Day",
    "Bank Holiday",
    "Nobel Day",
    "Man Day",
    "Woman Day",
    "Boyfriend Day",
    "Girlfriend Day",
    "Dog Day",
    "Cat Day",
    "Mouse Day",
    "Cow Day",
  ]
```

```
private func randomDay() -> Int{
  return Int(arc4random_uniform(20) + 1)
}
```

...

Then we move on to providing our instances of Holiday:

```
func allHolidays() -> [Holiday]{

  var all = [Holiday]()

  let now = NSDate()
  let cal = NSCalendar.currentCalendar()
  let units = NSCalendarUnit.Year.union(.Month).union(.Day)
  let comps = cal.components(units, fromDate: now)

  var dates = [NSDate]()

  for month in 1...12{
    comps.day = randomDay()
    comps.month = month
    dates.append(cal.dateFromComponents(comps)!)
  }

  var i = 0
  for date in dates{
    all.append(Holiday(date: date, name: holidayNames[i++]))
  }

  return all

}
```

It's worth noting that the allHolidays() function we just wrote simply goes through all months inside *this* year, and sets the day of the month to a random day. So we will get 12 holidays, one in each month, at a random day inside that month.

Over to our ComplicationController. When we get asked later when we would like to provide more data or updated data to watchOS, we are going to ask for 10 minutes in the future. So if our data changes, watchOS will have a chance to ask us for updated information:

```
extension NSDate{
  func plus10Minutes() -> NSDate{
    return self.dateByAddingTimeInterval(10 * 60)
  }
}
```

Because the template we are going to provide allows a maximum of three items, I would like to have methods on Array to return the second and the third items inside the array, just like the prebuilt first property that the class offers:

```
extension Array{
  var second : Generator.Element?{
    return self.count >= 1 ? self[1] : nil
  }
  var third : Generator.Element?{
    return self.count >= 2 ? self[2] : nil
  }
}
```

DataProvider's allHolidays() method returns 12 holidays. How about extending the built-in array type to always give us the next three holidays? It would have to read today's date, go through the items in our array, compare the dates, and give us just the upcoming three holidays:

```
extension CollectionType where Generator.Element : Holidayable {

  //may contain less than 3 holidays
  func nextThreeHolidays() -> Array<Self.Generator.Element>{
    let now = NSDate()

    let orderedArray = Array(self.filter{
      now.compare($0.date) == .OrderedAscending
    })

    let result = Array(orderedArray[0..<min(orderedArray.count , 3)])

    return result
  }

}
```

Now we start defining our complication:

```
class ComplicationController: NSObject, CLKComplicationDataSource {

  let dataProvider = DataProvider()

  ...
```

We need a method that can take in a Holiday object and give us a template of type CLKComplicationTemplate for that. Our specific template for this recipe is of type CLKComplicationTemplateModularLargeColumns. This template is like a 3 × 3 table. It has three rows and three columns (see Figure 2-45). If we are at the end of the year and we have no more holidays, we return a template that is of type CLKComplication TemplateModularLargeStandardBody and tell the user that there are no more upcoming holidays. Note that both templates have the words "ModularLarge" in their name. Because we have specified in our target setting that we support only modular large templates (see Figure 2-43), this example can return only templates that have those words in their name:

```swift
func templateForHoliday(holiday: Holiday) -> CLKComplicationTemplate{

    let next3Holidays = dataProvider.allHolidays().nextThreeHolidays()

    let headerTitle = "Next 3 Holidays"

    guard next3Holidays.count > 0 else{
        let template = CLKComplicationTemplateModularLargeStandardBody()
        template.headerTextProvider = CLKSimpleTextProvider(text: headerTitle)
        template.body1TextProvider = CLKSimpleTextProvider(text: "Sorry!")
        return template
    }

    let dateUnits = NSCalendarUnit.Month.union(.Day)
    let template = CLKComplicationTemplateModularLargeColumns()

    //first holiday
    if let firstHoliday = next3Holidays.first{
        template.row1Column1TextProvider =
            CLKSimpleTextProvider(text: firstHoliday.name)
        template.row1Column2TextProvider =
            CLKDateTextProvider(date: firstHoliday.date, units: dateUnits)
    }

    //second holiday
    if let secondHoliday = next3Holidays.second{
        template.row2Column1TextProvider =
            CLKSimpleTextProvider(text: secondHoliday.name)
        template.row2Column2TextProvider =
            CLKDateTextProvider(date: secondHoliday.date, units: dateUnits)
    }

    //third holiday
    if let thirdHoliday = next3Holidays.third{
        template.row3Column1TextProvider =
            CLKSimpleTextProvider(text: thirdHoliday.name)
        template.row3Column2TextProvider =
            CLKDateTextProvider(date: thirdHoliday.date, units: dateUnits)
    }

    return template
}
```

You need to provide a timeline entry (date plus template) for your holidays as well:

```swift
func timelineEntryForHoliday(holiday: Holiday) ->
    CLKComplicationTimelineEntry{
    let template = templateForHoliday(holiday)
    return CLKComplicationTimelineEntry(date: holiday.date,
        complicationTemplate: template)
}
```

Also provide the first and the last holidays:

```
func getTimelineStartDateForComplication(complication: CLKComplication,
  withHandler handler: (NSDate?) -> Void) {
    handler(dataProvider.allHolidays().first!.date)
}

func getTimelineEndDateForComplication(complication: CLKComplication,
  withHandler handler: (NSDate?) -> Void) {
    handler(dataProvider.allHolidays().last!.date)
}
```

Also support time travel and provide your content on the lock screen, because it is not private:

```
func getSupportedTimeTravelDirectionsForComplication(
  complication: CLKComplication,
  withHandler handler: (CLKComplicationTimeTravelDirections) -> Void) {
    handler([.Forward, .Backward])
}

func getPrivacyBehaviorForComplication(complication: CLKComplication,
  withHandler handler: (CLKComplicationPrivacyBehavior) -> Void) {
    handler(.ShowOnLockScreen)
}
```

Now let's give watchOS information about previous and upcoming holidays:

```
func getTimelineEntriesForComplication(complication: CLKComplication,
  beforeDate date: NSDate, limit: Int,
  withHandler handler: (([CLKComplicationTimelineEntry]?) -> Void)) {

    let entries = dataProvider.allHolidays().filter{
      date.compare($0.date) == .OrderedDescending
    }.map{
      self.timelineEntryForHoliday($0)
    }

    handler(entries)
}

func getTimelineEntriesForComplication(complication: CLKComplication,
  afterDate date: NSDate, limit: Int,
  withHandler handler: (([CLKComplicationTimelineEntry]?) -> Void)) {

    let entries = dataProvider.allHolidays().filter{
      date.compare($0.date) == .OrderedAscending
    }.map{
      self.timelineEntryForHoliday($0)
    }

    handler(entries)

}
```

Last but not least, provide the upcoming three holidays when you are asked to provide them *now*:

```
func getCurrentTimelineEntryForComplication(complication: CLKComplication,
  withHandler handler: ((CLKComplicationTimelineEntry?) -> Void)) {

    if let first = dataProvider.allHolidays().nextThreeHolidays().first{
      handler(timelineEntryForHoliday(first))
    } else {
      handler(nil)
    }

}

func getNextRequestedUpdateDateWithHandler(handler: (NSDate?) -> Void) {
  handler(NSDate().plus10Minutes());
}

func getPlaceholderTemplateForComplication(complication: CLKComplication,
  withHandler handler: (CLKComplicationTemplate?) -> Void) {
    if let holiday = dataProvider.allHolidays().nextThreeHolidays().first{
      handler(templateForHoliday(holiday))
    } else {
      handler(nil)
    }
}
```

See Also

Recipe 2.7 and Recipe 2.9

2.11 Displaying Times in Complications

Problem

You want to display a time on your watch UI and want it to look good regardless of available space on the watch.

Solution

Provide your time (in form of NSDate) to an instance of CLKTimeTextProvider and use it inside a template (see Figure 2-46). Our large and modular complication on the center of the screen is showing the next pause that we can take at work, which happens to be a coffee pause.

Figure 2-46. The time is displayed on the screen using an instance of CLKTime-TextProvider

 In this recipe, we are going to rely a lot on what we have learned in Recipe 2.8 and other complication recipes in this chapter. I suggest reading Recipe 2.8 at least to get an idea of how our data provider works. Otherwise, you will still be able to read this recipe; however, I will skip over some details that I've already explained in Recipe 2.8.

Discussion

This recipe uses a large-modular template, so make sure that your project is set up for that (see Figure 2-43). Here, I want to build an app that shows the different breaks or pauses that I can take at work, and when they occur: for instance, when the first pause is after I get to work, when lunch happens, when the next pause between lunch and dinner is, and if I want to have dinner as well, when that should happen.

So we have breaks at work and we need to define them. Create a Swift file in your watch extension and call it *DataProvider*. In there, define your break:

```swift
import Foundation

protocol Pausable{
  var name: String {get}
  var date: NSDate {get}
}

struct PauseAtWork : Pausable{
  let name: String
  let date: NSDate
}
```

Now in your `DataProvider` structure, create four pauses that we can take at work at different times and provide them as an array:

```
struct DataProvider{

  func allPausesToday() -> [PauseAtWork]{

    var all = [PauseAtWork]()

    let now = NSDate()
    let cal = NSCalendar.currentCalendar()
    let units = NSCalendarUnit.Year.union(.Month).union(.Day)
    let comps = cal.components(units, fromDate: now)
    comps.calendar = cal
    comps.minute = 30

    comps.hour = 11
    all.append(PauseAtWork(name: "Coffee", date: comps.date!))

    comps.minute = 30
    comps.hour = 14
    all.append(PauseAtWork(name: "Lunch", date: comps.date!))

    comps.minute = 0
    comps.hour = 16
    all.append(PauseAtWork(name: "Tea", date: comps.date!))

    comps.hour = 17
    all.append(PauseAtWork(name: "Dinner", date: comps.date!))

    return all

  }

}
```

Here we have just obtained the date and time of today and then gone from coffee break in the morning to dinner in the evening, adding each pause to the array. The method is called `allPausesToday()` and we are going to invoke it from our watch complication.

Before, we created a protocol called `Pausable` and now we have all our pauses in an array. When we are asked to provide a template for the next pause to show in the complication, we have to get the current time and find the pause whose time is after the current time. So let's bundle that up by extending `CollectionType` like we have done in other recipes in this chapter:

```
extension CollectionType where Generator.Element : Pausable {

  func nextPause() -> Self.Generator.Element?{
    let now = NSDate()
```

```
      for pause in self{
        if now.compare(pause.date) == .OrderedAscending{
          return pause
        }
      }

      return nil
    }

}
```

In our complication now, we instantiate our data provider:

```
class ComplicationController: NSObject, CLKComplicationDataSource {

  let dataProvider = DataProvider()

  ...
```

For every pause that we want to display to the user (see Figure 2-46), we need to provide a template of type CLKComplicationTemplate to the runtime. We never instantiate that class directly. Instead, we return an instance of a subclass of that class. In this particular example, we display an instance of CLKComplicationTemplateModularLargeTallBody. However, if there are no more pauses to take at work (e.g., if time is 21:00 and we are no longer at work), we display a placeholder to the user to tell her there are no more pauses. The template for that is of type CLKComplicationTemplateModularLargeStandardBody. The difference between the two templates is visible if you read their names. We set the time on our template by setting the bodyTextProvider property of our CLKComplicationTemplateModularLargeTallBody instance:

```
func templateForPause(pause: PauseAtWork) -> CLKComplicationTemplate{

  guard let nextPause = dataProvider.allPausesToday().nextPause() else{
    let template = CLKComplicationTemplateModularLargeStandardBody()
    template.headerTextProvider = CLKSimpleTextProvider(text: "Next Break")
    template.body1TextProvider = CLKSimpleTextProvider(text: "None")
    return template
  }

  let template = CLKComplicationTemplateModularLargeTallBody()
  template.headerTextProvider = CLKSimpleTextProvider(text: nextPause.name)
  template.bodyTextProvider = CLKTimeTextProvider(date: nextPause.date)

  return template
}
```

We also have to provide some of the other delegate methods of CLKComplicationDataSource, such as the timeline entry (date plus template) for every pause that we can take at work. We also need to support time travel for this example. On top of that, our information is not sensitive, so when asked whether we want to display our complication on the lock screen, we happily say yes:

```swift
func timelineEntryForPause(pause: PauseAtWork) ->
  CLKComplicationTimelineEntry{
  let template = templateForPause(pause)
  return CLKComplicationTimelineEntry(date: pause.date,
    complicationTemplate: template)
}

func getSupportedTimeTravelDirectionsForComplication(
  complication: CLKComplication,
  withHandler handler: (CLKComplicationTimeTravelDirections) -> Void) {
    handler([.Forward, .Backward])
}

func getPrivacyBehaviorForComplication(complication: CLKComplication,
  withHandler handler: (CLKComplicationPrivacyBehavior) -> Void) {
    handler(.ShowOnLockScreen)
}
```

When asked the beginning and the end range of dates for our complications, we will return the dates for the first and the last pause that we want to take at work *today*. Remember, in this complication, we will return *all* the pauses that we can take at work today. When the time comes to display the pauses to take at work tomorrow, we will provide a whole set of new pauses:

```swift
func getTimelineStartDateForComplication(complication: CLKComplication,
  withHandler handler: (NSDate?) -> Void) {
    handler(dataProvider.allPausesToday().first!.date)
}

func getTimelineEndDateForComplication(complication: CLKComplication,
  withHandler handler: (NSDate?) -> Void) {
    handler(dataProvider.allPausesToday().last!.date)
}
```

When the runtime calls the getTimelineEntriesForComplication(_:before Date:limit:withHandler:) method, provide all the pauses that are available *before* the given date:

```swift
func getTimelineEntriesForComplication(complication: CLKComplication,
  beforeDate date: NSDate, limit: Int,
  withHandler handler: (([CLKComplicationTimelineEntry]?) -> Void)) {

    let entries = dataProvider.allPausesToday().filter{
      date.compare($0.date) == .OrderedDescending
    }.map{
      self.timelineEntryForPause($0)
    }
```

```
      handler(entries)
  }
```

Similarly, when the getTimelineEntriesForComplication(_:after
Date:limit:withHandler:) method is called, return all the available pauses *after* the
given date:

```
func getTimelineEntriesForComplication(complication: CLKComplication,
  afterDate date: NSDate, limit: Int,
  withHandler handler: (([CLKComplicationTimelineEntry]?) -> Void)) {

    let entries = dataProvider.allPausesToday().filter{
      date.compare($0.date) == .OrderedAscending
    }.map{
      self.timelineEntryForPause($0)
    }

    handler(entries)

}
```

In the getCurrentTimelineEntryForComplication(_:withHandler:) method, you
will be asked to provide the template for the current data (the next pause) to show on
screen. We already have a method on CollectionType called nextPause(), so let's use
that to provide a template to watchOS:

```
func getCurrentTimelineEntryForComplication(complication: CLKComplication,
  withHandler handler: ((CLKComplicationTimelineEntry?) -> Void)) {

    if let pause = dataProvider.allPausesToday().nextPause(){
      handler(timelineEntryForPause(pause))
    } else {
      handler(nil)
    }

}
```

Because, in a typical watch app, our data would probably come from a backend, we
would like the runtime to task us for up-to-date information as soon as possible, but
not too soon. So let's do that after 10 minutes:

```
func getNextRequestedUpdateDateWithHandler(handler: (NSDate?) -> Void) {
  handler(NSDate().plus10Minutes());
}
```

Last but not least, we also need to provide a placeholder template when the user is
adding our complication to her watch face:

```
func getPlaceholderTemplateForComplication(complication: CLKComplication,
  withHandler handler: (CLKComplicationTemplate?) -> Void) {
    if let pause = dataProvider.allPausesToday().nextPause(){
      handler(templateForPause(pause))
    } else {
```

```
        handler(nil)
      }
  }
```

See Also

Recipe 2.9 and Recipe 2.11

2.12 Displaying Time Intervals in Complications

Problem

You want to display a time interval (start date–end date) on your watchOS UI (see Figure 2-47). Our template shows today's meetings on the screen. Right now, it's brunch time, so the screen shows the description and location of where we are going to have brunch, along with the time interval of the brunch (start–end).

Figure 2-47. Meeting with start and end times

Solution

Use an instance of `CLKTimeIntervalTextProvider` as your text provider (see Figure 2-47).

  I will base this recipe on other recipes such as Recipe 2.10 and Recipe 2.11.

Discussion

Let's say that we want to have an app that shows us all our meetings today. Every meeting has the following properties:

- Start and end times (the time interval)
- Name (e.g., "Brunch with Sarah")
- Location

Because text providers of type CLKSimpleTextProvider accept a short text in addition to the full text, we also have a short version of the location and the name. For instance, the location can be "Stockholm Central Train Station," whereas the short version of this could be "Central Station" or even "Centralen" in Swedish, which means the center. So let's define this meeting object:

```
protocol Timable{
  var name: String {get}
  var shortName: String {get}
  var location: String {get}
  var shortLocation: String {get}
  var startDate: NSDate {get}
  var endDate: NSDate {get}
  var previous: Timable? {get}
}

struct Meeting : Timable{
  let name: String
  let shortName: String
  let location: String
  let shortLocation: String
  let startDate: NSDate
  let endDate: NSDate
  let previous: Timable?
}
```

Create a Swift file in your project called *DataProvider*. Put all the meetings for today in there and return an array:

```
struct DataProvider{

  func allMeetingsToday() -> [Meeting]{

    var all = [Meeting]()

    let oneHour: NSTimeInterval = 1 * 60.0 * 60

    let now = NSDate()
    let cal = NSCalendar.currentCalendar()
    let units = NSCalendarUnit.Year.union(.Month).union(.Day)
    let comps = cal.components(units, fromDate: now)
    comps.calendar = cal
```

```
        comps.minute = 30

        comps.hour = 11
        let meeting1 = Meeting(name: "Brunch with Sarah", shortName: "Brunch",
            location: "Stockholm Central", shortLocation: "Central",
            startDate: comps.date!,
            endDate: comps.date!.dateByAddingTimeInterval(oneHour), previous: nil)
        all.append(meeting1)

        comps.minute = 30
        comps.hour = 14
        let meeting2 = Meeting(name: "Lunch with Gabriella", shortName: "Lunch",
            location: "At home", shortLocation: "Home",
            startDate: comps.date!,
            endDate: comps.date!.dateByAddingTimeInterval(oneHour),
            previous: meeting1)
        all.append(meeting2)

        comps.minute = 0
        comps.hour = 16
        let meeting3 = Meeting(name: "Snack with Leif", shortName: "Snack",
            location: "Flags Cafe", shortLocation: "Flags",
            startDate: comps.date!,
            endDate: comps.date!.dateByAddingTimeInterval(oneHour),
            previous: meeting2)
        all.append(meeting3)

        comps.hour = 17
        let meeting4 = Meeting(name: "Dinner with Family", shortName: "Dinner",
            location: "At home", shortLocation: "Home",
            startDate: comps.date!,
            endDate: comps.date!.dateByAddingTimeInterval(oneHour),
            previous: meeting3)
        all.append(meeting4)

        return all

    }

}
```

In your complication class, extend `CollectionType` so that it can return the upcoming meeting:

```
extension CollectionType where Generator.Element : Timable {

    func nextMeeting() -> Self.Generator.Element?{
        let now = NSDate()

        for meeting in self{
            if now.compare(meeting.startDate) == .OrderedAscending{
                return meeting
            }
```

```
        }

      return nil
    }

  }
```

 I have extended CollectionType, but only if the items are Timable. I explained this technique in Recipe 1.12.

In your complication handler, create an instance of the data provider:

```
class ComplicationController: NSObject, CLKComplicationDataSource {

  let dataProvider = DataProvider()


  ...
```

Our template is of type CLKComplicationTemplateModularLargeStandardBody, which has a few important properties that we set as follows:

headerTextProvider
> Shows the time range for the meeting.

body1TextProvider
> Shows the name of the meeting.

body2TextProvider
> Shows the location of the meeting.

To display the time range of the meeting, instantiate CLKTimeIntervalTextProvider:

```
    func templateForMeeting(meeting: Meeting) -> CLKComplicationTemplate{

      let template = CLKComplicationTemplateModularLargeStandardBody()

      guard let nextMeeting = dataProvider.allMeetingsToday().nextMeeting() else{
        template.headerTextProvider = CLKSimpleTextProvider(text: "Next Break")
        template.body1TextProvider = CLKSimpleTextProvider(text: "None")
        return template
      }

      template.headerTextProvider =
        CLKTimeIntervalTextProvider(startDate: nextMeeting.startDate,
          endDate: nextMeeting.endDate)

      template.body1TextProvider =
        CLKSimpleTextProvider(text: nextMeeting.name,
          shortText: nextMeeting.shortName)
```

```
template.body2TextProvider =
  CLKSimpleTextProvider(text: nextMeeting.location,
    shortText: nextMeeting.shortLocation)

  return template
}
```

Using this method, you can also create timeline entries (date plus template). In this example, I set every new event's start date to the end date of the previous event (if it is available). That way, as soon as the current ongoing meeting ends, the next meeting shows up on the list:

 If the event has no previous events, its timeline entry date will be its start date, instead of the end date of the previous event.

```
func timelineEntryForMeeting(meeting: Meeting) -> CLKComplicationTimelineEntry{
  let template = templateForMeeting(meeting)

  let date = meeting.previous?.endDate ?? meeting.startDate
  return CLKComplicationTimelineEntry(date: date,
    complicationTemplate: template)
}
```

Let's also participate in time travel and show our content on the lock screen as well:

```
func getSupportedTimeTravelDirectionsForComplication(
  complication: CLKComplication,
  withHandler handler: (CLKComplicationTimeTravelDirections) -> Void) {
    handler([.Forward, .Backward])
}

func getPrivacyBehaviorForComplication(complication: CLKComplication,
  withHandler handler: (CLKComplicationPrivacyBehavior) -> Void) {
    handler(.ShowOnLockScreen)
}
```

Then we have to provide the date range for which we have available meetings. The start of the range is the start date of the first meeting and the end date is the end date of the last meeting:

```
func getTimelineStartDateForComplication(complication: CLKComplication,
  withHandler handler: (NSDate?) -> Void) {
    handler(dataProvider.allMeetingsToday().first!.startDate)
}

func getTimelineEndDateForComplication(complication: CLKComplication,
  withHandler handler: (NSDate?) -> Void) {
```

```
        handler(dataProvider.allMeetingsToday().last!.endDate)
    }
```

We'll also be asked to provide all the available meetings before a certain date, so let's do that:

```
func getTimelineEntriesForComplication(complication: CLKComplication,
  beforeDate date: NSDate, limit: Int,
  withHandler handler: (([CLKComplicationTimelineEntry]?) -> Void)) {

    let entries = dataProvider.allMeetingsToday().filter{
      date.compare($0.startDate) == .OrderedDescending
    }.map{
      self.timelineEntryForMeeting($0)
    }

    handler(entries)
}
```

Similarly, we have to provide all our available meetings after a given date:

```
func getTimelineEntriesForComplication(complication: CLKComplication,
  afterDate date: NSDate, limit: Int,
  withHandler handler: (([CLKComplicationTimelineEntry]?) -> Void)) {

    let entries = dataProvider.allMeetingsToday().filter{
      date.compare($0.startDate) == .OrderedAscending
    }.map{
      self.timelineEntryForMeeting($0)
    }

    handler(entries)

}
```

Last but not least, provide your placeholder template, the template for now, and the next time we would like watchOS to ask us for updated information:

```
func getCurrentTimelineEntryForComplication(complication: CLKComplication,
  withHandler handler: ((CLKComplicationTimelineEntry?) -> Void)) {

    if let meeting = dataProvider.allMeetingsToday().nextMeeting(){
      handler(timelineEntryForMeeting(meeting))
    } else {
      handler(nil)
    }

}

func getNextRequestedUpdateDateWithHandler(handler: (NSDate?) -> Void) {
  handler(NSDate().plus10Minutes());
}

func getPlaceholderTemplateForComplication(complication: CLKComplication,
```

```
withHandler handler: (CLKComplicationTemplate?) -> Void) {
  if let pause = dataProvider.allMeetingsToday().nextMeeting(){
    handler(templateForMeeting(pause))
  } else {
    handler(nil)
  }
}
```

 We coded the `plus10Minutes()` method on `NSDate` in Recipe 2.10.

See Also

Recipe 2.9, Recipe 2.11, and Recipe 2.12

2.13 Recording Audio in Your Watch App

Problem

You want to allow your users to record audio while inside your watch app, and you want to get access to the recorded audio.

Solution

Use the `presentAudioRecorderControllerWithOutputURL(_:preset:options:com pletion:)` method of your `WKInterfaceController` class to present a system dialog that can take care of audio recording. If you want to dismiss the dialog, use the `dis missAudioRecordingController()` method of your controller.

The options parameter of the `presentAudioRecorderControllerWithOutpu tURL(_:preset:options:completion:)` method accepts a dictionary that can contain the following keys:

`WKAudioRecorderControllerOptionsActionTitleKey`
   This key, of type `String`, will be the title of our recorder.

`WKAudioRecorderControllerOptionsAlwaysShowActionTitleKey`
   This key, of type `NSNumber`, contains a `Bool` value to dictates whether the title should always be shown on the recorder.

`WKAudioRecorderControllerOptionsAutorecordKey`
   This key, of type `NSNumber`, contains a `Bool` value to indicate whether recording should begin automatically when the dialog is presented.

`WKAudioRecorderControllerOptionsMaximumDurationKey`

This key, of type `NSNumber`, contains an `NSTimeInterval` value to dictate the maximum duration of the audio content.

Discussion

For this recipe, we are going to create a watch app whose UI looks like that shown in Figure 2-48). It holds a label to show our current status (started recording, failed recording, etc.) and a button that, upon pressing, can show our recording dialog.

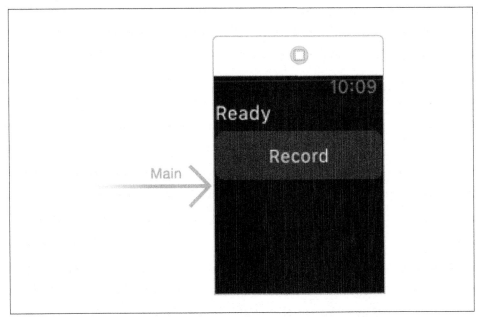

Figure 2-48. Label for status and button

Hook the label up to your code with the name `statusLbl`. Then hook your record button to your interface under a method named `record()`. Your interface code should look like this now:

```
class InterfaceController: WKInterfaceController {

@IBOutlet var statusLbl: WKInterfaceLabel!

...
```

Define the URL where your recording will be saved:

```
var url: NSURL{
  let fm = NSFileManager()
  let url = try! fm.URLForDirectory(NSSearchPathDirectory.MusicDirectory,
    inDomain: NSSearchPathDomainMask.UserDomainMask,
```

```
      appropriateForURL: nil, create: true)
      .URLByAppendingPathComponent("recording")
    return url
}
```

Also, because the completion block of our recording screen might not get called on the main thread, create a variable that can set the text inside our status label on the main thread:

```
var status = ""{
  willSet{
    dispatch_async(dispatch_get_main_queue()){
      self.statusLbl.setText(newValue)
    }
  }
}
```

When your record button is pressed, construct your options for the recording:

```
let oneMinute: NSTimeInterval = 1 * 60

let yes = NSNumber(bool: true)
let no = NSNumber(bool: false)

let options = [
  WKAudioRecorderControllerOptionsActionTitleKey : "Audio Recorder",
  WKAudioRecorderControllerOptionsAlwaysShowActionTitleKey : yes,
  WKAudioRecorderControllerOptionsAutorecordKey : no,
  WKAudioRecorderControllerOptionsMaximumDurationKey : oneMinute
]
```

Last but not least, present your audio recorder to the user and then set the status accordingly:

```
presentAudioRecorderControllerWithOutputURL(url,
  preset: WKAudioRecorderPreset.WideBandSpeech,
  options: options){
    success, error in

    defer{
      self.dismissAudioRecorderController()
    }

    guard success && error == nil else{
      self.status = "Failed to record"
      return
    }

    self.status = "Successfully recorded"

}
```

See Also

Recipe 12.3

2.14 Playing Local and Remote Audio and Video in Your Watch App

Problem

You want to play audio or video files, whether they are saved locally or online.

Solution

Use the `presentMediaPlayerControllerWithURL(_:options:completion:)` instance method of your interface controller (`WKInterfaceController`). Close the media player with the `dismissMediaPlayerController()` method.

Discussion

The first parameter to this method is just the URL from which the media must be loaded. The `options` parameter is a dictionary that can have the following keys:

WKMediaPlayerControllerOptionsAutoplayKey
:   A boolean value (wrapped inside an `NSNumber` instance) that dictates whether the media should autoplay when it is opened. This is set to `false` by default.

WKMediaPlayerControllerOptionsStartTimeKey
:   The number of seconds (of type `NSTimeInterval`) into the media where you want to start it.

WKMediaPlayerControllerOptionsVideoGravityKey
:   A value of type `WKVideoGravity` (place its raw integer value in your dictionary) that dictates the scaling of the video. You can, for instance, specify `WKVideoGravity.Resi zeAspectFill`.

WKMediaPlayerControllerOptionsLoopsKey
:   A boolean value (wrapped inside `NSNumber`) that specifies whether the media has to loop automatically. The default is `false`.

For this recipe, we are going to create a UI similar to that in Recipe 2.13 (see Figure 2-48). Our UI looks like Figure 2-49.

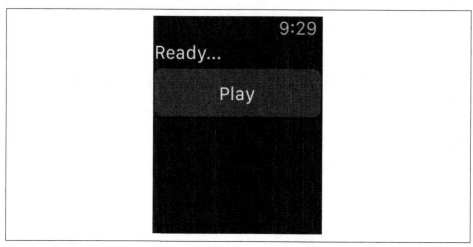

Figure 2-49. Label to show the current status, and a button to start the playback

Hook up the label to an outlet called `statusLbl` and the action of the button to a method called `play()`. Then create a variable in your code called `status` of type `String`, just as we did in Recipe 2.13. In the `play` method, first construct your URL:

```
guard let url = NSURL(string: "http://localhost:8888/video.mp4") else{
    status = "Could not create url"
    return
}
```

I am running MAMP (free version) on my computer and I'm hosting a video called *video.mp4*. You can download lots of public domain files by just searching online.

Now construct your options dictionary. I want the media player to do the following:

- Autoplay my video
- Loop the video
- Resize the video so that it fills the entire screen
- Start at 4 seconds into the video:

```
let gravity = WKVideoGravity.ResizeAspectFill.rawValue

let options = [
  WKMediaPlayerControllerOptionsAutoplayKey : NSNumber(bool: true),
  WKMediaPlayerControllerOptionsStartTimeKey : 4.0 as NSTimeInterval,
  WKMediaPlayerControllerOptionsVideoGravityKey : gravity,
  WKMediaPlayerControllerOptionsLoopsKey : NSNumber(bool: true),
]
```

Now start the media player and handle any possible errors:

```
presentMediaPlayerControllerWithURL(url, options: options) {
  didPlayToEnd, endTime, error in

  self.dismissMediaPlayerController()

  guard error == nil else{
    self.status = "Error occurred \(error)"
    return
  }

  if didPlayToEnd{
    self.status = "Played to end of the file"
  } else {
    self.status = "Did not play to end of file. End time = \(endTime)"
  }

}
```

See Also

Recipe 12.3 and Recipe 2.13

CHAPTER 3

The User Interface

Apple has added quite a few things to UIKit in iOS 9 worth knowing about. One of my favorites is stacked views. We'll check them out soon. We will also have a look at content sizes, unwind segues, layout guides, and more.

3.1 Arranging Your Components Horizontally or Vertically

Problem

You have vertical or horizontal view hierarchies that you find cumbersome to manage with constraints.

Solution

Stacked views are the solution.

Discussion

Imagine that you want to create a view that looks like Figure 3-1.

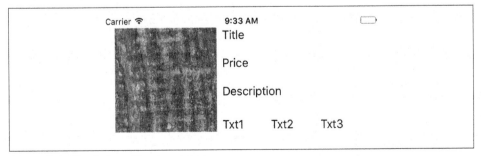

Figure 3-1. Vertical and horizontal views

Prior to Xcode 7 and its stacked views, we had to set up massive amounts of constraints just to achieve a simple layout like Figure 3-1. Well, no more. Let's head to IB and drop an image view, three labels arranged vertically, and three arranged horizontally, like the previous figure. Our image and labels look initially like Figure 3-2.

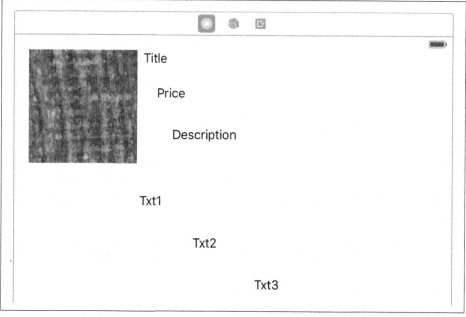

Figure 3-2. Stacked images

Grab the top three labels and press the little Stack button at the bottom of IB as shown in Figure 3-3.

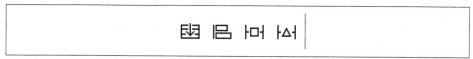

Figure 3-3. The stack button is the leftmost button

Now you will notice that your components are aligned as you wanted them. Now select the top stack (your vertical components). Then, from the Attributes inspector, under Spacing, choose 20. Then select your horizontal group and do the same. Bring your horizontal group up and align it to the bottom of the image view to end up with something like Figure 3-1.

See Also

Recipe 3.3, Recipe 3.2, and Recipe 3.7

3.2 Customizing Stack Views for Different Screen Sizes

Problem

You want to customize the way your stack views appear on the screen, based on the screen size they are running on.

Solution

Use size class customization features of Xcode, right in the Attributes inspector.

Discussion

You might have noticed tiny + buttons in various places inside IB. But what are they? Have you used them before? If not, you are missing out on a lot and I'm going to show you how to take advantage of them.

Size classes are encapsulated information about the dimensions of the current screen: possible values are regular, compact, and any. These sizes have been defined to stop us from thinking in terms of pixels. You either have a regular size or compact size.

Imagine your iPhone 6+ in portrait mode. The screen width is compact, and the screen height is regular. Once you go to landscape mode, your screen width is regular and your height is compact. Now imagine an iPad in portrait mode. Your screen width is regular and so is your height. Landscape, ditto.

Let's work on a project to get the idea more clearly. I want us to achieve the effect shown in Figure 3-4 when running our app on iPhone in portrait mode.

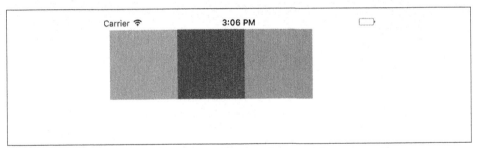

Figure 3-4. In portrait, our views have no spacing between them

And when we go to landscape, I want us to have 10 points spacing between the items, but only when the height of the screen is compact (Figure 3-5).

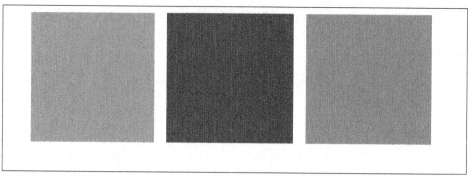

Figure 3-5. With compact screen height, we want spacing to be applied between our views

We get started by creating three colorful views on our main storyboard. I leave the colors to you to decide. Select all your views and then press the little stack button (Figure 3-3) in IB to group your views horizontally. Then place your stacked view on the top left of the view with proper top and left margin spacing (see Figure 3-6).

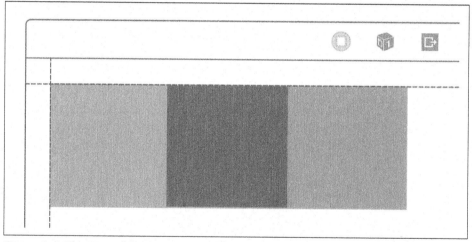

Figure 3-6. The IB guidelines appear when the view is on top left of the super view

Once done, make sure your stacked view is the selected view and then press the Resolve Auto Layout issues button (the rightmost button in Figure 3-3). Under Selected Views, choose "Reset to Suggested Constraints."

Now choose your stack view. In the Attributes inspector, under the Spacing section, find the little + button and press it. In the popup, choose Any Width and then under that choose Compact Height. This will give you an additional text field to write the desired spacing value for any screen width while the height of the screen is compact. Put the value of 10 in this box (see Figure 3-7).

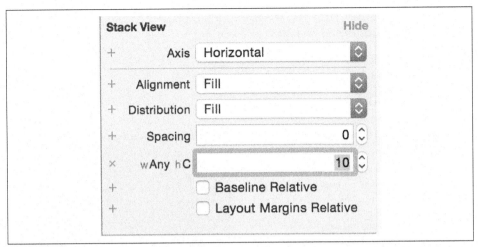

Figure 3-7. Place the value of 10 in the new text box

If you run your app on an iPhone 6+ and then switch to landscape, you *won't* see any spacing between the items—so what happened? The problem is that in landscape mode, we are not increasing the width of our stack view. It doesn't currently have extra width to show the spaces between the views. To account for this, let's first add a normal width constraint to our stack view. You can do that by selecting the stack view in the list of views that you have, holding down the Control button on your keyboard, and dragging from the stack view to the stack view itself. You will now get a popup. Choose Width in this popup (see Figure 3-8).

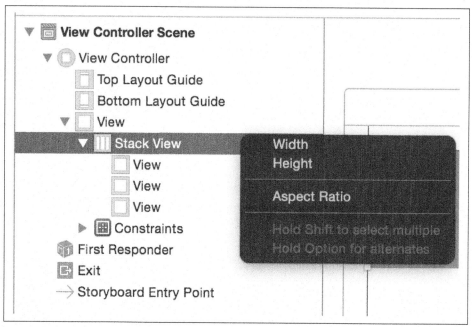

Figure 3-8. Choose the Width option in the popup to add a width constraint to the stack view

While your stack view is selected, go to the Size inspector and double-click the Width constraint that we just created. This will allow you to edit this constraint with size classes. How awesome is that? Next to the Constant text box, I can see the value of 300. You might see a different value based on the width of the views you placed in your stack view. My views were each 100 points wide, hence x3 comes to 300 points. I can also see a little + button next to the Constant box. Press that button and add a new constant for "Any Width and Compact Height" and set the value to N+20, where N is the value of your current constant. For me N is 300, so I'll enter the value of 320 in the new box (see Figure 3-9).

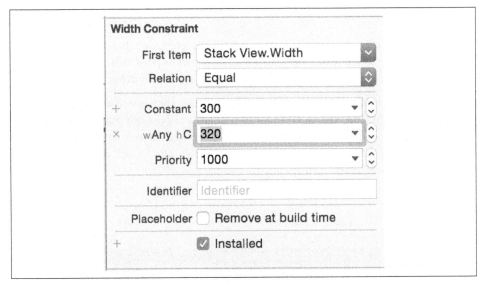

Figure 3-9. Add a new width constant class to the stack view

There is one more thing that we need to tell the stack view in order for it to stack our views correctly when its width changes. Select the stack view and, in attributes inspector, under the Distribution section, change the default value to Equal Spacing. Now run your app and enjoy the awesomeness that you just created. Rotate from portrait to landscape under any iPhone simulator (not iPad).

See Also

Recipe 3.1

3.3 Creating Anchored Constraints in Code

Problem

You want your code to use the same layout anchors that IB uses.

Solution

Start using the new anchor properties on `UIView`, such as `leadingAnchor` and `trailingAnchor`.

Discussion

Layout anchors are very useful for arranging your components on the screen. Let's say that you have two buttons on your view, arranged horizontally, and you want the second button to be placed 10 points to the right of the first button.

First create two buttons on your view using IB and then place them next to each other, horizontally. The horizontal space between them does not matter so much right now. Then select both of them and in the Resolve Auto Layout issues button (rightmost button in Figure 3-3), under the Selected Views, choose the Add Missing Constraints option (see Figure 3-10).

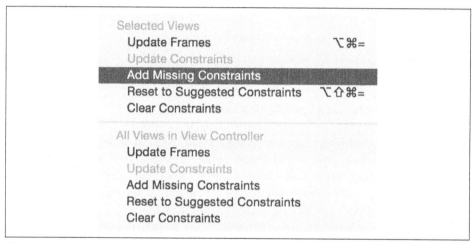

Figure 3-10. Adding the missing constraints to our buttons

Then select the second button (on the right). Under the Size inspector, find the "Leading Space to" constraint, double-click it, and choose the "Remove at build time" option (see Figure 3-11). This will make sure that the leading constraint, which we are going to create in code, will be present in IB while checking things out, but that during the project run the constraint will be removed, giving us the ability to replace it.

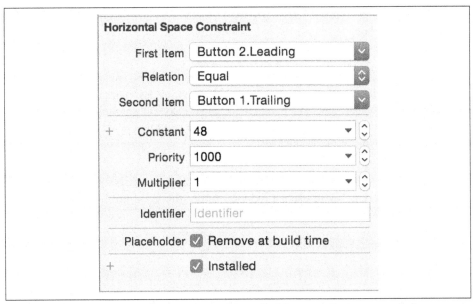

Figure 3-11. Removing the leading constraint at build time will give us a window to replace it at runtime

Now link your buttons into your code with names such as `btn1` and `btn2`. In the `view DidLoad` method of your view controller, write the following code:

```
override func viewDidLoad() {
  super.viewDidLoad()

  btn2.leadingAnchor.constraintEqualToAnchor(btn1.trailingAnchor,
    constant: 10).active = true

}
```

Now run your app and see how your second button is trailing your first button horizontally with a 10-point space between them. You can use the following anchors in your views:

- `bottomAnchor`
- `centerXAnchor`
- `centerYAnchor`
- `firstBaselineAnchor`
- `heightAnchor`
- `lastBaselineAnchor`
- `leadingAnchor`
- `leftAnchor`
- `rightAnchor`

- topAnchor
- trailingAnchor
- widthAnchor

 All of these anchors are direct or indirect subclasses of the NSLayou tAnchor class. The horizontal anchors specifically are subclasses of the NSLayoutXAxisAnchor class and the vertical ones are subclasses of NSLayoutYAxisAnchor.

Now, just to play with some more anchors, let's create a view hierarchy like the one in Figure 3-12. We are going to place a red view under the first button and set the width of this view to the width of the button in our code.

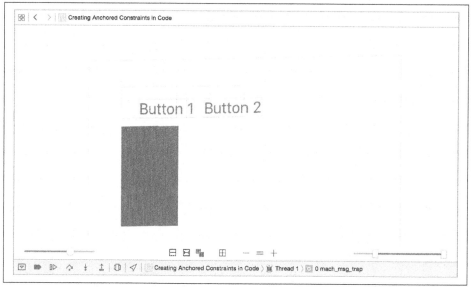

Figure 3-12. Two buttons and a view

In IB, drag and drop a view onto your main view and set the background color of it to red so that you can see it better. Drag and drop it so that it is aligned under the two buttons with proper left and top margins (see Figure 3-13).

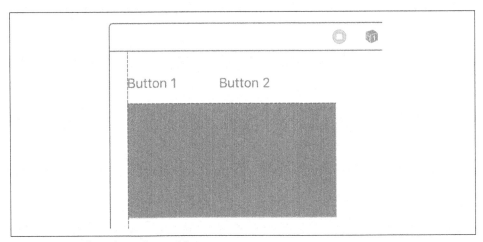

Figure 3-13. Align the red view like so

Anchor the views as follows:

1. Select the red view.
2. In IB, choose the Resolve Auto Layout issues button.
3. Under the Selected View section, choose Add Missing Constraints.
4. Go to the Size inspector. For the red view, find the "Trailing Space to" constraint and delete it by selecting it and pressing the delete button.
5. Select the red button in the view hierarchy, hold down the Control button on your keyboard, and drag and drop the button into itself.
6. A menu will appear. In the menu, choose Width to create a width constraint. Then find the new width constraint in the Size inspector, double-click it, and choose the "Remove at build time" option (see Figure 3-14).

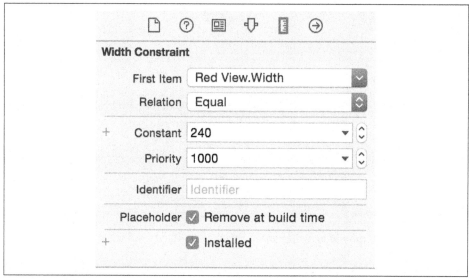

Figure 3-14. Remove the automatically built width constraint at build time so that we can replace it in code

Now create an outlet for this red view in your code (I've named mine "v") and add the following code to your viewDidLoad()method:

```
v.widthAnchor.constraintEqualToAnchor(btn2.widthAnchor,
    constant:0).active = true
```

See Also

Recipe 3.4

3.4 Allowing Users to Enter Text in Response to Local and Remote Notifications

Problem

You want to allow your users to enter some text in response to local or push notifications that you display. And you would additionally like to be able to read this text in your app and take action on it.

Solution

Set the new behavior property of the UIUserNotificationAction class to .TextInput (with a leading period).

Discussion

Let's say that we want our app to register for local notifications and then ask the user for her name once the app has been sent to the background. The user enters her name and then we come to the foreground and take action on that name.

We start by writing a method that allows us to register for local notifications:

```
func registerForNotifications(){

    let enterInfo = UIMutableUserNotificationAction()
    enterInfo.identifier = "enter"
    enterInfo.title = "Enter your name"
    enterInfo.behavior = .TextInput //this is the key to this example
    enterInfo.activationMode = .Foreground

    let cancel = UIMutableUserNotificationAction()
    cancel.identifier = "cancel"
    cancel.title = "Cancel"

    let category = UIMutableUserNotificationCategory()
    category.identifier = "texted"
    category.setActions([enterInfo, cancel], forContext: .Default)

    let settings = UIUserNotificationSettings(
        forTypes: .Alert, categories: [category])

    UIApplication.sharedApplication()
        .registerUserNotificationSettings(settings)

}
```

We set the `behavior` property on the `UIMutableUserNotificationAction` instance to `.TextInput` to allow this particular action to receive text input from the user. Now we will move on to calling this method when our app is launched:

```
func application(application: UIApplication,
    didFinishLaunchingWithOptions
    launchOptions: [NSObject : AnyObject]?) -> Bool {

    registerForNotifications()

    return true
}
```

We also need a method to schedule a local notification whenever asked for:

```
func scheduleNotification(){

    let n = UILocalNotification()
    let c = NSCalendar.autoupdatingCurrentCalendar()
    let comp = c.componentsInTimeZone(c.timeZone, fromDate: NSDate())
    comp.second += 3
```

```
    let date = c.dateFromComponents(comp)
    n.fireDate = date

    n.alertBody = "Please enter your name now"
    n.alertAction = "Enter"
    n.category = "texted"
    UIApplication.sharedApplication().scheduleLocalNotification(n)

}
```

And we'll call this method when our app is sent to the background:

```
func applicationDidEnterBackground(application: UIApplication) {
    scheduleNotification()
}
```

Once that is done, we will read the text that the user has entered and do our work with it (I'll leave this to you):

```
func application(application: UIApplication,
    handleActionWithIdentifier identifier: String?,
    forLocalNotification notification: UILocalNotification,
    withResponseInfo responseInfo: [NSObject : AnyObject],
    completionHandler: () -> Void) {

    if let text = responseInfo[UIUserNotificationActionResponseTypedTextKey]
      as? String{

        print(text)
        //TODO: now you have access to this text

    }

    completionHandler()

}
```

Let's run it and then send the app to the background and see what happens (see Figure 3-15).

Figure 3-15. A local notification is shown on the screen

Then take that little bar at the bottom of the notification and drag it down to show the actions that are possible on the notification (see Figure 3-16).

Figure 3-16. Possible actions on our local notification

Now if the user just taps the Enter button, she will see a text field and can then enter her information. Upon submitting the text, she will be redirected to our app where we will receive the text (see Figure 3-17).

Figure 3-17. Entering text in a local notification

See Also

Recipe 3.7

3.5 Dealing with Stacked Views in Code

Problem

You want to programmatically manipulate the contents of stack views.

Solution

Use an instance of the `UIStackView`.

Discussion

For whatever reason, you might want to construct your stack views programmatically. I do not recommend this way of working with stack views because IB already can handle most of the situations where you would want to use stack views, and then some. But if you absolutely have to use stack views in your app, simply instantiate `UIStackView` and pass it your arranged views.

You can also then set the `axis` property to either `Vertical` or `Horizontal`. Remember to set the `distribution` property as well, of type `UIStackViewDistribution`. Some of the values of this type are `Fill`, `FillEqually`, and `EqualSpacing`. I also like to set the spacing property of the stack view manually so that I know how much space there is between my items.

Let's say that we want to create a stack view like Figure 3-18. The stack view is tucked to the right side of the screen and every time we press the button, a new label will be appended to the stack view.

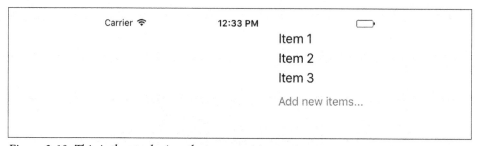

Figure 3-18. This is the stack view that we want to create

First define a stack view in your view controller:

```
var rightStack: UIStackView!
```

Then a few handy methods for creating labels and a button:

```
func lblWithIndex(idx: Int) -> UILabel{
  let label = UILabel()
  label.text = "Item \(idx)"
```

```
    label.sizeToFit()
    return label
}

func newButton() -> UIButton{
    let btn = UIButton(type: .System)
    btn.setTitle("Add new items...", forState: .Normal)
    btn.addTarget(self, action: "addNewItem",
        forControlEvents: .TouchUpInside)
    return btn
}

func addNewItem(){
    let n = rightStack.arrangedSubviews.count
    let v = lblWithIndex(n)
    rightStack.insertArrangedSubview(v, atIndex: n - 1)
}
```

 The addNewItem function will be called when the button is pressed.

When our view is loaded on the screen, we will create the stack view and fill it with the three initial labels and the button. Then we will set up its axis, spacing, and distribution. Once done, we'll create its constraints:

```
override func viewDidLoad() {
    super.viewDidLoad()

    rightStack = UIStackView(arrangedSubviews:
        [lblWithIndex(1), lblWithIndex(2), lblWithIndex(3), newButton()])

    view.addSubview(rightStack)

    rightStack.translatesAutoresizingMaskIntoConstraints = false

    rightStack.axis = .Vertical
    rightStack.distribution = .EqualSpacing
    rightStack.spacing = 5

    rightStack.trailingAnchor.constraintEqualToAnchor(view.trailingAnchor,
        constant: -20).active = true
    rightStack.topAnchor.constraintEqualToAnchor(
        topLayoutGuide.bottomAnchor).active = true

}
```

See Also

Recipe 3.2 and Recipe 3.3

3.6 Showing Web Content in Safari View Controller

Problem

You want to take advantage such awesome Safari functionalities as Reader Mode in your own apps.

Solution

Use the `SFSafariViewController` class in the `SafariServices.framework`. This view controller can easily be initialized with a URL and then displayed on the screen.

Discussion

Let's go ahead and build the UI. For this recipe, I am aiming for a UI like Figure 3-19.

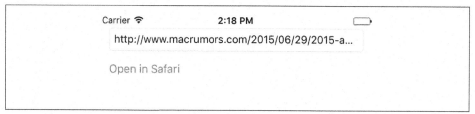

Figure 3-19. Create a UI that looks similar to this in your own storyboard

Then hook up the text field and button to your code. Once the button is tapped, the code that runs is:

```
@IBAction func openInSafari() {

  guard let t = textField.text where t.characters.count > 0,
    let u = NSURL(string: t)  else{
    //the url is missing, you can further code this method if you want
    return
  }

  let controller = SFSafariViewController(URL: u,
    entersReaderIfAvailable: true)
  controller.delegate = self
  presentViewController(controller, animated: true, completion: nil)

}
```

Now make your view controller conform to the `SFSafariViewControllerDelegate` protocol. Program the `safariViewControllerDidFinish(_:)` method to ensure that, when the user closes the Safari view controller, the view disappears:

```
func safariViewControllerDidFinish(controller: SFSafariViewController) {
  dismissViewControllerAnimated(true, completion: nil)
}
```

In the initializer of the Safari controller, I also specified that I would like to take advantage of the Reader Mode if it is available.

See Also

Recipe 11.1 and Recipe 5.1

3.7 Laying Out Text-Based Content on Your Views

Problem

You want to show text-based content to your users and want to lay it out on the screen in the optimal position.

Solution

Use the `readableContentGuide` property of `UIView`.

Discussion

The `readableContentGuide` property of `UIView` gives you the margins that you need to place your text content on the screen properly. On a typical iPhone 6 screen, this margin is around 20 points on both the left and the right. The top and bottom margins on the same device are usually set near 0. But don't take these numbers at face value. They might change and you should never think about them as hardcoded values. That is why we should use the `readableContentGuide` property to place our components correctly on the screen.

There isn't really much more to it than that, so let's just see an example. In this code, I will create a label and stretch it horizontally and vertically to fill the readable section of my view. I will also make sure the top and left positioning of the label is according to the readable section's guides:

```
let label = UILabel()
label.translatesAutoresizingMaskIntoConstraints = false
label.backgroundColor = UIColor.greenColor()
label.text = "Hello, World"
label.sizeToFit()
view.addSubview(label)
```

```
label.leadingAnchor.constraintEqualToAnchor(
  view.readableContentGuide.leadingAnchor).active = true

label.topAnchor.constraintEqualToAnchor(
  view.readableContentGuide.topAnchor).active = true

label.trailingAnchor.constraintEqualToAnchor(
  view.readableContentGuide.trailingAnchor).active = true

label.bottomAnchor.constraintEqualToAnchor(
  view.readableContentGuide.bottomAnchor).active = true
```

See Also

Recipe 3.4

3.8 Improving Touch Rates for Smoother UI Interactions

Problem

You want to be able to improve the interaction of the user with your app by decreasing the interval required between touch events.

Solution

Use the `coalescedTouchesForTouch(_:)` and the `predictedTouchesForTouch(_:)` methods of the `UIEvent` class. The former method allows you to receive coalesced touches inside an event, while the latter allows you to receive predicted touch events based on iOS's internal algorithms.

Discussion

On selected devices such as iPad Air 2, the display refresh rate is 60Hz like other iOS devices, but the touch scan rate is 120Hz. This means that iOS on iPad Air 2 scans the screen for updated touch events twice as fast as the display's refresh rate. These events obviously cannot be delivered to your app faster than the display refresh rate (60 times per second), so they are coalesced. At every touch event, you can ask for these coalesced touches and base your app's reactions on them..

In this recipe, imagine that we are just going to draw a line based on where the user's finger has been touching the screen. The user can move her finger over our view any way she wants and we just draw a line on that path.

Create a single-view app. In the same file as your view controller's Swift source file, define a new class of type `UIView` and name it `MyView`:

```
class MyView : UIView{

}
```

In your storyboard, set your view controller's view class to `MyView` (see Figure 3-20).

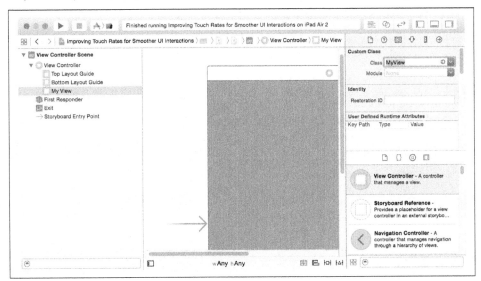

Figure 3-20. Your view is inside the view controller now

 Make sure that you are running this code on a device at least as advanced as an iPad Air 2. iPhone 6 and 6+ do *not* have a 120Hz touch scan rate.

Then in your view, define an array of points and a method that can take a set of touches and an event object, read the coalesced touch points inside the event, and place them inside our array:

```
var points = [CGPoint]()

func drawForFirstTouchInSet(s: Set<UITouch>, event: UIEvent?){

  guard let touch = s.first, event = event,
    allTouches = event.coalescedTouchesForTouch(touch)
    where allTouches.count > 0 else{
      return
  }

  points += allTouches.map{$0.locationInView(self)}

  setNeedsDisplay()
```

```
    }
```

Now when the user starts touching our view, we start recording the touch points:

```
override func touchesBegan(touches: Set<UITouch>,
    withEvent event: UIEvent?) {

    points.removeAll()
    drawForFirstTouchInSet(touches, event: event)

}
```

Should we be told that the touch events sent to our app were by accident, and that the user really meant to touch another UI component on the screen, such as the notification center, we have to clear our display:

```
override func touchesCancelled(touches: Set<UITouch>?,
    withEvent event: UIEvent?) {

    points.removeAll()
    setNeedsDisplayInRect(bounds)

}
```

Every time the touch location moves, we move with it and record the location:

```
override func touchesCancelled(touches: Set&lt;UITouch&gt;?,
    withEvent event: UIEvent?) {

    points.removeAll()
    setNeedsDisplayInRect(bounds)

}
```

Once the touches end, we also ask iOS for any predicted touch events that might have been calculated, and we will draw them too:

```
override func touchesEnded(touches: Set<UITouch>,
    withEvent event: UIEvent?) {

    guard let touch = touches.first, event = event,
      predictedTouches = event.predictedTouchesForTouch(touch)
      where predictedTouches.count > 0 else{
        return
    }

    points += predictedTouches.map{$0.locationInView(self)}
    setNeedsDisplay()

}
```

Our drawing code is simple. It goes through all the points and draws lines between them:

```
override func drawRect(rect: CGRect) {

    let con = UIGraphicsGetCurrentContext()

    //set background color
    CGContextSetFillColorWithColor(con, UIColor.blackColor().CGColor)
    CGContextFillRect(con, rect)

    CGContextSetFillColorWithColor(con, UIColor.redColor().CGColor)
    CGContextSetStrokeColorWithColor(con, UIColor.redColor().CGColor)

    for point in points{

      CGContextMoveToPoint(con, point.x, point.y)

      if let last = points.last where point != last{
        let next = points[points.indexOf(point)! + 1]
        CGContextAddLineToPoint(con, next.x, next.y)
      }

    }

    CGContextStrokePath(con)

  }

}
```

Now run this on an iPad Air 2 and compare the smoothness of the lines that you draw with those on an iPhone 6 or 6+, for instance.

See Also

Recipe 3.1

3.9 Supporting Right-to-Left Languages

Problem

You are internationalizing your app and, as part of this process, need to support right-to-left languages such as Persian or Arabic.

Solution

Use a combination of the following:

- Use IB's view properties to arrange your items with proper semantic properties.
- Ensure that you create your constraints correctly, preferably using IB.

- Use UIView's userInterfaceLayoutDirectionForSemanticContentAttri bute(_:) class method to find the direction of the user interface based on the semantic attributes that are part of the UISemanticContentAttribute enum.
- If arranging your items in code, use the semanticContentAttribute property of your views to set their semantic correctly.

Discussion

Let's create an app that has a text view on top and four buttons arranged like the arrow keys on the keyboard: up, left, down, right. When each one of these buttons is pressed, we will display the corresponding word in the text field. The text field will be read-only, and when displaying right-to-left languages, it will of course show the text on the righthand side. Make sure that your UI looks (for now) something like Figure 3-21. There are one text field and four buttons.

Figure 3-21. Initial layout

Now select the left, down, and right buttons on the UI (exclude the up button for now) and stack them up together. In the new stack that was created, set the spacing to 20 (see Figure 3-22). Set the horizontal stack view's spacing so that the buttons will be horizontally stacked with the proper distance from each other.

Then select the newly created stack and the up button on IB and stack *those* up together. This will create a vertical stack view for you. Set the spacing for this new stack view to 10. Place the main stack view at the center of the screen. Use IB's "Resolve Auto Layout Issues" feature to add all missing constraints for all the components. Also make sure that you disable editing of the text field. Then hook up the text field to your code as an outlet and hook up the four buttons' touch events to your view controller as well. Now your UI should look like Figure 3-23 on IB.

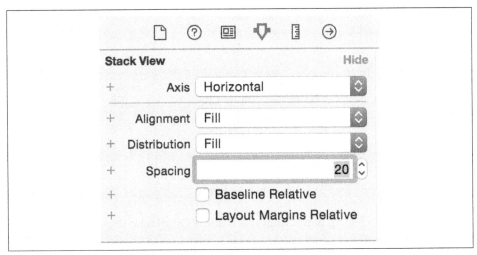

Figure 3-22. Horizontal spacing between buttons

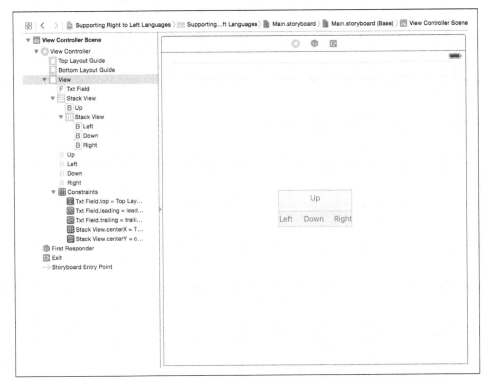

Figure 3-23. Your UI should look like this at the moment

Now choose the main stack view in your UI. In IB, in the Semantic section under Attributes inspector, choose Playback. This will ensure that the views inside this stack view will *not* be mirrored right to left when the language changes to a right-to-left language (see Figure 3-24).

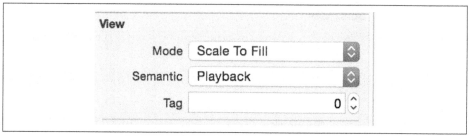

Figure 3-24. Choosing the Playback view semantic

Now from Xcode, create a new strings file, name it *Localizable.strings*, and place your string keys in there:

```
"up" = "Up";
"down" = "Down";
"right" = "Right";
"left" = "Left";
```

Under your main project's info page in Xcode, choose Localizations and add Arabic as a localization. Then move over to your newly created `strings` file and enable the Arabic language on it (see Figure 3-25).

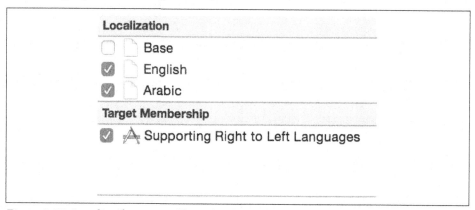

Figure 3-25. Localize the strings file so that you have both English and Arabic in the list

You will now have two strings files. Go into the Arabic one and localize the file:

```
"up" = "Up in Arabic";
"down" = "Down in Arabic";
"right" = "Right in Arabic";
"left" = "Left in Arabic";
```

In your code now, we have to set the text field's text direction based on the orientation that we get from UIView. That orientation itself depends on the semantics that we set on our text field before:

```
class ViewController: UIViewController {

  @IBOutlet var txtField: UITextField!

  @IBAction func up() {
    txtField.text = NSLocalizedString("up", comment: "")
  }

  @IBAction func left() {
    txtField.text = NSLocalizedString("left", comment: "")
  }

  @IBAction func down() {
    txtField.text = NSLocalizedString("down", comment: "")
  }

  @IBAction func right() {
    txtField.text = NSLocalizedString("right", comment: "")
  }

  override func viewDidAppear(animated: Bool) {

    let direction = UIView
      .userInterfaceLayoutDirectionForSemanticContentAttribute(
        txtField.semanticContentAttribute)

    switch direction{
    case .LeftToRight:
      txtField.textAlignment = .Left
    case .RightToLeft:
      txtField.textAlignment = .Right
    }

  }

}
```

Now run the app on an English device and you will see English content in the text field aligned from left to right. Run it on an Arabic localized device and you'll see the text aligned on the right hand side.

3.10 Associating Keyboard Shortcuts with View Controllers

Problem

You want to allow your application to respond to complex key combinations that a user can press on an external keyboard, to give the user more ways to interact with your app.

Solution

Construct an instance of the UIKeyCommand class and add it to your view controllers using the addKeyCommand(_:) method. You can remove key commands with the removeKeyCommand(_:) method.

Discussion

Keyboard shortcuts are very useful for users with external keyboards. Why? Since you asked, it's because they can use keyboard shortcuts. For instance, on a document editing iOS app, the user might expect to press Command-N to create a new document, whereas on an iOS device this may be achieved by the user pressing a button such as "New."

Let's say that we want to write a single-view app that allows users with an external keyboard to press Command-Alt-Control-N to see an alert controller. When our view is loaded, we will create the command and add it to our view controller:

```
override func viewDidLoad() {
  super.viewDidLoad()

  let command = UIKeyCommand(input: "N",
    modifierFlags: .Command + .Alternate + .Control,
    action: "handleCommand:")

  addKeyCommand(command)

}
```

As you can see, I am using the + operator between items of type UIKeyModifier Flags. This operator by default does not exist, so let's write a generic operator method that enables this functionality for us:

```
func +<T: OptionSetType where T.RawValue : SignedIntegerType>
  (lhs: T, rhs: T) -> T{
  return T(rawValue: lhs.rawValue | rhs.rawValue)
}
```

When the command is issued, iOS will attempt to call the method that we have specified. In there, let's show the alert:

```
func handleCommand(cmd: UIKeyCommand){

    let c = UIAlertController(title: "Shortcut pressed",
        message: "You pressed the shortcut key", preferredStyle: .Alert)

    c.addAction(UIAlertAction(title: "Ok!", style: .Destructive, handler: nil))

    presentViewController(c, animated: true, completion: nil)

}
```

Open this in the simulator. From the Hardware menu, select Keyboard, and then select the Connect Hardware Keyboard menu item (see Figure 3-26). While the focus is on the simulator, press the aforementioned key combinations and see the results for yourself.

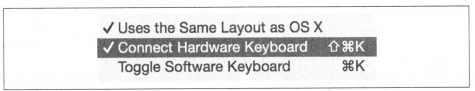

Figure 3-26. You can enable a hardware keyboard even in the simulator. This is necessary to test the output of this recipe.

3.11 Recording the Screen and Sharing the Video

Problem

You want your user to be able to record their screen while in your app and then edit and save the results. This is really important for games providing replay functionality to gamers.

Solution

Follow these steps:

1. Import `ReplayKit`.
2. Get a recorder of type `RPScreenRecorder` using `RPScreenRecorder.sharedRecorder()`.
3. Call the `available` property of the recorder to see whether recording is available.
4. Set the `delegate` property of the recorder to your code and conform to the `RPScreenRecorderDelegate` protocol.

5. Call the `startRecordingWithMicrophoneEnabled(_:handler:)` method of the recorder.
6. Wait until your handler method is called and then check for errors.
7. If no error occurred, once you are done with recording, call the `stopRecording WithHandler(_:)` on the same recorder object.
8. Wait for your handler to be called. In your handler, you'll get an instance of the `RPPreviewViewController` class.
9. Set the `previewControllerDelegate` property of the preview controller to your code and conform to the `RPPreviewViewControllerDelegate` protocol.
10. Preset your preview controller.

Discussion

When playing games, you might be given the option to record your screen for later playback or sharing with others. So let's define our view controller:

```
import UIKit
import ReplayKit

class ViewController: UIViewController, RPScreenRecorderDelegate,
RPPreviewViewControllerDelegate {
    ...
```

Set up your UI as shown in Figure 3-27. The start and stop buttons are self-explanatory. The segmented control is there just so you can play with it while recording and then see the results after you've stopped the playback.

Figure 3-27. Initial layout

I hook up the buttons to my code:

```
@IBOutlet var startBtn: UIButton!
@IBOutlet var stopBtn: UIButton!
```

And here I'll define my delegate methods:

```
func previewControllerDidFinish(previewController: RPPreviewViewController) {
  print("Finished the preview")
  dismissViewControllerAnimated(true, completion: nil)
  startBtn.enabled = true
  stopBtn.enabled = false
}

func previewController(previewController: RPPreviewViewController,
  didFinishWithActivityTypes activityTypes: Set<String>) {
    print("Preview finished activities \(activityTypes)")
}

func screenRecorderDidChangeAvailability(screenRecorder: RPScreenRecorder) {
  print("Screen recording availability changed")
}

func screenRecorder(screenRecorder: RPScreenRecorder,
  didStopRecordingWithError error: NSError,
  previewViewController: RPPreviewViewController?) {
```

```
        print("Screen recording finished")
    }
```

The `previewControllerDidFinish(_:)` method is important, because it gets called when the user is finished with the preview controller. Here you'll need to dismiss the preview controller.

Then I'll define my recorder object:

```
let recorder = RPScreenRecorder.sharedRecorder()
```

When the record button is pressed, I'll see whether recording is possible:

```
startBtn.enabled = true
stopBtn.enabled = false

guard recorder.available else{
  print("Cannot record the screen")
  return
}
```

If it is, I'll start recording:

```
recorder.delegate = self

recorder.startRecordingWithMicrophoneEnabled(true){err in
  guard err == nil else {
    if err!.code == RPRecordingErrorCode.UserDeclined.rawValue{
      print("User declined app recording")
    }
    else if err!.code == RPRecordingErrorCode.InsufficientStorage.rawValue{
      print("Not enough storage to start recording")
    }
    else {
      print("Error happened = \(err!)")
    }
    return
  }

  print("Successfully started recording")
  self.startBtn.enabled = false
  self.stopBtn.enabled = true

}
```

 I am checking the error codes for specific ReplayKit errors such as `RPRecordingErrorCode.UserDeclined` and `RPRecordingError Code.InsufficientStorage`.

The first time you attempt to record the user screen in any app, the user will be prompted to allow or disallow this with a dialog that looks similar to that shown in Figure 3-28.

Figure 3-28. Permission to record the screen is requested from the user

Now when the user is finished recording and presses the stop button, I'll stop the recording and present the preview controller:

```
recorder.stopRecordingWithHandler{controller, err in

    guard let previewController = controller where err == nil else {
        self.startBtn.enabled = true
        self.stopBtn.enabled = false
        print("Failed to stop recording")
        return
    }

    previewController.previewControllerDelegate = self

    self.presentViewController(previewController, animated: true,
        completion: nil)

}
```

The preview controller looks like this Figure 3-29.

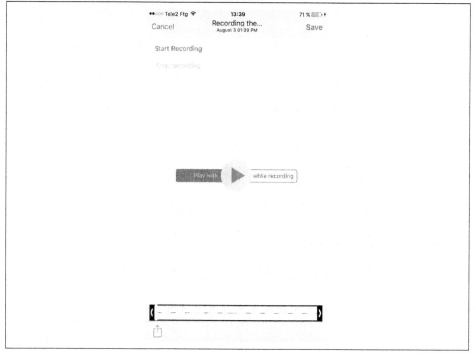

Figure 3-29. The user is previewing what she recorded on the screen earlier and can save and share the results

Throughout this whole process, your app doesn't get direct access to the recorded content. This protects the user's privacy.

See Also

Recipe 7.1

CHAPTER 4

Contacts

The Contacts framework is for those who want to import, show, select, modify, and save contacts on a user's iOS device. This framework is fully compatible with Swift's lingo and is very easy to work with. At the heart of the Contacts framework we have the `CNContact` object that represents a contact. You get access to the contacts' database using the `CNContactStore` class.

Every time you want to access the address book, whether you are trying to create a new contact or fetch an existing one, you need to ensure that you have sufficient access to the address book. You can check your access privileges using the `authoriza tionStatusForEntityType(_:)` class method of your contact store. This method takes in one parameter of type `CNEntityType`. You can pass the value of `Contacts` to this method, for instance, to ask for access to the user's contacts. If you do not have access, you can use the `requestAccessForEntityType(_:completionHandler:)` method of your contact store to request access.

The concept of a *partial contact* is important enough to cover now as well. A partial contact is a contact whose properties have not all been fetched from the store yet. For instance, perhaps you can fetch only a contact's first and last name, not her profile photo or email addresses. This is a partial contact. A partial contact's other information—such as email addresses—that have not been fetched yet can later be fetched from the store using her identifier (part of the `CNContact` object).

Some of the classes that are part of the Contacts framework have immutable and mutable flavors. An example is the `CNContact` and the `CNMutableContact` classes. The former is a contact that you have fetched from the store and just use in your app, while the latter is a contact that you have created in your app and want to save into the store.

Contact objects on iOS are thread-safe. I suggest that you do all your fetch operations on a background thread. Fetch the contacts in the background and safely display your contacts on your UI by accessing the same contact object on the main thread.

 In this chapter, it's best to always reset the contents of your address book on the simulator by resetting the simulator before testing the code in each recipe, unless I've explicitly specified not to. This is just to make sure that every recipe is working with a clear state of the address book database. You can find the Contacts app on your simulator. It should look like Figure 4-1 in a clear state.

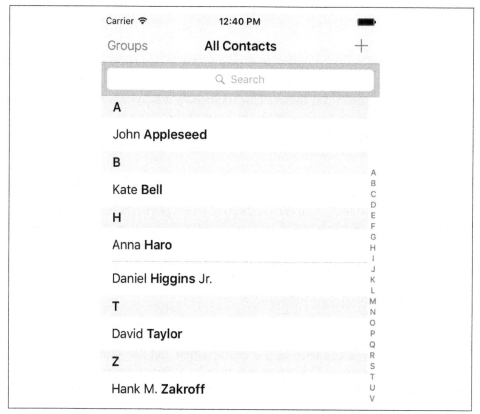

Figure 4-1. Clean state of the Contacts app on the simulator

4.1 Creating Contacts

Problem

You want to insert a new contact into the contacts database.

Solution

Follow these steps:

1. Request access to the database if you don't already have it.
2. Create an instance of the CNMutableContact class.
3. Set its various properties, such as givenName, middleName, and familyName.
4. Instantiate CNSaveRequest, call the addContact(_:toContainerWithIdenti fier:) method on it, and pass your contact to it. Set the container ID to nil.
5. Once you have the request, execute it on your store instance using executeSa veRequest(_:).

Discussion

Create a single-view app and first ask for permission to access contacts on the user's device:

```
switch CNContactStore.authorizationStatusForEntityType(.Contacts){
case .Authorized:
  createContact()
case .NotDetermined:
  store.requestAccessForEntityType(.Contacts){succeeded, err in
    guard err == nil && succeeded else{
      return
    }
    self.createContact()
  }
default:
  print("Not handled")
}
```

After I get the permission here, I am calling the createContact() method that we are just about to code. Also, I am using a property on my class that is my instance of the contact store:

```
var store = CNContactStore()
```

In the createContact() method, first let's create the basics of the contact object with the basic name and such:

```
let fooBar = CNMutableContact()
fooBar.givenName = "Foo"
fooBar.middleName = "A."
fooBar.familyName = "Bar"
fooBar.nickname = "Fooboo"
```

Then we set the profile photo:

```
//profile photo
if let img = UIImage(named: "apple"),
```

```
let data = UIImagePNGRepresentation(img){
    fooBar.imageData = data
}
```

 I've included a profile photo that I can use in the app. You don't have to do that if you don't want to. This code will work even if you don't have a profile photo by jumping over this section if the image cannot be found.

Now I am going to set the user's phone numbers. This can be done by setting an array of CNLabeledValue on the phoneNumbers property of the contact object. Labeled values are instances of the aforementioned class and can have a label and a value. The label is a string such as CNLabelHome or CNLabelWork and the value, in case of a phone number, is an instance of the CNPhoneNumber class:

```
//set the phone numbers
let homePhone = CNLabeledValue(label: CNLabelHome,
  value: CNPhoneNumber(stringValue: "123"))
let workPhone = CNLabeledValue(label: CNLabelWork,
  value: CNPhoneNumber(stringValue: "567"))
fooBar.phoneNumbers = [homePhone, workPhone]
```

I am then going to set the email addresses for this person by manipulating the email Addresses property of the contact. This property also accepts an array of CNLabeled Value and the values of this labeled object are the email addresses, as string objects:

```
//set the email addresses
let homeEmail = CNLabeledValue(label: CNLabelHome,
  value: "foo@home")
let workEmail = CNLabeledValue(label: CNLabelWork,
  value: "bar@home")
fooBar.emailAddresses = [homeEmail, workEmail]
```

Next up, I am going to write some information in this contact about her job using the jobTitle, organizationName, and departmentName properties:

```
//job info
fooBar.jobTitle = "Chief Awesomeness Manager (CAM)"
fooBar.organizationName = "Pixolity"
fooBar.departmentName = "IT"
```

After that, I want to set the Facebook and Twitter profiles of this user. I do that by setting the value of the socialProfiles array on the contact. This array takes items of type CNLabeledValue and the value of each one of these labeled objects should be of type CNSocialProfile. You can set the service for each of the profiles using constants such as the following:

• CNSocialProfileServiceFacebook

- CNSocialProfileServiceTwitter
- CNSocialProfileServiceLinkedIn
- CNSocialProfileServiceFlickr

```
//social media
let facebookProfile = CNLabeledValue(label: "FaceBook", value:
  CNSocialProfile(urlString: nil, username: "foobar",
  userIdentifier: nil, service: CNSocialProfileServiceFacebook))
let twitterProfile = CNLabeledValue(label: "Twitter", value:
  CNSocialProfile(urlString: nil, username: "foobar",
    userIdentifier: nil, service: CNSocialProfileServiceTwitter))
fooBar.socialProfiles = [facebookProfile, twitterProfile]
```

I am also going to set some instant messaging information for my contact, such as her Skype and AIM information. I can do that by setting the value of the `instantMessa geAddresses` property that takes in an array of, you guessed it, `CNLabeledValue`. Each of these values should be of type `CNInstantMessageAddress` and service inside each message address object can be a string such as:

- CNInstantMessageServiceSkype
- CNInstantMessageServiceAIM
- CNInstantMessageServiceMSN
- CNInstantMessageServiceYahoo

```
//instant messaging
let skypeAddress = CNLabeledValue(label: "Skype", value:
CNInstantMessageAddress(username: "foobar",
  service: CNInstantMessageServiceSkype))
let aimAddress = CNLabeledValue(label: "AIM", value:
CNInstantMessageAddress(username: "foobar",
  service: CNInstantMessageServiceAIM))
fooBar.instantMessageAddresses = [skypeAddress, aimAddress]
```

I can also set some notes on my contact using the `note` property that is just a string:

```
//some additional notes
fooBar.note = "Some additional notes"
```

Next step is to set the `birthday` property. This is a property of type `NSDate Components`:

```
//birthday
let birthday = NSDateComponents()
birthday.year = 1980
birthday.month = 9
birthday.day = 27
fooBar.birthday = birthday
```

Every contact also has a property named `dates` that can contain dates such as the user's anniversary. This is an array of `CNLabeledValue` objects. Here I am going to set the anniversary for this user:

```
//anniversary
let anniversaryDate = NSDateComponents()
anniversaryDate.month = 6
anniversaryDate.day = 13
let anniversary = CNLabeledValue(label: "Anniversary",
  value: anniversaryDate)
fooBar.dates = [anniversary]
```

I did not set the year for the anniversary because an anniversary is a repeating event.

I am finally done with my contact and will save her into the contact store:

```
//finally save
let request = CNSaveRequest()
request.addContact(fooBar, toContainerWithIdentifier: nil)
do{
  try storeo.executeSaveRequest(request)
  print("Successfully stored the contact")
} catch let err{
  print("Failed to save the contact. \(err)")
}
```

If you run this code *n* times on the same device, you will get *n* of the same contacts. The Contacts database does not prevent multiple saves on the same contact. They become different contacts eventually. It is our responsibility to avoid this.

And now my contact appears in the list (Figure 4-2).

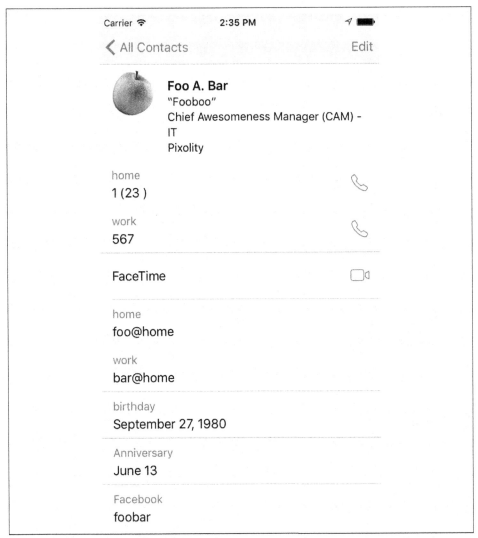

Figure 4-2. The new contact in all its glory

4.2 Searching for Contacts

Problem

You want to search the contacts available on a device.

Solution

There are various ways of fetching contacts from a store. Here are some of them, in no particular order:

`unifiedContactsMatchingPredicate(_:keysToFetch:)` *method of* `CNContactStore`
This allows you to fetch all contacts that match a certain predicate.

`enumerateContactsWithFetchRequest(_:usingBlock:)` *method of* `CNContactStore`
This allows you to enumerate through all contacts that match a fetch request. The fetch request can have a predicate if you want it to. Otherwise, you can use this method with a request object that does *not* have a predicate, in order to fetch *all* contacts.

`unifiedContactWithIdentifier(_:keysToFetch:)` *method of* `CNContactStore`
This fetches only a single contact with a given identifier, if it can find one. Use this method to fetch properties for a partially fetched contact.

 The term "unified contacts" is iOS's way of showing that the contact objects that we get are intelligently merged from different sources, if available. If you have "Foo bar" in your contacts and then you sign into Facebook with its iOS app and bring your Facebook contacts into your phone, and you have "Foo bar" on Facebook as well, iOS will merge that contact for you into one contact. Foo bar is now a unified contact.

Discussion

Let's have a look at a few examples. First, let's write some code that will find anybody in our address book whose name matches "John". We start off by creating a predicate using the `predicateForContactsMatchingName(_:)` class method of the `CNContact` class:

```
let predicate = CNContact.predicateForContactsMatchingName("john")
```

Then we are going to specify that we need the first and the last name of the contacts that match that name:

```
let toFetch = [CNContactGivenNameKey, CNContactFamilyNameKey]
```

Once that is done, use the `unifiedContactsMatchingPredicate(_:keysToFetch:)` method of the contact store to fetch the contacts matching our predicate. Go through all matching contacts and print their first and last name alongside their `identifier` property:

```
do{
  let contacts = try store.unifiedContactsMatchingPredicate(
    predicate, keysToFetch: toFetch)
```

```
    for contact in contacts{
      print(contact.givenName)
      print(contact.familyName)
      print(contact.identifier)
    }

} catch let err{
  print(err)
}
```

 I've wrapped this whole code inside NSOperationQueue().addOper
ationWithBlock(_:) to make sure that I am doing the search on a
background thread. I suggest that you do that too.

Every contact object has a handy property called identifier. This identifier usually
looks like a UUID. If you keep an identifier to a contact, you can always refetch that
contact using the unifiedContactWithIdentifier(_:keysToFetch:) method of
CNContactStore. You do not have to explicitly fetch the identifier property of a
contact. This identifier is fetched whether you want it or not, for every contact that
you get from a store. So you can omit that in your keysToFetch.

Let's look at another example. This time we are going to do the same thing that we did
in the previous example, but instead, use the CNContactFetchRequest class mixed
with the enumerateContactsWithFetchRequest(_:usingBlock:) method of CNCon
tactStore to achieve the same results.

First, again I am going to specify what properties in the contacts I am interested in
reading:

```
let toFetch = [CNContactGivenNameKey, CNContactFamilyNameKey]
```

I will now construct my fetch request using these properties:

```
let request = CNContactFetchRequest(keysToFetch: toFetch)
```

Then I will fetch the contacts with the aforementioned method:

```
do{
  try store.enumerateContactsWithFetchRequest(request) {
    contact, stop in
    print(contact.givenName)
    print(contact.familyName)
    print(contact.identifier)
  }
} catch let err{
  print(err)
}
```

The block that you pass to this method has two parameters. The first is the contact. The second is a Boolean *pointer* that you can set to true whenever you want to exit this enumeration. You can do that like this:

```
stop.memory = true
```

How about looking at another example. Let's say that you want to fetch all contacts whose name is similar to "Foo". You then want to find out whether they have a profile photo. If they do, we will refetch those contacts and get their profile photo. The purpose of this exercise is to show you that if you are interested in contacts with photos, it is best to first see whether they have photos and only if they do, fetch their profile photos. I'll start off by defining the keys that I want to fetch and I ask for a key that tells me whether a contact has a photo:

```
var toFetch = [CNContactImageDataAvailableKey]
```

Then I will define my predicate:

```
let predicate = CNContact.predicateForContactsMatchingName("foo")
```

Next, I will find all contacts that match my predicate:

```
let contacts = try store.unifiedContactsMatchingPredicate(predicate,
    keysToFetch: toFetch)
```

The previous statement must be wrapped inside a do{}catch{} block, otherwise it won't compile. I am not writing that statement here in the book because I want to explain the code step by step. If I paste the do{}catch{}, I'll have to paste the whole code in a gigantic block and that's not very good.

Now that we have our contacts, let's go through them and only find the ones that *do* have an image:

```
for contact in contacts{
  guard contact.imageDataAvailable else{
    continue
  }

    ...
```

The CNContact class offers an isKeyAvailable(_:) method that returns true or false depending on whether or not a given key is available for access on a contact. So here I am going to ask whether my contacts have images (the CNContactImageDataKey key) and if they do, I am going to read the image:

```
//have we fetched image data?
if contact.isKeyAvailable(CNContactImageDataKey){
  print(contact.givenName)
  print(contact.identifier)
```

```
        print(UIImage(data: contact.imageData!))
    } else {

        ...
```

 None of our contacts at this point will have images because we have
not fetched the images yet in our original fetch request. This is for
demonstration purposes really and to teach you how to use the
isKeyAvailable(_:) method.

If the contacts don't have their image data available at this point (which they won't!),
we will use the identifier of each one of them and re-fetch them, but this time by
specifying that we need the image data as well:

```
else {
    toFetch += [CNContactImageDataKey, CNContactGivenNameKey]
    do{
        let contact = try store.unifiedContactWithIdentifier(
            contact.identifier, keysToFetch: toFetch)
        print(contact.givenName)
        print(UIImage(data: contact.imageData!))
        print(contact.identifier)
    } catch let err{
        print(err)
    }
}
```

And that was it, really. If you have the identifier of a contact, you can fetch that contact quite easily, as we saw. Now let's say that you do have this identifier saved some-
where inside your app and you want to directly fetch that contact. You do that using
the unifiedContactWithIdentifier(_:keysToFetch:) method of the contact store:

```
NSOperationQueue().addOperationWithBlock{[unowned store] in
    let id = "AECF6A0E-6BCB-4A46-834F-1D8374E6FE0A:ABPerson"
    let toFetch = [CNContactGivenNameKey, CNContactFamilyNameKey]

    do{

        let contact = try store.unifiedContactWithIdentifier(id,
            keysToFetch: toFetch)

        print(contact.givenName)
        print(contact.familyName)
        print(contact.identifier)

    } catch let err{
        print(err)
    }
}
```

See Also

Recipe 4.1

4.3 Updating Contacts

Problem

You have an existing contact whose properties you want to update.

Solution

Call the `mutableCopy()` method of your `CNContact` class. This will give you an instance of the `CNMutableContact`. Once you have a mutable contact, you can change her properties as you would with a contact of type `CNContact`. Once done editing, instantiate `CNSaveRequest`, issue the `updateContact(_:)` method on it, and pass your mutable contact to that method. Now that you have the request object, pass it to the `executeSaveRequest(_:)` method of your store to update the contact.

Discussion

Let's check an example. Let's say that we want to find a contact named "John" and then add a new email address to it, if it doesn't already have it. I am not going to explain the things that we learned in Recipe 4.2, so let's dive in. Figure 4-3 shows the contact we will change. The contact comes prefilled in your iOS simulator, with only one work email address. We are going to add another work email to this list:

Figure 4-3. Current state of the contact

```
NSOperationQueue().addOperationWithBlock{[unowned store] in
  let predicate = CNContact.predicateForContactsMatchingName("john")
  let toFetch = [CNContactEmailAddressesKey]

do{
  let contacts = try store.unifiedContactsMatchingPredicate(predicate,
    keysToFetch: toFetch)

  guard contacts.count > 0 else{
    print("No contacts found")
    return
  }

  //only do this to the first contact matching our criteria
  guard let contact = contacts.first else{
    return
  }

  ...
```

We are only adding this new email to the *first* contact that matches our criteria.

Now we have a contact object that matches our criteria. Let's see whether he already has this email address, and bail out if he does:

```
let newEmail = "newemail@work.com"

for email in contact.emailAddresses{
  if email.value as! String == newEmail{
    print("This contact already has this email")
    return
  }
}
```

Now that we are sure he didn't have this email address already in the list, we will add it:

```
let john = contact.mutableCopy() as! CNMutableContact

let emailAddress = CNLabeledValue(label: CNLabelWork,
  value: "newemail@work.com")

john.emailAddresses.append(emailAddress)

let req = CNSaveRequest()
req.updateContact(john)

try store.executeSaveRequest(req)
```

```
print("Successfully added an email")
```

Now if we look at our contact in the list, we can see the new email address added (see Figure 4-4).

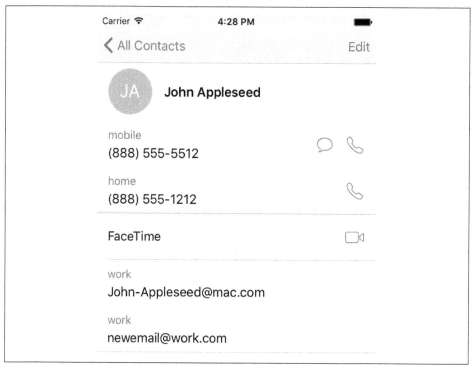

Figure 4-4. The new email address is added to our contact

See Also

Recipe 4.1

4.4 Deleting Contacts

Problem

You want to delete a contact on a device.

Solution

Follow these steps:

1. Find your contact using what you learned in Recipe 4.2.

2. Instantiate an object of type CNSaveRequest.
3. Issue the deleteContact(_:) function on the request and pass your mutable contact to it.
4. Execute your request using the executeSaveRequest(_:) method of your contact store.

Discussion

 Deleting a contact from a store is irreversible. I suggest that you test your code on the simulator first and as much as possible, ask the user first whether they allow a contact to be deleted.

Let's have a look at an example. We want to find all contacts named John and then delete the first one that we find. I am not showing an alert asking the user whether this is okay or not, because that's not the focus of this recipe. I suggest that you do so, though.

```
NSOperationQueue().addOperationWithBlock{[unowned store] in
    let predicate = CNContact.predicateForContactsMatchingName("john")
    let toFetch = [CNContactEmailAddressesKey]

do{

    let contacts = try store.unifiedContactsMatchingPredicate(predicate,
      keysToFetch: toFetch)

    guard contacts.count > 0 else{
      print("No contacts found")
      return
    }

    //only do this to the first contact matching our criteria
    guard let contact = contacts.first else{
      return
    }

    let req = CNSaveRequest()
    let mutableContact = contact.mutableCopy() as! CNMutableContact
    req.deleteContact(mutableContact)

    do{
      try store.executeSaveRequest(req)
      print("Successfully deleted the user")

    } catch let e{
      print("Error = \(e)")
```

```
        }

    } catch let err{
        print(err)
    }
}
```

See Also

Recipe 4.1

4.5 Formatting Contact Data

Problem

You want to present a local contact's name and postal address in a localized and read-able way, regardless of the current language on the user's device.

Solution

Use an instance of the `CNContactFormatter` or the `CNPostalAddressFormatter` classes. The former one can easily be used to format the contact's name, and the latter is self-explanatory.

Discussion

The `CNContactFormatter` class allows you to format the name of any contact, accord-ing to the localization settings of the current device. For instance, in some languages, the last name of a person may be mentioned first. You can use the `stringFromCon tact(_:)` function of this method to get the full name.

 You must fetch the full name of a contact from the store for this method to work at all. Otherwise, you might get an exception.

Because we have already talked about Recipe 4.2, I have written a simple extension on `CNContactStore` that allows me to fetch the first contact that it finds with a given name. I've named this method `firstUnifiedContactMatchingName(_:toFetch:out put:)` and it calls my output block when it finds the contact or if an error occurs. You don't have to know the full implementation of this method because you already know how you can fetch a contact with a given name.

So let's look at an example where we fetch a contact from the store and print his full name to the console:

```
let toFetch =
CNContactFormatter.descriptorForRequiredKeysForStyle(.FullName)

store.firstUnifiedContactMatchingName("john", toFetch: [toFetch]){
  guard let contact = $0 else{
    return
  }

  guard let name = CNContactFormatter().stringFromContact(contact) else{
    return
  }

  print("The name of the contact is \(name)")

}
```

Note that I am using the descriptorForRequiredKeysForStyle(_:) class method of the CNContactFormatter class to get an object of type CNKeyDescriptor and then pass the results to firstUnifiedContactMatchingName(_:toFetch:output:) when fetching the contact. The aforementioned method on CNContactFormatter tells the system what properties of the contact to fetch; in this case, all the properties that are required for the full name, including the first, middle, and last names.

Now imagine that we want to find a contact's localized phonetic name. A phonetic name is the name of a person, written as it is pronounced, rather than how the name is spelled. For instance, a person's name might be Julian, but in Swedish, because the J is pronounced as "you,"this name will eventually be pronounced as "you-lian." So "you-lian" is the phonetic equivalent of the name "Julian" in Swedish. These phonetic names are very useful for Siri. So a Swedish speaker will ask Siri to phone up "you-lian" and Siri will have no idea who that is unless the phonetic name has been set for that user.

Create a contact in your list. Set his first name to "Julian" and last name to "Julianson." Then tap the "add field" button at the bottom of the create-contact screen and add the phonetic first and last name fields to the contact (see Figure 4-5).

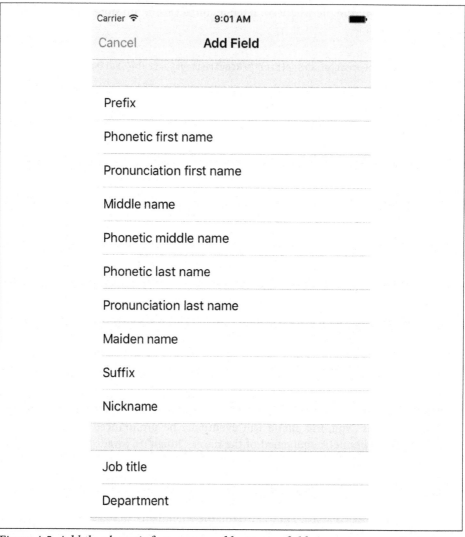

Figure 4-5. Add the phonetic first name and last name fields to your new contact

Set the phonetic first name to "Youlian" and the phonetic last name to "Youlianson" until your contact looks like Figure 4-6.

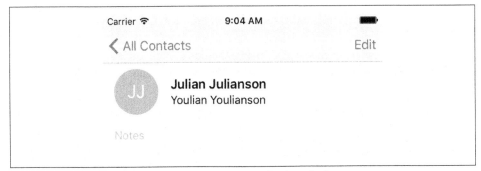

Figure 4-6. Your contact's phonetic name is also displayed, if set

Let's now look at an example where we fetch the phonetic name of a contact and then format it according to the localization on the current device. First, we need to find the fields in the contact store for phonetic name. We do that using the descriptorForRe quiredKeysForStyle(_:) class method of CNContactFormatter and this time pass the value of PhoneticFullName to it. Because the stringFromContact(_:) *class* method of the CNContactFormatter class by default reads the full name, and not the phonetic full name, we will have to start using the stringFromContact(_:style:) instance method of this class instead. The last parameter to this function allows us to pass a style of type CNContactFormatterStyle that can be set to FullName or Phone ticFullName:

```
let style = CNContactFormatterStyle.PhoneticFullName

let toFetch =
CNContactFormatter.descriptorForRequiredKeysForStyle(style)

store.firstUnifiedContactMatchingName("julian", toFetch: [toFetch]){

  guard let contact = $0 else{
    return
  }
  guard let name = CNContactFormatter
    .stringFromContact(contact, style: style) else{
    return
  }

  print("The phonetic name of the contact is \(name)")

}
```

Aside from getting the localized full name of a contact, you can also get her address information, again, properly localized, using the CNPostalAddressFormatter class. Follow these steps:

1. Fetch your contact and make sure you include the `CNContactPostalAddresse sKey` key.
2. Get the address from the contact using the `postalAddresses` property of `CNCon tact`. This will give you a value of type `CNLabeledValue`. Get the `value` of this labeled value and cast it to `CNPostalAddress`.
3. Instantiate `CNPostalAddressFormatter`.
4. Pass the postal address to the `stringFromPostalAddress(_:)` method of your postal address formatter to get the formatted address:

```
let toFetch = [CNContactPostalAddressesKey]

store.firstUnifiedContactMatchingName("john", toFetch: toFetch){
  guard let contact = $0 else{
    return
  }

  guard let firstAddress = contact.postalAddresses.first else{
    print("no postal address could be found")
    return
  }

  guard let address = firstAddress.value as? CNPostalAddress
    where firstAddress.value is CNPostalAddress else{
    return
  }

  let formatter = CNPostalAddressFormatter()
  let formattedAddress = formatter.stringFromPostalAddress(address)

  print("The address is \(formattedAddress)")

}
```

See Also

Recipe 4.1

4.6 Picking Contacts with the Prebuilt System UI

Problem

You want to use a built-in system dialog to allow your users to pick contacts from their contact store.

Solution

Use an instance of the `CNContactPickerViewController` class inside the `ContactsUI` framework.

Instances of the `CNContactPickerViewController` cannot be pushed to the stack. They need to be presented modally. Use the `presentViewController(_:animated:completion:)` method of your view or navigation controller to display the contact picker modally.

Discussion

Let's say that you want to allow the user to pick a contact. You will then attempt to read the phone numbers from that contact. Instances of the `CNContactPickerView Controller` class have a property called `delegate` that is of type `CNContactPickerDe legate`. Some of the interesting methods in this delegate are:

`contactPickerDidCancel(_:)`
> This gets called when the user cancels his request to pick a contact.

`contactPicker(_:didSelectContact:)`
> This gets called when the user picks a contact from the list.

In this example, I want to allow the user to pick a contact, whereupon I will read all the phone numbers from that contact. I have placed a button in my storyboard and hooked that button to a method in my code called `pickaContact()`. In that code, I present a simple contact picker:

```
let controller = CNContactPickerViewController()

controller.delegate = self

navigationController?.presentViewController(controller,
    animated: true, completion: nil)
```

I'm doing all this code inside a view controller and I've made my view controller conform to `CNContactPickerDelegate`.

Then, when the user picks a contact, I just print out all the phone numbers of that contact, if any, to the console:

```
func contactPickerDidCancel(picker: CNContactPickerViewController) {
    print("Cancelled picking a contact")
```

```
        }

        func contactPicker(picker: CNContactPickerViewController,
          didSelectContact contact: CNContact) {

          print("Selected a contact")

          if contact.isKeyAvailable(CNContactPhoneNumbersKey){
            //this is an extension I've written on CNContact
            contact.printPhoneNumbers()
          } else {
            /*
              TOOD: partially fetched, use what you've learnt in this chapter to
              fetch the rest of this contact
            */
            print("No phone numbers are available")
          }

        }
```

 The printPhoneNumbers() function is a custom extension on CNContact that I've written. You don't have to know the implementation of that as it's not relevant to this recipe. You already know how to do that using what you learned in Recipe 4.2.

In this example, we are looking for contacts with phone numbers, but the user is allowed to pick any contact, even if that contact has no phone numbers. How do we remedy this? A property called predicateForEnablingContact of type NSPredicate, on instances of CNContactPickerViewController, allows us to specify which contacts should be enabled and which ones should be disabled. Here we can create a predicate that checks the @count of the phoneNumbers property. Also, for fun, let's say that we only want to allow contacts whose names starts with "John" to be selectable (see Figure 4-7).

```
        let controller = CNContactPickerViewController()

        controller.delegate = self

        controller.predicateForEnablingContact =
          NSPredicate(format:
            "phoneNumbers.@count > 0 && givenName BEGINSWITH 'John'",
            argumentArray: nil)

        navigationController?.presentViewController(controller,
          animated: true, completion: nil)
```

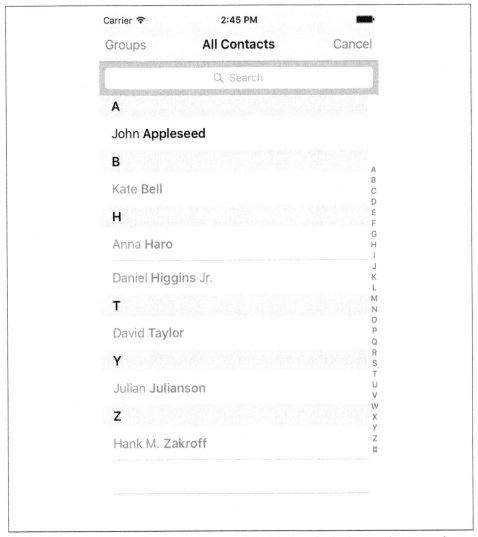

Figure 4-7. Only people whose names start with "John" and who have at least one phone number are retrieved

The `predicateForEnablingContact` property disables all contacts who do not pass the predicate so that the user won't even be able to select those contacts. There is another property on `CNContactPickerViewController` that does something more interesting: `predicateForSelectionOfContact`. The contacts that pass this predicate will be selectable by the user so that when the user taps that contact, the controller is dismissed and we get access to the contact object. The contacts that do not pass this predicate will still be selectable, but upon selection, their details will be shown to the user using the system UI. They won't be returned to our app:

```
let controller = CNContactPickerViewController()

controller.delegate = self

controller.predicateForSelectionOfContact =
  NSPredicate(format:
    "phoneNumbers.@count > 0",
    argumentArray: nil)

navigationController?.presentViewController(controller,
  animated: true, completion: nil)
```

There is another funky property on CNContactPickerViewController named predi
cateForSelectionOfProperty. This is a predicate that dictates which property for
any contact the user should be able to pick. If you want to allow the user to pick a
specific property—say the first phone number—of any contact to be passed to your
app, you also have to implement the contactPicker(_:didSelectContactProp
erty:) method of the CNContactPickerDelegate protocol. Let's write sample code
that allows the user to pick any contact as long as that contact has at least one phone
number, and then be able to pick the first phone number of that contact to be
returned to our app:

```
let controller = CNContactPickerViewController()

controller.delegate = self

controller.predicateForEnablingContact =
  NSPredicate(format:
    "phoneNumbers.@count > 0",
    argumentArray: nil)

controller.predicateForSelectionOfProperty =
  NSPredicate(format: "key == 'phoneNumbers'", argumentArray: nil)

navigationController?.presentViewController(controller,
  animated: true, completion: nil)
```

And then we provide an implementation of the contactPicker(_:didSelectContact
Property:) method:

```
func contactPicker(picker: CNContactPickerViewController,
  didSelectContactProperty contactProperty: CNContactProperty) {

  print("Selected a property")

}
```

In addition to all of this, you can also allow the user to pick multiple contacts. Do that
by implementing the contactPicker(_:didSelectContacts:) method of the CNCon
tactPickerDelegate protocol (see Figure 4-8):

```
func contactPicker(picker: CNContactPickerViewController,
  didSelectContacts contacts: [CNContact]) {
  print("Selected \(contacts.count) contacts")
}

//allows multiple selection mixed with contactPicker:didSelectContacts:
func example5(){
  let controller = CNContactPickerViewController()

  controller.delegate = self

  navigationController?.presentViewController(controller,
    animated: true, completion: nil)
}
```

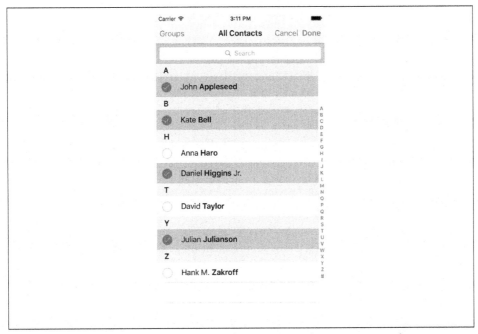

Figure 4-8. The user is able to select multiple contacts at the same time and return to our app at the end

See Also

Recipe 4.2

4.7 Creating Contacts with a Prebuilt System UI

Problem

You want to specify some basic information for a new contact and let a system UI and the user take care of the creation of this contact.

Solution

Follow these steps:

1. Create an instance of `CNContactStore` and ask for permission to use the store (see Recipe 4.1).
2. Create a contact of type `CNMutableContact` and put your default values in it. This is an optional step. You might want the user to create a whole new contact on her own, with no predefined values from your side.
3. Instantiate an object of type `CNContactViewController` using the `forNewContact` initializer and pass your contact to it.
4. Set the `contactStore` property of this view controller to a valid contact store instance.
5. Optionally, set the `delegate` property of this view controller to a valid delegate object that conforms to the `CNContactViewControllerDelegate` protocol.

Discussion

You have Recipe 4.1 to create a contact programmatically. What if you have some basic information about a contact, or no information at all, and you want your user to supply the rest of the information? Of course you could create a UI to allow the user to do that, but why do so if the SDK already comes with a prebuilt UI called `CNContactViewController`?

You can simply push an instance of the `CNContactViewController` class on your navigation controller. When you become the delegate of this view controller, a delegate method named `contactViewController(_:didCompleteWithContact:)` will get called if the user cancels or accepts the contact creation. Use this method to dismiss (pop) the contact view controller:

```
func contactViewController(viewController: CNContactViewController,
  didCompleteWithContact contact: CNContact?) {

  //whatever happens, pop back to our view controller
  defer{navigationController?.popViewControllerAnimated(true)}

  guard let contact = contact else{
    print("The contact creation was cancelled")
```

```
        return
    }

    print("Contact was created successfully \(contact)")

}
```

Let's look at a simple example now. Create a simple contact with some basic information and then ask the user to complete the creation process:

```
let contact = CNContact().mutableCopy() as! CNMutableContact
contact.givenName = "Anthony"
contact.familyName = "Appleseed"

let controller = CNContactViewController(forNewContact: contact)
controller.contactStore = store
controller.delegate = self

navigationController?
    .pushViewController(controller, animated: true)
```

Then our user will see a UI similar to Figure 4-9.

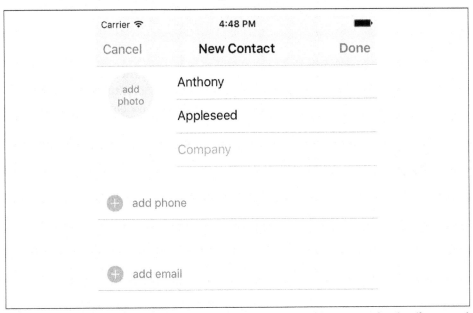

Figure 4-9. The new-contact system UI is displayed, asking the user to finish off or cancel the contact creation

The contact that you pass to the aforementioned initializer of CNContactViewController is optional. If you pass nil, the new-contact dialog that the user will see will be empty and the user will have to fill out every field in the UI.

See Also

Recipe 4.1

4.8 Displaying Contacts with a Prebuilt System UI

Problem

You want to use a built-in system UI to display an existing contact's information.

Solution

Use the forContact initializer of the CNContactViewController class and pass this method an instance of the CNContact that you want to display.

Discussion

Sometimes, you might want to display information for a particular contact but don't want to write the whole UI yourself. Why would you? It's a lot of work to display *all* the information. That's where you can use the CNContactViewController class again.

In this example, I am going to use my custom firstUnifiedCon tactMatchingName(_:toFetch:output:) method to fetch an existing contact. You don't have to know the implementation of this method because you already learned how to in Recipe 4.2

So this is what we are going to do: we fetch a contact whose name matches "John" and display his information on the screen. Make sure that you fetch all the required keys for your contact. Otherwise, the controller won't be able to display the contact's infor-mation. You can get the list of required keys by calling the descriptorForRequired Keys() class function of the CNContactViewController:

```
let toFetch = [CNContactViewController.descriptorForRequiredKeys()]
store.firstUnifiedContactMatchingName("john", toFetch: toFetch){

  guard let contact = $0 else{
    print("No contact was found")
    return
  }
```

```
let controller = CNContactViewController(forContact: contact)
controller.contactStore = self.store
controller.allowsEditing = false

controller.displayedPropertyKeys =
  [CNContactEmailAddressesKey, CNContactPostalAddressesKey]

self.navigationController?
  .pushViewController(controller, animated: true)
}
```

By default, when a contact is displayed, the contact controller allows the user to edit that contact. You can disable that behavior by setting the `allowsEditing` property of the controller to `false`. Also bear in mind that you have to set the `contactStore` property of the controller to the same store from where you fetched your contact.

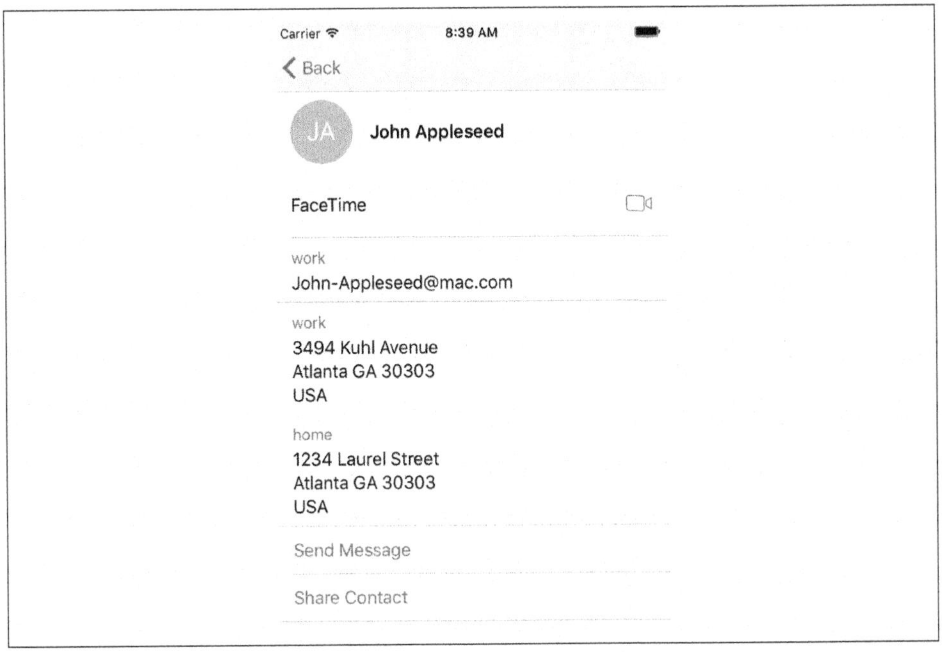

Figure 4-10. Displaying a contact

There is another interesting property on the controller: displayedPropertyKeys. As its name implies, it allows you to pass a series of contact property keys that have to be displayed. Other properties will be hidden. I have, in our code, enabled only email and postal addresses. The results are shown in Figure 4-10. Some other information such as full name are shown by default.

See Also

Recipe 4.2

CHAPTER 5

Extensions

Apple increased the number of extensions that we developers can write in the new iOS. One of the hot extensions that everybody seems to be talking about is the Safari Content Blocker, which allows a developer to specify which URLs or resources should get blocked in Safari tabs.

Extensions are separate binaries that sit inside your app's bundle. They usually have their own naming convention and sit inside reserved folders inside your app bundle. It's best not to mention what they are called on disk because Apple can change that at any time without us knowing. Because extensions sit in their own folders and have their own bundles, they do *not* share the same physical space as their container app. But, through some work, they *can* access the container app's resources such as images and text.

5.1 Creating Safari Content Blockers

Problem

You want to create a content blocker that the user can add to her Safari browser for blocking specific web content.

Solution

Use the Safari Content Blocker extension.

Discussion

This is something I am very excited about. You can ignore the long list of content blockers popping up on App Store every day from now on.

This is how the Apple blocker works. When you create an app, you can add a Safari Content Blocker extension to it. In that extension, you define the rules for your content blocking; e.g., whether you want to block images, style sheets, etc. The user can then, after opening your app at least once, go into the settings on her device and enable your content blocker. From now on, if she visits a web page that your content blocker applies to, she will see only the content that passes your filters.

Let's create a simple single-view controller app and then add a new target to your app. From the iOS main section, choose Application Extension and then Content Blocker Extension (see Figure 5-1).

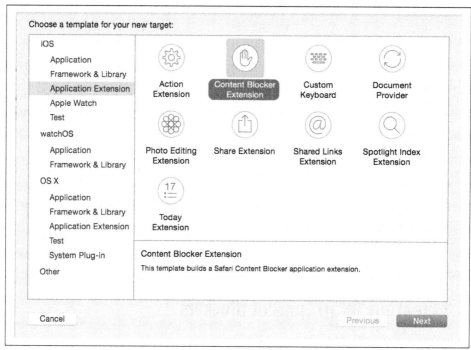

Figure 5-1. Adding a new content blocker extension to our existing app

Give any name that you want to your extension. It doesn't really matter so much for this exercise.

Now go to the new extension's new file called *blockerList.json* and place the following content in it:

```
[
    {
```

```
    "action": {
      "type": "block"
      },
      "trigger": {
        "url-filter": ".*",
        "resource-type" : ["image"],
        "if-domain" : ["edition.cnn.com"]
      }
    }
  ]
```

Even though there is a specific type of formatting to this file, I think you can just read this as I've written it and understand what it is doing. It is blocking all images that are under the edition.cnn.com domain name. Now head to your app delegate and import the SafariServices framework. Every time you change your content blocker, you will have to go to the Settings application on the simulator and turn it off and on again so that the simulator understands that the extension is updated. We are now going to write a piece of code that automates that for us:

```
func applicationDidBecomeActive(application: UIApplication) {

  //TODO: replace this with your own content blocker's identifier
  let id = "se.pixolity.Creating-Safari-Content-Blockers.Image-Blocker"
  SFContentBlockerManager.reloadContentBlockerWithIdentifier(id) {error in
    guard error == nil else {
      //an error happened, handle it
      print("Failed to reload the blocker")
      return
    }
    print("Reloaded the blocker")
  }
}
```

Then reset your simulator and run your app. Send your app to the background, open Safari on the simulator, and type in **cnn.com**. This will redirect you to *http:// edition.cnn.com/* (at the time of writing this book). Safari will hit the filter we wrote and will discard all the images. The results will be lovely. Well, I don't know whether a website without images is lovely or not, but it's what we set out to do.

A user can always enable or disable a content blocker. To do that, you can go to the Settings app on your device and in the search field type in **blocker**. Then tap the Content Blockers item that pops up (see Figure 5-2).

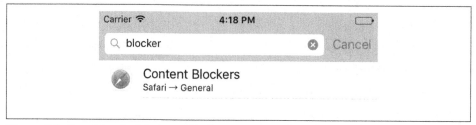

Figure 5-2. Searching for blocker will allow you to go directly to the Content Blockers settings section of Safari

Once there, you can enable or disable available Safari Content Blockers (see Figure 5-3).

Figure 5-3. The list of our Safari Content Blockers is shown here

Now that you have seen an example, let me bug you with some more details on that *json* file. That file contains an array of dictionaries with various configurations that you can enter. This book would grow very large if I wanted to describe everything there thoroughly, so I am going to explain the options for each field through some pseudo-json code if that's OK:

```
[
  {
    "action": {
      "type": "block" | "block-cookies" | "css-display-none",
      "selector" : This is a CSS selector that the action will be applied to
    },
    "trigger": {
      "url-filter": "this is a filter that will be applied on the WHOLE url",
      "url-filter-is-case-sensitive" : same as url-filter but case sensitive,
      "resource-type" : ["image" | "style-sheet" | "script" | "font" | etc],
      "if-domain" : [an array of actual domain names to apply filter on],
```

```
        "unless-domain" : [an array of domain names to exclude from filter],
        "load-type" : "first-party" | "third-party"
      }
    }
  ]
```

Armed with this knowledge, let's do some more experiments. Let's now block all `a` tags in macrumors.com:

```
{
  "action": {
    "type": "css-display-none",
    "selector" : "a"
  },
  "trigger": {
    "url-filter": ".*",
    "if-domain" : ["macrumors.com"]
  }
}
```

 I have no affiliation with nor any hate toward macrumors.com. I find that website quite informative, actually. Check it out for yourself. I am using this website as an example only and I am *not* suggesting that content on that website is worthy of blocking.

Or how about removing the `a` tag on top of the macrumors.com page that is an `id` attribute equal to `logo`?

```
{
  "action": {
    "type": "css-display-none",
    "selector" : "a[id='logo']"
  },
  "trigger": {
    "url-filter": ".*",
    "if-domain" : ["macrumors.com"]
  }
}
```

Now let's have a look at another example. Let's start blocking all images on all websites except for reddit.com:

```
{
  "action": {
    "type": "block"
  },
  "trigger": {
    "url-filter": ".*",
    "resource-type" : ["image"],
    "unless-domain" : ["reddit.com"]
```

```
    }
  }
```

Or how about blocking all elements of type a that have an href attribute on Apple's website?

```
{
  "action": {
    "type": "css-display-none",
    "selector" : "a[href]"
  },
  "trigger": {
    "url-filter": ".*",
    "if-domain" : ["apple.com"]
  }
}
```

See Also

Recipe 3.6

5.2 Creating Shared Links for Safari

Problem

You want to display your own links inside Safari's shared links on users' devices.

Solution

Add the new Shared Links Extension target to your existing app and code the extension. It is already prepopulated, so you don't really have to do much.

Discussion

Shared links are like bookmarks, but lead to content defined in your app or *a* website. The links are visible inside Safari on iOS when the user taps the bookmarks button and then the shared links icon. To get started, create a single-view controller project and then add a new target to your project. In the target selection screen, under the iOS main section, choose Application Extension and then Shared Links Extension (see Figure 5-4).

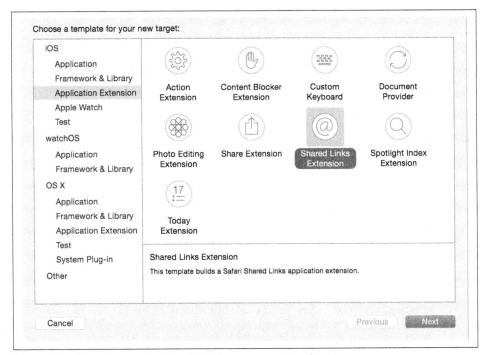

Figure 5-4. Creating a new shared link extension in Xcode

I suggest that you also add some proper icons to your app's bundle, because your app's icon will also appear in the list of shared links when iOS shows your shared link. You can just enter "public domain icon" into Google and find some really awesome icons that you can use in your app. Also make sure to add a simple icon to your shared link extension, because our code will show this icon in the list. Your extension's icon will appear on the left side of the link and your app icon on top right (see Figure 5-5).

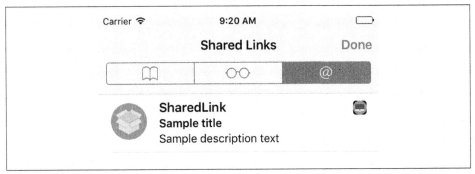

Figure 5-5. You can see our shared link's icon on the left and our app's icon on the upper-right corner

Then head to the new file called *RequestHandler.swift* that has been created in your extension. Xcode has already populated this file with all the code that you need to display your shared link. Uncomment the line that starts with extensionItem.attachments, load your extensions' icon, and attach it to the extension item like so:

```
import Foundation

class RequestHandler: NSObject, NSExtensionRequestHandling {

    func beginRequestWithExtensionContext(context: NSExtensionContext) {
        let extensionItem = NSExtensionItem()

        extensionItem.userInfo = [
            "uniqueIdentifier": "uniqueIdentifierForSampleItem",
            "urlString": "http://reddit.com/r/askreddit",
            "date": NSDate()
        ]

        extensionItem.attributedTitle = NSAttributedString(string: "Reddit")

        extensionItem.attributedContentText = NSAttributedString(
            string: "AskReddit, one of the best subreddits there is")

        guard let img = NSBundle.mainBundle().URLForResource("ExtIcon",
            withExtension: "png") else {
            context.completeRequestReturningItems(nil, completionHandler: nil)
            return
        }

        extensionItem.attachments = [NSItemProvider(contentsOfURL: img)!]

        context.completeRequestReturningItems([extensionItem], completionHandler: nil)
    }

}
```

Run your code and then open Safari on the device. Navigate to the bookmarks button and then shared links to see your link displayed (Figure 5-6).

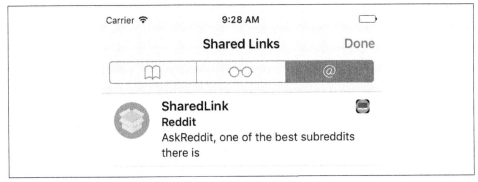

Figure 5-6. Our shared link is displayed in the list

The user can also subscribe or unsubscribe from various shared link providers by tapping the Subscriptions button (see Figure 5-7).

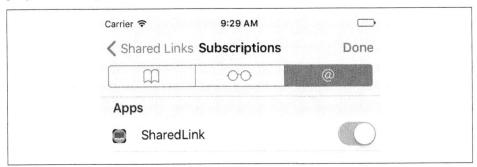

Figure 5-7. The user can subscribe to or unsubscribe from shared links providers right in Safari

5.3 Maintaining Your App's Indexed Content

Problem

You want to know when iOS is about to delete your indexed items and you would like to be able to provide new content to the search index.

Solution

This is an extension to the search capability explained in Recipe 6.1.

Add a Spotlight Index Extension to your app and update the index right in your extension (see Figure 5-8).

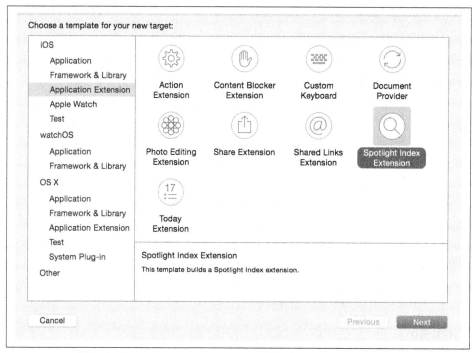

Figure 5-8. Adding a Spotlight Index Extension will allow us to re-index our app's searchable content

Discussion

Every now and then, iOS has to clean up the search index on a device. When this happens, apps that have provided searchable content will be given a chance to reindex their items. To get started, create a Spotlight index extension as shown in Figure 5-8. I've given mine the name of `Reindex`. It's up to you what you want to name your extension. Now you will get a class called `IndexRequestHandler` in your extension. It offers two methods:

- `searchableIndex(_:reindexAllSearchableItemsWithAcknowledgementHan dler:)`
- `searchableIndex(_:reindexSearchableItemsWithIdentifiers:acknowledge mentHandler:)`

The first method gets called when you are asked to reindex *all* your previously indexed items. This can happen if the index is corrupted on the device and you are asked to reindex all of your content. The second method will be called on your extension if you have to index specific items with the given identifiers. You will be given a function called an *acknowledgement handler* to call when you are done indexing again.

 In both of these methods, the first parameter that you are given is an index into which you have to index your items. Use that index instead of the default index.

Here is an example. Let's define a protocol that dictates what indexable items have to look like:

```
protocol Indexable{
    var id: String {get set}
    var title: String {get set}
    var description: String {get set}
    var url: NSURL? {get set}
    var thumbnail: UIImage? {get set}
}
```

And then a structure that conforms to our protocol:

```
struct Indexed : Indexable{
    //Indexable conformance
    var id: String
    var title: String
    var description: String
    var url: NSURL?
    var thumbnail: UIImage?
}
```

Later on we are going to go through an array of `Indexed` instances, grab all the IDs, and put those in an array. Then, when we are asked by iOS to index certain items with given IDs, we can just find that ID in our array, and then find the associated indexed item using the ID. For this, we can use protocol extensions on sequence types. I wrote about this in Recipe 1.12:

```
extension SequenceType where Generator.Element : Indexable{
    func allIds() -> [String]{
        var ids = [String]()
```

```
        for (_, v) in self.enumerate(){
          ids.append(v.id)
        }
        return ids
    }
}
```

And now the juicy part: our extension. We construct an array of indexed items:

```
lazy var indexedItems: [Indexed] = {

    var items = [Indexed]()
    for n in 1...10{
      items.append(Indexed(id: "id \(n)", title: "Item \(n)",
        description: "Description \(n)", url: nil, thumbnail: nil))
    }
    return items

}()
```

When we are asked to reindex all our items, we just go through this array and reindex them (see Recipe 6.1):

```
override func searchableIndex(searchableIndex: CSSearchableIndex,
  reindexAllSearchableItemsWithAcknowledgementHandler
  acknowledgementHandler: () -> Void) {

    for _ in indexedItems{
      //TODO: you can index the item here.
    }

    //call this handler once you are done
    acknowledgementHandler()
}
```

When we are asked to reindex only specific items with given identifiers, we use our sequence type extension to find all the IDs of our indexed items. Then we search through these IDs for the IDs that iOS gave us. Should we find a match, we will rein-dex that item. Code for reindexing is not shown here, but Recipe 6.1 shows you how to do it:

```
override func searchableIndex(searchableIndex: CSSearchableIndex,
  reindexSearchableItemsWithIdentifiers identifiers: [String],
  acknowledgementHandler: () -> Void) {

    //get all the identifiers strings that we have
    let ourIds = indexedItems.allIds()

    //go through the items that we have and look for the given id
    var n = 0
    for i in identifiers{
      if let index = ourIds.indexOf(i){
        let _ = indexedItems[index]
```

```
        //TODO: reindex this item.
      }
      n++
    }

    acknowledgementHandler()
  }
```

See Also

Recipe 3.6 and Recipe 5.1

CHAPTER 6

Web and Search

iOS 9 brings with it some really exciting functionality, such as indexing contents inside your app as searchable content on an iOS device. Even better, you can contribute to iOS's public search index so that your searchable content appears on devices that don't even have your app installed. That's pretty cool, don't you agree? In this chapter we'll have a look at all these great features.

6.1 Making Your App's Content Searchable

Problem

You want the user to be able to search within the contents *inside* your app, from iOS's search functionality (see Figure 6-1).

Solution

First construct an object of type `CSSearchableItemAttributeSet`. This will represent the metadata for any one item that you want to index in the search. Having the metadata, construct an instance of the `CSSearchableItem` class with your metadata and expiration date, plus some other properties that you will see soon. Index an item using the `CSSearchableIndex` class. You'll get a completion block that will let you know whether or not things went well.

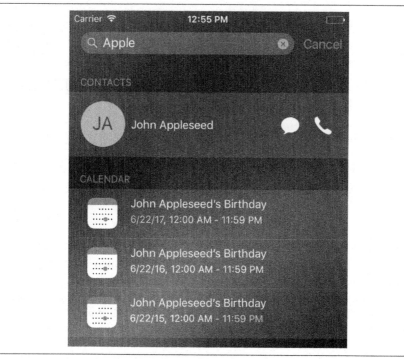

Figure 6-1. iOS 9 has improved search functionality

Discussion

You have to keep quite a few things in mind when indexing items in the local device search functionality. I'll walk you through them one by one. Always keep this index in a useful state. Don't index stuff that you don't need, and make sure you delete the old items. You can specify an expiration date for your content, so I suggest that you always do that.

Let's look at an example. We will start off by including the two required frameworks that we are going to use and a handy extension:

```
import CoreSpotlight
import MobileCoreServices

extension String{
  func toFoundationString() -> NSString{
    return NSString(string: self)
  }
}
```

Then we will proceed to deleting all existing indexed items using the `deleteAll SearchableItemsWithCompletionHandler(_:)` method of the `CSSearchableIndex` class. This method takes in a closure that gives you an optional error. Check this error if you want to find out whether something went wrong:

```
//delete the existing indexed items
CSSearchableIndex.defaultSearchableIndex()
  .deleteAllSearchableItemsWithCompletionHandler {err in
    if let err = err{
      print("Error in deleting \(err)")
    }
  }
```

Now let's instantiate our metadata of type `CSSearchableItemAttributeSet` and give it a title, description, path and URL, keywords, and a thumbnail:

```
let attr = CSSearchableItemAttributeSet(
  itemContentType: kUTTypeText as String)

attr.title = "My item"
attr.contentDescription = "My description"
attr.path = "http://reddit.com"
attr.contentURL = NSURL(string: attr.path!)!
attr.keywords = ["reddit", "subreddit", "today", "i", "learned"]

if let url = NSBundle(forClass: self.dynamicType)
  .URLForResource("Icon", withExtension: "png"){
    attr.thumbnailData = NSData(contentsOfURL: url)
}
```

Then let's create the actual searchable item of type `CSSearchableItem` and set its expiration date 20 seconds into the future:

```
//searchable item
let item = CSSearchableItem(
  uniqueIdentifier: attr.contentURL!.absoluteString,
  domainIdentifier: nil, attributeSet: attr)

let cal = NSCalendar.currentCalendar()

//our content expires in 20 seconds
item.expirationDate = cal.dateFromComponents(cal
  .componentsInTimeZone(cal.timeZone, fromDate:
    NSDate().dateByAddingTimeInterval(20)))
```

Last but not least, use the `indexSearchableItems(_:)` method of the `CSSearcha bleIndex` class to index the item that we just created. You can index an array of items, but we have just one item, so let's index that for now:

```
//now index the item
CSSearchableIndex.defaultSearchableIndex()
  .indexSearchableItems([item]) {err in
    guard err == nil else{
      print("Error occurred \(err!)")
      return
```

```
        }

            print("We successfully indexed the item. Will expire in 20 seconds")

    }
```

When the user taps your item in the results list, your app will be opened and iOS will call the `application(_:continueUserActivity:restorationHandler:)` method on your app delegate. In this method, you have to do a few things:

1. Check the activity type that is given to you and make sure it is `CSSearchableIte
   mActionType`. The aforementioned method gets called under various circumstances, for example, with HandOff, so we have to make sure we are responding only to activities that concern indexed items:
2. Check the `userInfo` property of the activity and read the value of the `CSSearcha
   bleItemActivityIdentifier` key from it. This should be the identifier for your indexed item.

```
    func application(application: UIApplication,
        continueUserActivity userActivity: NSUserActivity,
        restorationHandler: ([AnyObject]?) -> Void) -> Bool {

        guard userActivity.activityType == CSSearchableItemActionType,
        let userInfo = userActivity.userInfo,
        let id = userInfo[CSSearchableItemActivityIdentifier
          .toFoundationString()] as? String
        else{
            return false
        }

        //now we have access to id of the activity. and that is the URL
        print(id)

        return true

    }
```

Run your code and then send your app to the background. Open a search in your iPhone and do a search on the item that we just indexed (see Figure 6-2).

Figure 6-2. Our item is listed in the search results

See Also

Recipe 5.3

6.2 Making User Activities Searchable

Problem

You want to allow user activities inside your app to be searchable. User activities are of type `NSUserActivity`.

Solution

Use the `eligibleForSearch` and `eligibleForPublicIndexing` properties of the `NSUserActivity` class to mark your activities as searchable.

Discussion

Let's say that the user is inside your app and is editing the text inside a text field. You start a user activity and want the user to be able to search for this activity in her home screen, then continue with that activity later. Start with the UI. Drop a text field and a text view on your view controller to make it look like Figure 6-3.

Figure 6-3. Put a text field and a text view on your UI

The text field will allow the user to enter whatever text she wants, and we will use the text view to write log messages so that we know what is going on under the hood of our app and so will the user. Hook these up to your code. I've named the text field textField and the text view status. Also set the delegate of your text field to your view controller, because you are going to want to know when the text field becomes active and inactive. That lets you update the user activity accordingly.

Make your view controller conform to UITextFieldDelegate and NSUserActivityDelegate protocols and implement the user activity delegate methods:

```
func userActivityWasContinued(userActivity: NSUserActivity) {
  log("Activity was continued")
}

func userActivityWillSave(userActivity: NSUserActivity) {
  log("Activity will save")
}
```

Let's also write a handy method that allows us to log messages into our text view:

```
func log(t: String){
  dispatch_async(dispatch_get_main_queue()) {
    self.status.text = t + "\n" + self.status.text
  }
}
```

We need another method that can read the contents of our text field and, if it's nil, give us an empty string:

```
func textFieldText() -> String{
  if let txt = self.textField.text{
    return txt
  } else {
    return ""
  }
}
```

Then create your user activity as a lazy variable and mark it as searchable:

```
//TODO: change this ID to something relevant to your app
let activityType = "se.pixolity.Making-User-Activities-Searchable.editText"
let activityTxtKey = "se.pixolity.Making-User-Activities-Searchable.txt"

lazy var activity: NSUserActivity = {
  let a = NSUserActivity(activityType: self.activityType)
  a.title = "Text Editing"
  a.eligibleForHandoff = true
  a.eligibleForSearch = true
  //do this only if it makes sense
  //a.eligibleForPublicIndexing = true
  a.delegate = self
  a.keywords = ["txt", "text", "edit", "update"]

  let att = CSSearchableItemAttributeSet(
    itemContentType: kUTTypeText as String)
  att.title = a.title
  att.contentDescription = "Editing text right in the app"
  att.keywords = Array(a.keywords)

  if let u = NSBundle.mainBundle().URLForResource("Icon",
    withExtension: "png"){
      att.thumbnailData = NSData(contentsOfURL: u)
  }
  a.contentAttributeSet = att

  return a
}()
```

 Make sure that you import the CoreSpotlight and MobileCore Services frameworks.

Once your text field becomes active, mark the activity as the current one:

```
func textFieldDidBeginEditing(textField: UITextField) {
  log("Activity is current")
  userActivity = activity
  activity.becomeCurrent()
}

func textFieldDidEndEditing(textField: UITextField) {
  log("Activity resigns being current")
  activity.resignCurrent()
  userActivity = nil
}
```

When the text field's content changes, mark that the user activity needs to be updated:

```
func textField(textField: UITextField,
  shouldChangeCharactersInRange range: NSRange,
  replacementString string: String) -> Bool {

    activity.needsSave = true

    return true

}
```

A method in your view controller named updateUserActivityState(_:) gets called periodically when the current activity needs to be updated. Here you get the chance to update the user info dictionary of the activity:

```
override func updateUserActivityState(a: NSUserActivity) {

  log("We are asked to update the activity state")

  a.addUserInfoEntriesFromDictionary(
    [self.activityTxtKey : self.textFieldText()])

  super.updateUserActivityState(a)

}
```

That's it, really. Now when the user starts writing text in the text field, and then sends the app to background, she will be able to search for the activity that she had started right on her home screen and then continue where she left off. I leave the details where we handle the request to continue the user activity up to you, because they are *not* new APIs.

See Also

Recipe 5.3 and Recipe 6.1

6.3 Deleting Your App's Searchable Content

Problem

You have indexed some items in Spotlight and you would like to get rid of that now.

Solution

Use a combination of the following methods on CSSearchableIndex:

- deleteAllSearchableItemsWithCompletionHandler(_:)
- deleteSearchableItemsWithDomainIdentifiers(_:completionHandler:)
- deleteSearchableItemsWithIdentifiers(_:completionHandler:)

Discussion

Let's have a look at an example. Say that you have already indexed some items (see Recipe 6.1) and you want to delete that content. The first thing is to get a handle to the `CSSearchableIndex` class:

```
let identifiers = [
  "com.yourcompany.etc1",
  "com.yourcompany.etc2",
  "com.yourcompany.etc3"
]

let i = CSSearchableIndex(name: NSBundle.mainBundle().bundleIdentifier!)
```

Then use the `fetchLastClientStateWithCompletionHandler(_:)` method on the index to get the latest application state that you had submitted to the index. After that, you can begin deleting the items inside the `identifiers` array by using the `beginIndexBatch()` function on the index. Then use the `deleteSearchableItemsWithIdentifiers(_:)` function, which returns a completion handler. This handler will return an optional error that dictates whether the deletion went OK or not. Once we are done, we end the batch updates on the index with the `endIndexBatchWithClientState(_:completionHandler:)` method:

```
i.fetchLastClientStateWithCompletionHandler {clientState, err in
  guard err == nil else{
    print("Could not fetch last client state")
    return
  }

  let state: NSData
  if let s = clientState{
    state = s
  } else {
    state = NSData()
  }

  i.beginIndexBatch()

  i.deleteSearchableItemsWithIdentifiers(identifiers) {err in
    if let e = err{
      print("Error happened \(e)")
    } else {
      print("Successfully deleted the given identifiers")
    }
  }
  i.endIndexBatchWithClientState(state, completionHandler: {err in
    guard err == nil else{
      print("Error happened in ending batch updates = \(err!)")
      return
    }
    print("Successfully batch updated the index")
```

```
            })

        }
```

 The content identifiers that I've put in the `identifiers` array are just an example. I don't know what identifiers you want to use, but make sure that you update this array before attempting to delete the existing indexed items.

See Also

Recipe 5.3 and Recipe 6.2

CHAPTER 7

Multitasking

iOS 9 added some really cool multitasking functionalities to select devices, such as the latest iPads. One of these functionalities is PiP, or Picture in Picture. In this chapter, we'll have a look at some of these exciting features.

7.1 Adding Picture in Picture Playback Functionality

Problem

You want to let a user shrink a video to occupy a portion of the screen, so that she can view and interact with other content in other apps.

Solution

I'll break the process down into small and digestible steps:

1. You need a view that has a layer of type `AVPlayerLayer`. This layer will be used by a view controller to display the video.
2. Instantiate an item of type `VPlayerItem` that represents the video.
3. Take the player item and place it inside an instance of `AVPlayer`.
4. Assign this player to your view's layer player object. (Don't worry if this sounds confusing. I'll explain it soon.)
5. Assign this view to your view controller's main view and issue the `play()` function on the player to start normal playback.
6. Using KVO, listen to changes to the `currentItem.status` property of your player and wait until the status becomes `ReadyToPlay`, at which point you create an instance of the `AVPictureInPictureController` class.

7. Start a KVO listener on the `pictureInPicturePossible` property of your controller. Once this value becomes `true`, let the user know that she can now go into Picture in Picture mode.

8. Now when the user presses a button to start Picture in Picture, read the value of `pictureInPicturePossible` from your controller for safety's sake, and if it checks out, call the `startPictureInPicture()` function on the controller to start the Picture in Picture eventually.

Discussion

Picture in Picture is finally here. Let's get started. Armed with what you learned in the solution section of this recipe, let's start defining our view. Create a view class and call it `PipView`. Go into the *PipView.swift* file and start importing the right frameworks:

```
import Foundation
import UIKit
import AVFoundation
```

Then define what a "pippable" item is. It is any type that has a PiP layer and a PiP player:

```
protocol Pippable{
  var pipLayer: AVPlayerLayer{get}
  var pipLayerPlayer: AVPlayer? {get set}
}
```

Extend `UIView` to make it pippable:

```
extension UIView : Pippable{

  var pipLayer: AVPlayerLayer{
    get{return layer as! AVPlayerLayer}
  }

  //shortcut into pipLayer.player
  var pipLayerPlayer: AVPlayer?{
    get{return pipLayer.player}
    set{pipLayer.player = newValue}
  }

  override public func awakeFromNib() {
    super.awakeFromNib()
    backgroundColor = .blackColor()
  }

}
```

Last but not least for this view, change the view's layer class to `AVPlayerLayer`:

```
class PipView : UIView{
```

```
override class func layerClass() -> AnyClass{
  return AVPlayerLayer.self
}


}
```

Go to your view controller's storyboard and change the main view's class to `PipView`. Also embed your view controller in a navigation controller and put two bar button items on the nav bar, namely:

- Play (give it a play button style)
- PiP (by pressing this we enable PiP; disable this button by default and hook it to an outlet in your code.)

So you'll end up with something like Figure 7-1.

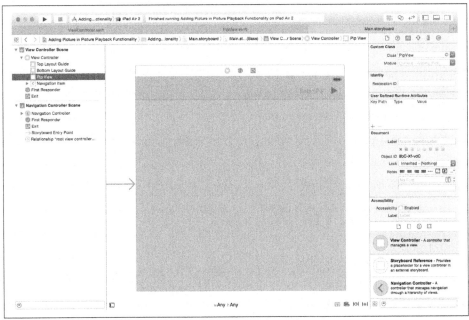

Figure 7-1. Your view controller should look like this (should is too strong a word really!)

Hook up the two buttons to your view controller's code. The Play button will be hooked to a method called `play()` and the PiP button to `beginPip()`. Now let's head to our view controller and import some frameworks we need:

```
import UIKit
import AVKit
import AVFoundation
import SharedCode
```

Define the KVO context for watching the properties of our player:

```
private var kvoContext = 0
let pipPossible = "pictureInPicturePossible"
let currentItemStatus = "currentItem.status"
```

Then our view controller becomes pippable:

```
protocol PippableViewController{
  var pipView: PipView {get}
}
extension ViewController : PippableViewController{
  var pipView: PipView{
    return view as! PipView
  }
}
```

 If you want to, you can define your view controller as conformant to AVPictureInPictureControllerDelegate to get delegate messages from the PiP view controller.

I'll also define a property for the PiP button on my view controller so that I can enable this button when PiP is available:

```
@IBOutlet var beginPipBtn: UIBarButtonItem!
```

We also need a player of type AVPlayer. Don't worry about its URL; we will set it later:

```
lazy var player: AVPlayer = {
  let p = AVPlayer()
  p.addObserver(self, forKeyPath: currentItemStatus,
    options: .New, context: &kvoContext)
  return p
}()
```

Here we define the PiP controller and the video URL. As soon as the URL is set, we construct an asset to hold the URL, place it inside the player, and set the player on our view's layer:

```
var pipController: AVPictureInPictureController?

var videoUrl: NSURL? = nil{
  didSet{
    if let u = videoUrl{
      let asset = AVAsset(URL: u)
      let item = AVPlayerItem(asset: asset,
        automaticallyLoadedAssetKeys: ["playable"])
      player.replaceCurrentItemWithPlayerItem(item)
      pipView.pipLayerPlayer = player
    }
```

```
    }
  }
```

I also need a method that returns the URL of the video I am going to play. I've embedded a public domain video to my app and it resides in my app bundle. Check out this book's GitHub repo for sample code:

```
var embeddedVideo: NSURL?{
  return NSBundle.mainBundle().URLForResource("video", withExtension: "mp4")
}
```

We need to find out whether PiP is supported by calling the isPictureInPictureSupported() class method of the AVPictureInPictureController class:

```
func isPipSupported() -> Bool{
  guard AVPictureInPictureController.isPictureInPictureSupported() else{
    //no pip
    return false
  }

  return true
}
```

When we start our PiP controller, we also need to make sure that the audio plays well even though the player is detached from our app. For that, we have to set our app's audio playback category:

```
func setAudioCategory() -> Bool{
  //set the audio category
  do{
    try AVAudioSession.sharedInstance().setCategory(
      AVAudioSessionCategoryPlayback)
    return true
  } catch {
    return false
  }
}
```

When PiP playback is available, we can finally construct our PiP controller with our player's layer. Remember, if the layer is not ready yet to play PiP, constructing the PiP view controller will fail:

```
func startPipController(){
  pipController = AVPictureInPictureController(playerLayer: pipView.pipLayer)
  guard let controller = pipController else{
    return
  }

  controller.addObserver(self, forKeyPath: pipPossible,
    options: .New, context: &kvoContext)
}
```

Write the code for play() now. We don't have to check for availability of PiP just because we want to play a video:

```
@IBAction func play() {
    guard setAudioCategory() else{
        alert("Could not set the audio category")
        return
    }

    guard let u = embeddedVideo else{
        alert("Cannot find the embedded video")
        return
    }

    videoUrl = u
    player.play()

}
```

As soon as the user presses the PiP button, we start PiP if the pictureInPicturePos sible() method of our PiP controller returns true:

```
@IBAction func beginPip() {

    guard isPipSupported() else{
        alert("PiP is not supported on your machine")
        return
    }

    guard let controller = pipController else{
        alert("Could not instantiate the pip controller")
        return
    }

    controller.addObserver(self, forKeyPath: pipPossible,
        options: .New, context: &kvoContext)

    if controller.pictureInPicturePossible{
        controller.startPictureInPicture()
    } else {
        alert("Pip is not possible")
    }

}
```

Last but not least, we listen for KVO messages:

```
override func observeValueForKeyPath(keyPath: String?,
    ofObject object: AnyObject?,
    change: [String : AnyObject]?,
    context: UnsafeMutablePointer<Void>) {

    guard context == &kvoContext else{
```

```
      return
    }

    if keyPath == pipPossible{
      guard let possibleInt = change?[NSKeyValueChangeNewKey]
        as? NSNumber else{
          beginPipBtn.enabled = false
          return
      }

      beginPipBtn.enabled = possibleInt.boolValue

    }

    else if keyPath == currentItemStatus{

      guard let statusInt = change?[NSKeyValueChangeNewKey] as? NSNumber,
        let status = AVPlayerItemStatus(rawValue: statusInt.integerValue)
        where status == .ReadyToPlay else{
          return
      }

      startPipController()

    }

  }
```

Give this a go in an iPad Air 2 or a similar device that has PiP support.

See Also

Recipe 3.11

7.2 Handling Low Power Mode and Providing Alternatives

Problem

You want to know whether the device is in low power mode and want to be updated on the status of this mode as the user changes it.

Solution

Read the value of the `lowPowerModeEnabled` property of your process (of type `NSPro cessInfo`) to find out whether the device is in low power mode, and listen to NSPro cessInfoPowerStateDidChangeNotification notifications to find out when this state changes.

Discussion

Low power mode is a feature that Apple has placed inside iOS so that users can preserve battery whenever they wish to. For instance, if you have 10% battery while some background apps are running, you can save power by:

- Disabling background apps
- Reducing network activity
- Disabling automatic mail pulls
- Disabling animated backgrounds
- Disabling visual effects

And that's what low power mode does. In Figure 7-2, low power mode is disabled at the moment because there is a good amount of battery left on this device. Should the battery reach about 10%, the user will automatically be asked to enable low power mode.

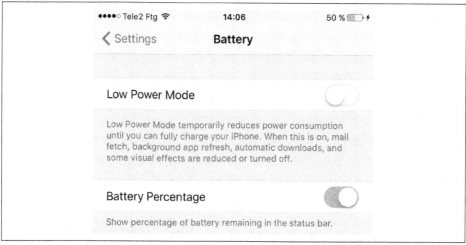

Figure 7-2. Low power mode in the Settings app

Let's create an app that wants to download a URL but won't do so when low power mode is enabled. Instead, the app will defer the download until this mode is disabled. So let's start by listening to NSProcessInfoPowerStateDidChangeNotification notifications:

```
override func viewDidLoad() {
    super.viewDidLoad()

    NSNotificationCenter.defaultCenter().addObserver(self,
```

```
    selector: "powerModeChanged:",
    name: NSProcessInfoPowerStateDidChangeNotification, object: nil)

  downloadNow()

}
```

Our custom downloadNow() method has to avoid downloading the file if the device is
in low power mode:

```
func downloadNow(){

  guard let url = NSURL(string: "http://localhost:8888/video.mp4") where
    !processInfo.lowPowerModeEnabled else{
    return
  }

  //do the download here
  print(url)

  mustDownloadVideo = false

}
```

Last but not least, write the powerModeChanged(_:) method that we have hooked to
our notification:

```
class ViewController: UIViewController {

  var mustDownloadVideo = true
  let processInfo = NSProcessInfo.processInfo()

  func powerModeChanged(notif: NSNotification){

    guard mustDownloadVideo else{
      return
    }

    downloadNow()

  }

  ...
```

CHAPTER 8

Maps and Location

In this chapter, we will have a look at some awesome updates to the MapKit and Core Location frameworks.

8.1 Requesting the User's Location a Single Time

Problem

You want an optimized and energy-efficient way of requesting the current location of the user only once.

Solution

Use the requestLocation() method of the CLLocationManager class. The new location will be sent to your location manager's locationManager(_:didUpdateLocations:) delegate method. Errors will be reported on locationManager(_:didFailWithError:). You can make only one request to this method at any given time. A new request will cancel the previous one.

Discussion

Place a button on your interface inside IB and then hook it up to a method in your code called requestLocation(). Then go into your *Info.plist* file and set the value of the NSLocationWhenInUseUsageDescription key to a valid string that explains to the user why you want to get her location. You will also have to import the CoreLocation framework and make your view controller conform to CLLocationManagerDelegate.

Implement a variable in your view controller to represent the location manager:

```
lazy var locationManager: CLLocationManager = {
  let m = CLLocationManager()
  m.delegate = self
  m.desiredAccuracy = kCLLocationAccuracyNearestTenMeters
  return m
}()
```

When your button is pressed, request access to the user's location. This requests users location to be delivered to your app only when it is the foreground app. As soon as your app is sent to the background, iOS stops delivering location updates to you:

```
@IBAction func requestLocation() {

    locationManager.requestWhenInUseAuthorization()

}
```

Then wait for the user to accept or reject the request. If everything is going smoothly, request the user's location:

```
func locationManager(manager: CLLocationManager,
  didChangeAuthorizationStatus status: CLAuthorizationStatus) {

    if case .AuthorizedWhenInUse = status{
      manager.requestLocation()
    } else {
      //TODO: we didn't get access, handle this
    }

}
```

Last but not least, wait for the location gathering mechanism to fail or succeed:

```
func locationManager(manager: CLLocationManager,
  didUpdateLocations locations: [CLLocation]) {
    //TODO: now you have access to the location. do your work
}

func locationManager(manager: CLLocationManager,
  didFailWithError error: NSError) {
  //TODO: handle the error
}
```

See Also

Recipe 8.2

8.2 Requesting the User's Location in Background

Problem

You want to receive updates on the user's location while in the background. Being a good iOS citizen, you won't ask for this unless you *really* need it for the *main* functionality of your app.

Solution

Set the `allowsBackgroundLocationUpdates` property of your location manager to `true` and ask for location updates using the `requestAlwaysAuthorization()` function.

Discussion

When linked against iOS 9, apps that want to ask for a user's location when the app is in the background have to set the `allowsBackgroundLocationUpdates` property of their location manager to `true`. We are going to have to have a look at an example. Start a single view controller app, place a button on your UI with IB, and give it a title similar to "Request background location updates". Then hook it to a method in your view controller and name the method `requestBackgroundLocationUpdates()`. In your `Info.plist` file, set the string value of the `NSLocationAlwaysUsageDescription` key and make sure that it explains exactly why you want to access the user's location even in the background. Then go into the Capabilities section of your target, and under Background Modes, enable "Location updates" (see Figure 8-1).

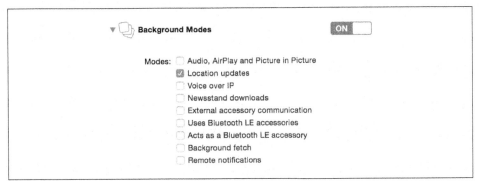

Figure 8-1. Enabling location updates in Background Modes in your project

Now import `CoreLocation` in your code and make your view controller conformant to `CLLocationManagerDelegate`. Create your location manager and make sure that the `allowsBackgroundLocationUpdates` property is set to `true`.

```
lazy var locationManager: CLLocationManager = {
  let m = CLLocationManager()
  m.delegate = self
  m.desiredAccuracy = kCLLocationAccuracyNearestTenMeters
  m.allowsBackgroundLocationUpdates = true
  return m
}()
```

When the user presses the button, ask for location updates:

```
@IBAction func requestBackgroundLocationUpdates() {
  locationManager.requestAlwaysAuthorization()
}
```

Wait until the user accepts the request and then start looking for location updates:

```
func locationManager(manager: CLLocationManager,
  didChangeAuthorizationStatus status: CLAuthorizationStatus) {
    if case CLAuthorizationStatus.AuthorizedAlways = status{
      manager.startUpdatingLocation()
    }
}
```

Last but not least, implement the usual location manager methods to get to know when the user's location has changed:

```
func locationManager(manager: CLLocationManager,
  didUpdateLocations locations: [CLLocation]) {
    //TODO: now you have access to the location. do your work

}

func locationManager(manager: CLLocationManager,
  didFailWithError error: NSError) {
    //TODO: handle the error
}
```

See Also

Recipe 8.1

8.3 Customizing the Tint Color of Pins on the Map

Problem

You want to set the tint color of pin annotations on your map manually.

Solution

Use the pinTintColor property of the MKPinAnnotationView class like so:

```
let view = MKPinAnnotationView(annotation: annotation,
  reuseIdentifier: color.toString())

view.pinTintColor = color
```

Discussion

Let's check out an example. Create a single view controller project and dump a map view on top of your view. Make sure that you set the delegate of this map view to your view controller. Also link it to a variable named map in your view controller.

In the view controller, we are going to create annotations with reusable identifiers, so let's use the color as the ID:

```
import MapKit

extension UIColor{
  final func toString() -> String{

    var red = 0.0 as CGFloat
    var green = 0.0 as CGFloat
    var blue = 0.0 as CGFloat
    var alpha = 0.0 as CGFloat
    getRed(&red, green: &green, blue: &blue, alpha: &alpha)

    return "\(Int(red))\(Int(green))\(Int(blue))\(Int(alpha))"
  }
}
```

Now we create our annotation:

```
class Annotation : NSObject, MKAnnotation{
  var coordinate: CLLocationCoordinate2D
  var title: String?
  var subtitle: String?

  init(coordinate: CLLocationCoordinate2D, title: String, subtitle: String){
    self.coordinate = coordinate
    self.title = title
    self.subtitle = subtitle
  }

}
```

Now ensure that your view controller conforms to the MKMapViewDelegate protocol, define the location that you want to display on the map, and create an annotation for it:

```
let color = UIColor(red: 0.4, green: 0.8, blue: 0.6, alpha: 1.0)
let location = CLLocationCoordinate2D(latitude: 59.33, longitude: 18.056)

lazy var annotations: [MKAnnotation] = {
```

```
    return [Annotation(coordinate: self.location,
      title: "Stockholm Central Station",
      subtitle: "Stockholm, Sweden")]
  }()
```

When your view appears on the screen, add the annotation to the map:

```
override func viewDidAppear(animated: Bool) {
  super.viewDidAppear(animated)

  map.removeAnnotations(annotations)
  map.addAnnotations(annotations)

}
```

And when the map view asks for an annotation view for your annotation, return an annotation view with the custom color (see Figure 8-2):

```
func mapView(mapView: MKMapView,
  viewForAnnotation annotation: MKAnnotation) -> MKAnnotationView? {

    let view: MKPinAnnotationView
    if let v = mapView.dequeueReusableAnnotationViewWithIdentifier(
      color.toString()) where v is MKPinAnnotationView{
        view = v as! MKPinAnnotationView
    } else {
      view = MKPinAnnotationView(annotation: annotation,
        reuseIdentifier: color.toString())
    }

    view.pinTintColor = color

    return view

}
```

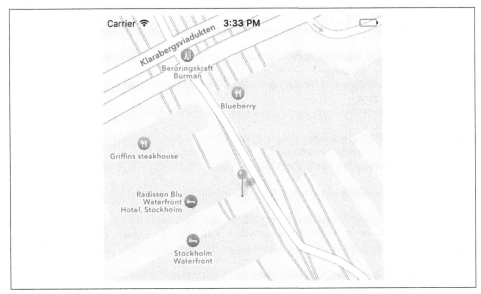

Figure 8-2. Our custom color pin is displayed on the map

See Also

Recipe 8.4 and Recipe 8.5

8.4 Providing Detailed Pin Information with Custom Views

Problem

When the user taps on an annotation in a map, you want to display details for that annotation in a view.

Solution

Set the detailCalloutAccessoryView property of your MKAnnotationView instances to a valid UIView instance.

Discussion

Create your project just as you did in Recipe 8.3. In this recipe, I am going to reuse a lot of code from the aforementioned recipe, *except* for the implementation of the map View(_:viewForAnnotation:) delegate method of our view controller. Instead, we are going to construct instances here of MKAnnotationView and then set the detail callout accessory view:

```
func mapView(mapView: MKMapView,
    viewForAnnotation annotation: MKAnnotation) -> MKAnnotationView? {

    let view: MKAnnotationView
    if let v = mapView
        .dequeueReusableAnnotationViewWithIdentifier(identifier){
        //reuse
        view = v
    } else {
        //create a new one
        view = MKAnnotationView(annotation: annotation,
            reuseIdentifier: identifier)

        view.canShowCallout = true

        if let img = UIImage(named: "Icon"){
            view.detailCalloutAccessoryView = UIImageView(image: img)
        }

        if let extIcon = UIImage(named: "ExtIcon"){
            view.image = extIcon
        }
    }

    return view

}
```

Figure 8-3 shows the image of an annotation on a map. The image inside the callout is the detail callout accessory view.

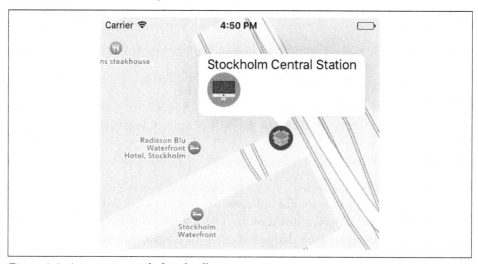

Figure 8-3. Annotation with detail callout accessory

I am using two public domain images in this recipe. You also can find public domain images on Google.

See Also

Recipe 8.3 and Recipe 8.5

8.5 Displaying Traffic, Scale, and Compass Indicators on the Map

Problem

You want to display traffic as well as the little compass and scale indicators on the map view.

Solution

Set the following properties of your map view to `true`:

- `showsCompass`
- `showsTraffic`
- `showsScale`

Discussion

Place a map view on your view and set the appropriate constraints on it so that it stretches across the width and height of your view controller's view. This is really optional, but useful so the user can see the map view properly on all devices. Then follow what I talked about in Recipe 8.3 to place an annotation on the map. Write a code similar to the following in a method such as `viewDidLoad`:

```
map.showsCompass = true
map.showsTraffic = true
map.showsScale = true
```

The results will be similar to those shown in Figure 8-4. The scale is shown on top left and the compass on the top right. You have to rotate the map for the compass to appear.

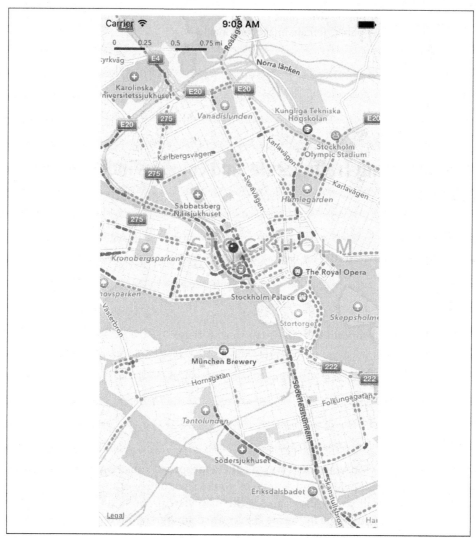

Figure 8-4. Map with scale, compass, and traffic

See Also

Recipe 8.3 and Recipe 8.4

8.6 Providing an ETA for Transit Transport Type

Problem

You want your app to provide routing options to the user when she is in the iOS maps app.

Solution

Mark your app as a routing app and construct an instance of the `MKDirectionsRe quest` class. Set the `transportType` property of that request to `Transit` and send your request to Apple to calculate an estimated time of arrival (ETA), using the `calcula teETAWithCompletionHandler(_:)` method of the `MKDirections` class.

> We use Geo JSON files (*http://geojson.org/geojson-spec.html*) in this recipe, so read the spec for that format first, please.

Discussion

Create a single-view application. Then head to the Capabilities tab in Xcode, enable the Maps section, and mark the routing options that you believe your app will be able to provide (see Figure 8-5). I've enabled all these items for demonstration purposes. You probably wouldn't want to enable *all* of these in your app.

Figure 8-5. Transportation routing options

Create a new *Directions.geoJson* file in your app and then head over to GeoJson.io (*http://geojson.io/*) to create the polygon that defines your routing coverage area. Then copy and paste the generated content and place it in the aforementioned file in your project. Now go and edit your target's scheme. Under Run and then Options, find the Routing App Coverage file section and select your file (see Figure 8-6).

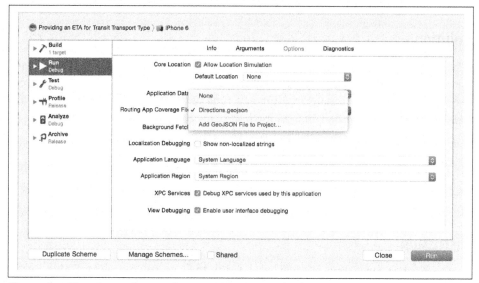

Figure 8-6. Here I am selecting the routing coverage file for my project

 You can always go to GeoJsonLint (*http://geojsonlint.com/*) to validate your Geo JSON files.

This will allow the maps app to open my app whenever the user asks for transit information on the iOS maps app. Now code the `application(_:openURL:options:)` method of your app delegate and handle the routing request there:

```
func application(app: UIApplication, openURL url: NSURL,
  options: [String : AnyObject]) -> Bool {

    guard MKDirectionsRequest.isDirectionsRequestURL(url) else{
      return false
    }

    //now we have the url
    let req = MKDirectionsRequest(contentsOfURL: url)

    guard req.source != nil && req.destination != nil else{
      return false
```

```
    }

    req.transportType = .Transit
    req.requestsAlternateRoutes = true

    let dir = MKDirections(request: req)

    dir.calculateETAWithCompletionHandler {response, error in
      guard let resp = response where error == nil else{
        //handle the error
        print(error!)
        return
      }

      print("ETA response = \(resp)")

    }

    return true
  }
```

Now open the maps app and ask for directions from one location to another. If the maps app couldn't handle the request, it will show a little "View Routing Apps" button. Regardless of whether the maps app could or couldn't show the routing options, the user can always press the little navigation button to open alternative routing apps (see Figure 8-7). Your app will be displayed in the list of routing apps if the user asks for a routing option you support, and if the starting and stopping points are within the shape you defined in your Geo JSON file. When the user opens your app, your app delegate will be informed and will calculate an ETA.

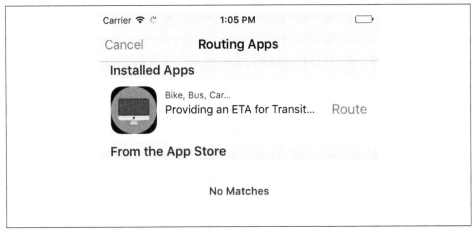

Figure 8-7. Our app, displayed in the list of routing apps

See Also

Recipe 8.5

8.7 Launching the iOS Maps App in Transit Mode

Problem

You want to launch iOS's maps app in transit mode.

Solution

When calling the `openMapsWithItems(_:launchOptions:)` class method of `MKMapI tem`, in the options collection, set the value of the `MKLaunchOptionsDirectionsMode Key` key to `MKLaunchOptionsDirectionsModeTransit`.

Discussion

Let's create a single-view controller app and place a button on the view controller to open a map. Set the title of this button to something like "Open maps app in transit mode." Then hook it up to your view controller. For every coordinate of type `CLLoca tionCoordinate2D`, you have to create an instance of `MKPlacemark` and then from the placemark, create an instance of `MKMapItem`.

Here is the source map item:

```
let srcLoc = CLLocationCoordinate2D(latitude: 59.328564,
    longitude: 18.061448)
let srcPlc = MKPlacemark(coordinate: srcLoc, addressDictionary: nil)
let src = MKMapItem(placemark: srcPlc)
```

Followed by the destination map item:

```
let desLoc = CLLocationCoordinate2D(latitude: 59.746148,
    longitude: 18.683281)
let desPlc = MKPlacemark(coordinate: desLoc, addressDictionary: nil)
let des = MKMapItem(placemark: desPlc)
```

You can use the Get Latitude Longitude website (*http://www.latlong.net/*) to find the latitude and longitude of any point on the map.

Now we can launch the app, under transit mode, with the source and the destination points:

```
let options = [
  MKLaunchOptionsDirectionsModeKey : MKLaunchOptionsDirectionsModeTransit
]

MKMapItem.openMapsWithItems([src, des], launchOptions: options)
```

See Also

Recipe 8.5 and Recipe 8.6

8.8 Showing Maps in Flyover Mode

Problem

You want to display your maps in a flyover state, where the regions on the map are translated onto a 3D globe, rather than a 2D flattened map.

Solution

Set the `mapType` property of your `MKMapView` to either `HybridFlyover` or `Satellite Flyover`.

Discussion

The flyover mode of a map view represents the map as if it were on a globe, rather than flat. So keep that in mind when placing a camera on the map to show to the user.

Let's start off with a single-view controller app. Place a map view on your view and hook it up to your code. I've named mine "map." When your view gets loaded, make sure that your map type is one of the aforementioned flyover modes:

```
map.mapType = .SatelliteFlyover
map.showsBuildings = true
```

Then when your view appears on the screen, set the camera on your map:

```
let loc = CLLocationCoordinate2D(latitude: 59.328564,
  longitude: 18.061448)

let altitude: CLLocationDistance  = 500
let pitch = CGFloat(45)
let heading: CLLocationDirection = 90

let c = MKMapCamera(lookingAtCenterCoordinate: loc,
  fromDistance: altitude, pitch: pitch, heading: heading)

map.setCamera(c, animated: true)
```

Run this code on a real device (this doesn't work very well on simulator) and you'll get a display along the lines of Figure 8-8.

Figure 8-8. The Stockholm central station is shown here under satellite flyover mode

See Also

Recipe 8.5, Recipe 8.6, and Recipe 8.7

CHAPTER 9

UI Testing

Apple added quite a good framework for UI testing in Xcode 7. This is so much fun, I am sure you are going to enjoy writing UI tests. UI tests go hand-in-hand with accessibility, so knowing a bit about that is very useful, if not necessary.

When you are debugging accessibility-enabled apps on the simulator, you may want to use a really handy dev tool that comes with Xcode: the Accessibility inspector (Figure 9-1). You can find it by right-clicking Xcode's icon in the Dock and then choosing Accessibility Inspector from Open Developer Tool. The Accessibility inspector allows you to move your mouse over items on the screen and then get information about their accessibility properties, such as their values, identifiers, etc. I suggest that you use this program whenever you want to figure out the identifiers, labels, and values of UI components on your views.

In this chapter we will have a look at how to write UI tests and evaluate the results. We will use Xcode's automated UI tests and also write some tests by hand.

9.1 Preparing Your Project for UI Testing

Problem

You either have an existing app or want to create a new app, and you want to ensure that you have some UI testing capabilities built into your app so that you can get started writing UI tests.

Figure 9-1. The Accessibility inspector shows information for a button on the screen, in the simulator

Solution

If you have an existing project, simply add a new UI Test target to your project. If you are creating a new project from scratch, you can add a UI Test target in the creation process.

Discussion

If you are starting a new app from scratch, upon setting your project's properties, you will be given a chance to create a UI testing target (see Figure 9-2). Enable the "Include UI Tests" option.

If you have an existing project and want to add a new UI testing target to it, create a new target. In the templates screen, under iOS, choose Test and then "Cocoa Touch UI Testing Bundle" (see Figure 9-3).

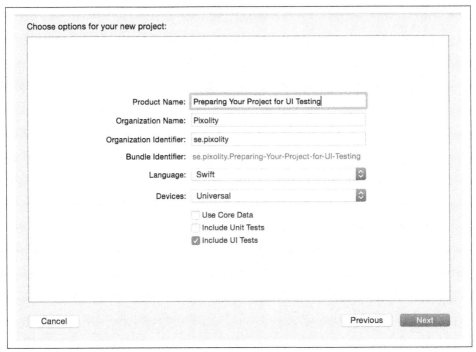

Figure 9-2. The "Include UI Tests" option in the Xcode's new project sheet

In the next screen, you will then be asked on which target inside your project you want to create the UI testing target. Make sure that you choose the right target. You can change this later, if you want, from the properties of your UI Test target (see Figure 9-4).

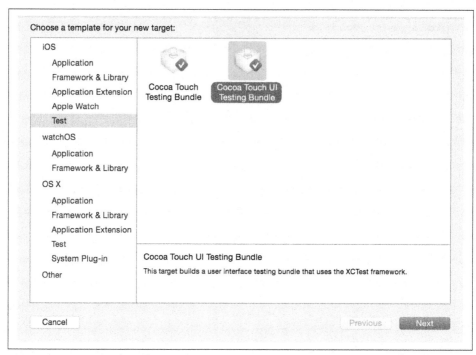

Figure 9-3. You can also add a new UI testing bundle to your existing apps

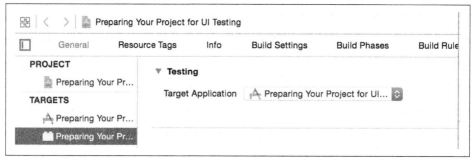

Figure 9-4. You can change the target to which your UI tests are attached even after the creation of your UI Test target

9.2 Automating UI Test Scripts

Problem

You want Xcode to generate most, if not all, of your UI testing code. You can write more UI testing code in Swift, but it's useful to take advantage of what Xcode gives you for free.

Solution

Use the new record button in Xcode when you are in your UI testing target's code (see the red circle near the upper-left corner of Figure 9-5). This will really be handy if you want to automatically get all your UI test codes written for you (but sometimes you'll still have to write some yourself).

Figure 9-5. The little circular record button on the debugger section of Xcode's window automatically gets UI test codes

 You can write all your UI tests in pure Swift code. No more mocking around with JavaScript. Jeez, isn't that a relief?!

Discussion

Let's say that you have a UI that looks similar to that shown in Figure 9-6. In this UI, the user is allowed to enter some text in the text field at the top of the screen. Once she is done, she can just press the button and the code will translate her input into its equivalent capitalized string and place it in the label at the bottom.

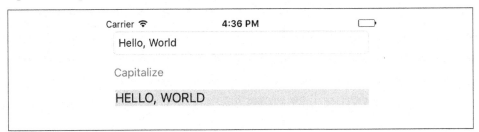

Figure 9-6. Sample UI with text fields and button

I assume that you have arranged these UI components inside a storyboard. In the Identity inspector in IB, set the accessibility label of your text field to "Full Name," the label for your button to "Capitalize," and your label to "Capitalized String." Now hook up your text field and your label to your code under the names of "lbl" and "txtField" as I've done. It just makes understanding the code easier. Otherwise you can name them what you want. Then hook the action of your button to your code. I've named this action method `capitalize()`. Now when the user presses the button, we read the text and capitalize it:

```
@IBAction func capitalize() {
    guard let txt = txtField.text where txt.characters.count > 0 else{
        return
    }
    lbl.text = txt.uppercaseString
    lbl.accessibilityValue = lbl.text
}
```

Now head over to the main Swift file for your UI tests and you should see a simple and empty method usually named `testExample()`. Put your cursor inside that method and then press the record button. Xcode will open your app and you will be able to interact with your app as you would normally. Acting as a user would be expected to act, select the text field by tapping on it and then type some text in it like "Hello, World!" Finally, press the capitalize button. Xcode will generate a test that looks more or less like:

```
let app = XCUIApplication()
let fullNameTextField = app.textFields["Full Name"]
fullNameTextField.tap()
fullNameTextField.typeText("Hello, World")
app.buttons["Capitalize"].tap()
```

We have a problem, Watson! We now need to make sure that the capitalized text inside our label is correctly capitalized. How can we do that in Xcode and get Xcode to generate the code for us? Well, the answer is: we can't! This is a logical task that you cannot automate with Xcode, so let's do it ourselves. In the app object, there is a property called `staticTexts`, so let's get our label from there:

```
let lbl = app.staticTexts["Capitalized String"]
```

This will give us an item of type `XCUIElement`. The app object is of type `XCUIApplication`, just so you know. Every element has a `value` property that is an optional value of type `AnyObject`. For our label, this is going to contain a string. So let's read its value as a string and then compare it with the string that we expect it to be:

```
let enteredString = "Hello, World!"
let expectedString = enteredString.uppercaseString

let app = XCUIApplication()
let fullNameTextField = app.textFields["Full Name"]
fullNameTextField.tap()
fullNameTextField.typeText(enteredString)
app.buttons["Capitalize"].tap()
```

```
let lbl = app.staticTexts["Capitalized String"]
XCTAssert(lbl.value as! String == expectedString)
```

 I took the opportunity to put the entered and expected strings inside string objects so that we don't have to write them multiple times.

Now press the little play button next to your test method and let Xcode do its thing. You should now see that the text has succeeded if everything went well.

9.3 Testing Text Fields, Buttons, and Labels

Problem

You want to create UI tests to work with instances of UITextField, UIButton, and UILabel.

Solution

All the aforementioned items are instances of type XCUIElement. That means that you can work with some really cool properties of them in UI testing, such as the followings:

- exists
- title
- label
- enabled
- frame
- debugDescription
- descendantsMatchingType(_:)
- childrenMatchingType(_:)

The last two in the list are a bit more advanced than what I'd like to discuss in this recipe, so we are going to talk about them later in this chapter when we discuss queries.

Discussion

Let's say that you have a label and a button. When the button is pressed, you are hiding the label (by setting its hidden property to true). You now want to write a UI test to see whether the desired effect actually happens. I assume that you've already set up your UI and you've given an accessibility label of "Button" to the button and "Label" to the label.

 I recommend that you do as much as possible in Xcode's automated recording system, where you can just visually see your UI and then let Xcode write your UI test code for you. So I will do that, not only in this recipe, but as much as possible in all other recipes in this book if appropriate.

So open the recording section of UI tests (see Figure 9-5) and press the button. The code that you'll get will be similar to this:

```
let app = XCUIApplication()
app.buttons["Button"].tap()
```

You can see that the app object has a property called buttons that returns an array of all buttons that are on the screen. That itself is awesome, in my opinion. Then the tap() method is called on the button. We want to find the label now:

```
let lbl = app.staticTexts["Label"]
```

As you can see, the app object has a property called staticTexts that is an array of labels. Any label, anywhere. That's really cool and powerful. Regardless of where the label is and who is the parent of the label, this property will return that label. Now we want to find whether that label is on screen:

```
XCTAssert(lbl.exists == false)
```

You can, of course, also read the value of a text field. You can also use the debugger to inspect the value property of a text field element using the po command. You can find all text fields that are currently on the screen using the textFields property of the app that you instantiated with XCUIApplication().

Here is an example where I try to find a text field on the screen with a specific accessibility label that I have set in my storyboard:

```
let app = XCUIApplication()

let txtField = app.textFields["MyTextField"]
XCTAssert(txtField.exists)
XCTAssert(txtField.value != nil)

let txt = txtField.value as! String

XCTAssert(txt.characters.count > 0)
```

See Also

Recipe 9.1 and Recipe 9.2

9.4 Finding UI Components

Problem

You want to be able to find your UI components wherever they are, using simple to complex queries.

Solution

Construct queries of type `XCUIElementQuery`. Link these queries together to create even more complicated queries and find your UI elements.

The `XCUIElement` class conforms to the `XCUIElementTypeQueryProvider` protocol. I am not going to waste space here and copy/paste Apple's code in that protocol, but if you have a look at it yourself, you'll see that it is made out of a massive list of properties such as `groups`, `windows`, `dialogs`, `buttons`, etc.

Here is how I recommend going about finding your UI elements using this knowledge:

1. Instantiate your app with `XCUIApplication()`.
2. Refer to the `windows` property of the app object to get all the windows in the app as a query object of type `XCUIElementQuery`.
3. Now that you have a query object, use the `childrenMatchingType(_:)` method to find children inside this query.

Let's say that you have a simple view controller. Inside that view controller's view, you dump another view, and inside that view you dump a button so that your view hierarchy looks something like Figure 9-7.

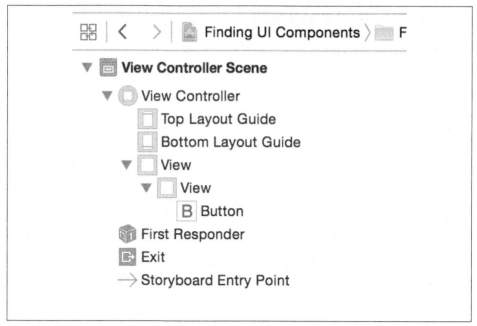

Figure 9-7. Hierarchy of views in this sample app

This hierarchy was created by placing a view inside the view controller's view, and placing a button inside that view. We are now going to try to find that button and tap it:

```
let app = XCUIApplication()
let view = app.windows.childrenMatchingType(.Unknown)
let innerView = view.childrenMatchingType(.Unknown)
let btn = innerView.childrenMatchingType(.Button).elementBoundByIndex(0)
XCTAssert(btn.exists)
btn.tap()
```

Discussion

Let's write the code that we wrote just now, but in a more direct and compact way using the descendantsMatchingType(_:) method:

```
let app = XCUIApplication()

let btn = app.windows.childrenMatchingType(.Unknown)
  .descendantsMatchingType(.Button).elementBoundByIndex(0)

XCTAssert(btn.exists)
btn.tap()
```

Here I am looking at the children of all my windows that are of type Unknown (view) and then finding *a* button inside that view, wherever that button may be and in whichever subview it may have been bundled up. Can this be written in a simpler way? You betcha:

```
let btn = XCUIApplication().buttons.elementBoundByIndex(0)
XCTAssert(btn.exists)
btn.tap()
```

The buttons property of our app object is a query that returns all the buttons that are descendants of any window inside the app. Isn't that awesome?

Those of you with a curious mind are probably thinking, "Can this be written in a more *complex* way?" Well yes, I am glad that you asked:

```
let mainView = XCUIApplication().windows.childrenMatchingType(.Unknown)

let viewsWithButton = mainView.descendantsMatchingType(.Unknown)
  .containingType(.Button, identifier: nil)

XCTAssert(viewsWithButton.count > 0)

let btn = viewsWithButton.childrenMatchingType(.Button)
  .elementBoundByIndex(0)

XCTAssert(btn.exists)

btn.tap()
```

Here I am first finding the main view inside the view controller that is on screen. Then I am finding *all* views that have a button inside them as a first child using the awesome containingType(_:identifier:) method. After I have all the views that have buttons in them, I find the first button inside the first view and then tap it.

Now let's take the same view hierarchy, but this time we will use predicates of type NSPredicate to find our button. There are two handy methods on XCUIElementQuery that we can use to find elements with predicates:

- elementMatchingPredicate(_:)
- matchingPredicate(_:)

The first method will find *an* element that matches a given predicate (so your result has to be unique) and the second method finds *all* elements that match a given predicate. I now want to find a button inside my UI with a specific title:

```
let app = XCUIApplication()

let btns = app.buttons.matchingPredicate(
  NSPredicate(format: "title like[c] 'Button'"))
```

```
XCTAssert(btns.count >= 1)

let btn = btns.elementBoundByIndex(0)

XCTAssert(btn.exists)
```

Now another example. Let's say we want to write a test script that goes through all the disabled buttons on our UI:

```
let app = XCUIApplication()

let disabledBtns = app.buttons.containingPredicate(
  NSPredicate(format: "enabled == false"))

XCTAssert(disabledBtns.count > 1)

for n in 0..<disabledBtns.count{
  let btn = disabledBtns.elementBoundByIndex(n)
  XCTAssert(btn.exists)
}
```

See Also

Recipe 9.1, Recipe 9.2, and Recipe 9.3

9.5 Long-Pressing on UI Elements

Problem

You want to be able to simulate long-pressing on a UI element using UI tests.

Solution

Use the pressForDuration(_:) method of XCUIElement.

Discussion

Create a single-view app and when your view gets loaded, add a long gesture recognizer to your view. The following code waits until the user long-presses the view for 5 seconds:

```
override func viewDidLoad() {
  super.viewDidLoad()

  view.isAccessibilityElement = true

  let gr = UILongPressGestureRecognizer(target: self,
    action: "handleLongPress")
```

```
    gr.minimumPressDuration = 5

    view.addGestureRecognizer(gr)

}
```

The gesture recognizer is hooked to a method. In this method, we will show an alert controller and ask the user for her name. Once she has answered the question and pressed the Save button on the alert, we will set the entered value as the accessibility value of our view so that we can read it in our UI tests:

```
func handleLongPress(){
    let c = UIAlertController(title: "Name", message: "What is your name?",
        preferredStyle: .Alert)

    c.addAction(UIAlertAction(title: "Cancel", style: .Destructive,
        handler: nil))

    c.addAction(UIAlertAction(title: "Save", style: .Destructive){
        action in

        guard let fields = c.textFields where fields.count == 1 else{
            return
        }

        let txtField = fields[0]
        guard let txt = txtField.text where txt.characters.count > 0 else{
            return
        }

        self.view.accessibilityValue = txt

    })

    c.addTextFieldWithConfigurationHandler {txt in
        txt.placeholder = "Foo Bar"
    }

    presentViewController(c, animated: true, completion: nil)

}
```

Now let's go to our UI test code and do the following:

1. Get an instance of our app.
2. Find our view object with the `childrenMatchingType(_:)` method of our app.
3. Call the `pressForDuration(_:)` method on it.
4. Call the `typeText(_:)` method of our app object and find the Save button on the dialog.
5. Programmatically press the save button using the `tap()` method.

6. Check the value of our view and check it against the value that we entered earlier. They should match:

```
let app = XCUIApplication()
let view = app.windows.childrenMatchingType(.Unknown).elementBoundByIndex(0)
view.pressForDuration(5)

XCTAssert(app.alerts.count > 0)

let text = "Foo Bar"
app.typeText(text)

let alert = app.alerts.elementBoundByIndex(0)
let saveBtn = alert.descendantsMatchingType(.Button).matchingPredicate(
  NSPredicate(format: "title like[c] 'Save'")).elementBoundByIndex(0)

saveBtn.tap()

XCTAssert(view.value as! String == text)
```

 I highly recommend that you always start by using the auto recorded and written UI tests that Xcode can create for you. This will give you an insight into how you can find your UI elements better on the screen. Having said that, Xcode isn't always so intelligent in finding the UI elements.

See Also

Recipe 9.1 and Recipe 9.2

9.6 Typing Inside Text Fields

Problem

You want to write UI tests for an app that contains text fields. You want to be able to activate a text field, type some text in it, deactivate it, and then run some tests on the results, or a combination of the aforementioned scenarios.

Solution

Follow these steps:

1. Find your text field with the `textFields` property of your app or one of the other methods mentioned in Recipe 9.4.
2. Call the `tap()` method on your text field to activate it.
3. Call the `typeText(_:)` method on the text field to type whatever text that you want.

---

4. Call the `typeText(_:)` method of your app with the value of `XCUIKeyboardKeyRe`turn as the parameter. This will simulate pressing the Enter button on the keyboard. Check out other `XCUIKeyboardKey` constant values such as `XCUIKeyboardKeySpace` or `XCUIKeyboardKeyCommand`.

5. Once you are done, read the `value` property of your text field element as `String` and do your tests on that.

Discussion

Create a single-view app and place a text field on it. Set the accessory label of that text field to "myText." Set your text field's delegate as your view controller and make your view controller conform to `UITextFieldDelegate`. Then implement the notoriously redundant delegate method named `textFieldShouldReturn(_:)` so that pressing the return button on the keyboard will dismiss the keyboard from the screen:

```
import UIKit

class ViewController: UIViewController, UITextFieldDelegate {

  func textFieldShouldReturn(textField: UITextField) -> Bool {
    textField.resignFirstResponder()
    return true
  }

}
```

Then inside your UI tests, let's write the code similar to what I suggested in the solution section of this recipe:

```
let app = XCUIApplication()
let myText = app.textFields["myText"]
myText.tap()

let text1 = "Hello, World!"

myText.typeText(text1)
myText.typeText(XCUIKeyboardKeyDelete)
app.typeText(XCUIKeyboardKeyReturn)

XCTAssertEqual((myText.value as! String).characters.count,
  text1.characters.count - 1)
```

See Also

Recipe 9.1 and Recipe 9.3

9.7 Swiping on UI Elements

Problem

You want to simulate swiping on various UI components in your app.

Solution

Use the various swipe methods on XCUIElement such as the following:

- swipeUp()
- swipeDown()
- swipeRight()
- swipeleft()

Discussion

Let's set our root view controller to a table view controller and program the table view controller so that it shows 10 hardcoded cells inside it:

```
class ViewController: UITableViewController {

  let id = "c"

  lazy var items: [String] = {
    return Array(0..<10).map{"Item \($0)"}
  }()

  override func tableView(tableView: UITableView,
    numberOfRowsInSection section: Int) -> Int {
    return items.count
  }

  override func tableView(tableView: UITableView,
    cellForRowAtIndexPath indexPath: NSIndexPath) -> UITableViewCell {

      let c = tableView.dequeueReusableCellWithIdentifier(id,
        forIndexPath: indexPath)

      c.textLabel!.text = items[indexPath.row]

      return c

  }

  override func tableView(tableView: UITableView,
    commitEditingStyle editingStyle: UITableViewCellEditingStyle,
    forRowAtIndexPath indexPath: NSIndexPath) {
```

```
        items.removeAtIndex(indexPath.row)
        tableView.deleteRowsAtIndexPaths([indexPath],
          withRowAnimation: .Automatic)

    }

}
```

With this code, the user can swipe left on any cell and then press the Delete button to delete that cell. Let's test this in our UI test. This is what I am going to do:

1. Get the handle to the app.
2. Using the `cells` property of the app, I am going to first count to make sure there are initially 10 items in the table view.
3. I am then going to find the fifth item and swipe left on it.
4. I will then find the "Delete" button using the `buttons` property of the app object and tap on it with the `tap()` method.
5. Then I will assert that the cell was deleted for sure by making sure the cell's count is now 9 instead of 10:

```
let app = XCUIApplication()
let cells = app.cells
XCTAssertEqual(cells.count, 10)
app.cells.elementBoundByIndex(4).swipeLeft()
app.buttons["Delete"].tap()
XCTAssertEqual(cells.count, 9)
```

See Also

Recipe 9.2

9.8 Tapping UI Elements

Problem

You want to be able to simulate various ways of tapping UI elements when writing your UI tests.

Solution

Use one or a combination of the following methods of the XCUIElement class:

- `tap()`
- `doubleTap()`
- `twoFingerTap()`

Double tapping is two taps, with one finger. The two-finger tap is one tap, but with two fingers.

Discussion

Create a single-view app and then add a gesture recognizer to the view that sets the accessibility of the view whenever two fingers have been tapped on the view:

```
class ViewController: UIViewController {

  func handleTap(){
    view.accessibilityValue = "tapped"
  }

  override func viewDidLoad() {
    super.viewDidLoad()

    view.isAccessibilityElement = true
    view.accessibilityValue = "untapped"
    view.accessibilityLabel = "myView"

    let tgr = UITapGestureRecognizer(target: self, action: "handleTap")
    tgr.numberOfTapsRequired = 1
    tgr.numberOfTouchesRequired = 2
    view.addGestureRecognizer(tgr)

  }

}
```

Now our UI tests will do a two-finger tap on the view and check its value before and after to make sure it checks out:

```
let app = XCUIApplication()
let view = app.descendantsMatchingType(.Unknown)["myView"]

XCTAssert(view.exists)
XCTAssert(view.value as! String == "untapped")

view.twoFingerTap()

XCTAssert(view.value as! String == "tapped")
```

See Also

Recipe 9.3

CHAPTER 10

Core Motion

This year, Apple finally brought some long-awaited features into the Core Motion framework. It's especially exciting that the same capabilities, or some version of them, is also available on the Apple Watch. This is great news for us developers because we can program for the watch in a more native way, rather than reading this data from the user's iPhone and sending it to the watch with Bluetooth.

There are a couple key terms I'll be using throughout this chapter that you need to know about:

Cadence

I use a cadence sensor on my bicycle. It helps me figure out how many times I spin my pedals, which can be crucial knowledge. Think about riding downhill on a bicycle, at a 45-degree angle, for 20 minutes, out of a total 40-minute bike ride. Your total calories burned and effort will be miscalculated because you might not even have pedaled when going downhill. The watch actually includes a cadence sensor for *running.*

Pace

This is a ratio, dividing the time you have moved by the distance. If you're counting in meters, for instance, your pace might be 0.5 seconds per meter, meaning that you travelled 1 meter in half a second.

iOS devices can provide pace and cadence information when it's available from the pedometer. Some pedometers might not have this information available. You can call the `isPaceAvailable()` class function of `CMPedometer` to find out whether pace information is available. Similarly, the `isCadenceAvailable()` class method of `CMPedometer` can tell you whether cadence information is available.

Import the CoreMotion framework into your project before attempting to run the code we write in this chapter.

10.1 Querying Pace and Cadence Information

Problem

You want to get cadence and pace information from the pedometer on an iOS device.

Solution

Follow these steps:

1. Find out whether cadence and pace are available.
2. Call the `startPedometerUpdatesFromDate(_:withHandler:)` function of `CMPedometer`.
3. In your handler block, read the `currentPace` and `currentCadence` properties of the incoming optional `CMPedometerData` object.

Discussion

Let's check out an example:

```
guard CMPedometer.isCadenceAvailable() &&
  CMPedometer.isPaceAvailable() else{
  print("Pace and cadence data are not available")
  return
}

let oneWeekAgo = NSDate(timeIntervalSinceNow: -(7 * 24 * 60 * 60))
pedometer.startPedometerUpdatesFromDate(oneWeekAgo) {data, error in

  guard let pData = data where error == nil else{
    return
  }

  if let pace = pData.currentPace{
    print("Pace = \(pace)")
  }

  if let cadence = pData.currentCadence{
    print("Cadence = \(cadence)")
  }

}
```

When you finish querying pedometer data, always remember to call the stopPedometerUpdates() function on your instance of CMPedometer.

10.2 Recording and Reading Accelerometer Data

Problem

You want iOS to accumulate some accelerometer data for a specific number of seconds and then batch update your app with all the accelerometer data in one go.

Solution

Follow these steps:

1. Call the isAccelerometerRecordingAvailable() class function on CMSensorRe corder and abort if it returns false, because that means that accelerometer recording is not available
2. Instantiate CMSensorRecorder.
3. Call the recordAccelerometerFor(_:) function on your sensor recorder and pass the number of seconds for which you want to record accelerometer data.
4. Go into a background thread and wait for your data if you want.
5. Call the accelerometerDataFrom(_:to:) function on your sensor recorder to get the accelerometer data from a given date to another date. The return value of this function is a CMSensorDataList object, which is enumerable. Each item in this enumeration is of type CMRecordedAccelerometerData.
6. Read the value of each CMRecordedAccelerometerData. You'll have properties such as startDate, timestamp, and acceleration, which is of type CMAccelera tion.

Discussion

I mentioned that CMSensorDataList is enumerable. That means it conforms to the NSFastEnumeration protocol, but you can not use the for x in ... syntax on this type of enumerable object. You'll have to make it conform to the SequenceType protocol and implement the generate() function like so:

```
extension CMSensorDataList : SequenceType{
  public func generate() -> NSFastGenerator {
    return NSFastGenerator(self)
  }
}
```

So I'm going to first define a lazily allocated sensor recorder. If sensor information is not available, my object won't hang around in the memory:

```
lazy var recorder = CMSensorRecorder()
```

Then I check whether sensor information is available:

```
guard CMSensorRecorder.isAccelerometerRecordingAvailable() else {
  print("Accelerometer data recording is not available")
  return
}
```

Next I will record my sensor data for a period:

```
let duration = 3.0
recorder.recordAccelerometerFor(duration)
```

Then I will go to the background and read the data:

```
  NSOperationQueue().addOperationWithBlock{[unowned recorder] in

NSThread.sleepForTimeInterval(duration)
let now = NSDate()
let past = now.dateByAddingTimeInterval(-(duration))
guard let data = recorder.accelerometerDataFrom(past, to: now) else{
  return
}

let accelerationData: [CMAcceleration] = data.map{
  //every $0 is CMRecordedAccelerometerData
  $0.acceleration
}

print(accelerationData)

}
```

It is important to enumerate the result of accelerometerData From(_:to:) on a non-UI thread, because there may be thousands of data points in the results.

CHAPTER 11

Security

iOS 9 didn't change much with regard to the Security framework. A few things were added, mainly about the keychain. There are also some additions that are about Application Transport Security, or ATS. ATS is now incorporated into iOS 9, so all apps compiled with Xcode 7, linked against iOS 9, and running under iOS 9 will by default use HTTPS for all their network traffic. This is really good, and not so good. It is good because it strongly encourages the use of secure connections for everything, but sometimes it can be annoying to *force* using a secure connection for *everything*!

There are also some changes that affect the way we can store values in the keychain, but overall, not much to worry about.

11.1 Protecting Your Network Connections with ATS

Problem

You want to control the details about the HTTPS channels through which your network connections go, or use a non-secure channel (HTTP).

I do not personally suggest using non-secure connections. However, in some cases, if you are using a backend that does not provide an HTTPS variant, you will be eventually forced to go through HTTP. In this chapter, I'll help you figure out how to do that as well.

Solution

As I said, by default, all domain names that you use in your URLs will be going through secure channels. But you can indicate specific exceptions. ATS has a dictionary key in your *Info.plist* file called `NSAppTransportSecurity`. Under that, you have another dictionary key called NSExceptionDomains. Under this key you can list specific domain names that don't use ATS.

Discussion

If you want to disable ATS entirely so that all your network connections go through channels specified in your code, simply insert the NSAllowsArbitraryLoads key under the NSExceptionDomains key. The NSAllowsArbitraryLoads key accepts a Boolean value. If set to true, your HTTP connections will be HTTP and HTTPS will be HTTPS.

Alternatively, under the NSExceptionDomains key, you can specify the name of your domain and set its data type to be a dictionary. Under this dictionary, you can have the following keys:

NSExceptionAllowsInsecureHTTPLoads
:   If set to true, allows HTTP loads on the given domain.

NSIncludesSubdomains
:   If set to true, includes all the subdomains of the given domain as an exception from ATS.

NSRequiresCertificateTransparency
:   Dictates that the SSL certificate of the given URL has to include certificate-transparency information. Check certificate transparency out on the Web for more information.

NSExceptionMinimumTLSVersion
:   This is a key to which you assign a string value to specify the minimum TLS version for the connection. Values can be TLSv1.0, TLSv1.1, or TLSv1.2.

So if I want to disable ATS completely, my plist will look like this:

```
<plist version="1.0">
<dict>
        <key>NSExceptionDomains</key>
        <dict>
                <key>NSAllowsArbitraryLoads</key>
                <true/>
        </dict>
</dict>
</plist>
```

How about if I want to have ATS enabled but not for *mydomain.com*? I'd also like to request certificate transparency and I'd like ATS to be disabled for subdomains as well:

```
<plist version="1.0">
<dict>
```

```
<key>NSExceptionDomains</key>
<dict>
        <key>NSAllowsArbitraryLoads</key>
        <false/>
        <key>mydomain.com</key>
        <dict>
                <key>NSExceptionAllowsInsecureHTTPLoads</key>
                <true/>
                <key>NSIncludesSubdomains</key>
                <true/>
                <key>NSRequiresCertificateTransparency</key>
                <true/>
        </dict>
</dict>
</dict>
</plist>
```

How about if I want to enable ATS *only* for *mydomain.com*?

```
<plist version="1.0">
<dict>
        <key>NSExceptionDomains</key>
        <dict>
                <key>NSAllowsArbitraryLoads</key>
                <true/>
                <key>mydomain.com</key>
                <dict>
                        <key>NSExceptionAllowsInsecureHTTPLoads</key>
                        <false/>
                        <key>NSIncludesSubdomains</key>
                        <true/>
                </dict>
        </dict>
</dict>
</plist>
```

See Also

Recipe 3.6

11.2 Binding Keychain Items to Passcode and Touch ID

Problem

You want to create a secure item in the keychain that is accessible only if the user has set a passcode on her device *and* has enrolled into using the device with Touch ID. So at least one finger has to have been registered.

Solution

Follow these steps:

1. Create your access control flags with the SecAccessControlCreateWithFlags function. Pass the value of kSecAttrAccessibleWhenPasscodeSetThisDevi ceOnly as the protection parameter and the value of SecAccessControlCreate Flags.TouchIDAny as the flags parameter.
2. In your secure dictionary, add a key named kSecUseAuthenticationUI and set its value to kSecUseAuthenticationUIAllow. This allows the user to unlock the secure key with her device passcode or Touch ID.
3. In your secure dictionary, add a key named kSecAttrAccessControl and set its value to the return value of the SecAccessControlCreateWithFlags function that you called earlier.

Discussion

For extra security, you might want to sometimes bind secure items in the keychain to Touch ID and a passcode on a device. As explained before, you'd have to first create your access control flags with the SecAccessControlCreateWithFlags function and then proceed to use the SecItemAdd function as you normally would, to add the secure item to the keychain.

The following example saves a string (as a password) into the keychain, and binds it to the user's passcode and Touch ID. First, start off by creating the access control flags:

```
guard let flags =
  SecAccessControlCreateWithFlags(kCFAllocatorDefault,
    kSecAttrAccessibleWhenPasscodeSetThisDeviceOnly,
    SecAccessControlCreateFlags.TouchIDAny, nil) else{
      print("Could not create the access control flags")
      return
}
```

Then define the data that you want to store in the keychain:

```
let password = "some string"

guard let data = password.dataUsingEncoding(NSUTF8StringEncoding) else{
  print("Could not get data from string")
  return
}
```

The next step is to create the dictionary that you need to pass to the SecItemAdd function later with all your flags:

```
let service = "onlinePasswords"

let attrs = [
  kSecClass.str() : kSecClassGenericPassword.str(),
  kSecAttrService.str() : service,
  kSecValueData.str() : data,
  kSecUseAuthenticationUI.str() : kSecUseAuthenticationUIAllow.str(),
  kSecAttrAccessControl.str() : flags,
]
```

Last but not least, asynchronously add the item to the keychain:

```
NSOperationQueue().addOperationWithBlock{
  guard SecItemAdd(attrs, nil) == errSecSuccess else{
    print("Could not add the item to the keychain")
    return
  }

  print("Successfully added the item to keychain")
}
```

Earlier, we used the value of SecAccessControlCreateFlags.TouchIDAny in the flags parameter of the SecAccessControlCreateWithFlags function to specify that we need Touch ID to be enabled on the current device before our secure item can be read. There is another value in SecAccessControlCreateFlags that you might find useful: TouchIDCurrentSet. If you use this value, your secure item will still require Touch ID, but it will be invalidated by a change to the current set of enrolled Touch ID fingers. If the user adds a new finger to Touch ID or removes an existing one, your item will be invalidated and won't be readable.

11.3 Opening URLs Safely

Problem

You want to find out whether an app on the user's device can open a specific URL.

Solution

Follow these steps:

1. Define the key of LSApplicationQueriesSchemes in your *plist* file as an array.
2. Under that array, define your URL schemes as strings. These are the URL schemes that you want your app to be able to open.
3. In your app, issue the canOpenUrl(_:) method on your shared app.
4. If you can open the URL, proceed to open it using the openUrl(_:) method of the shared app.
5. If you cannot open the URL, offer an alternative to your user if possible.

Discussion

In iOS, previously, apps could issue the `canOpenUrl(_:)` call to find out whether a URL could be opened on the device by another application. For instance, I could find out whether I can open "instagram://app" (see iPhone Hooks : Instagram Documentation (*https://instagram.com/developer/mobile-sharing/iphone-hooks/*)). If that's possible, I would know that Instagram is installed on the user's device. This technique was used by some apps to find which other apps are installed on the user's device. This information was then used for marketing, among other things.

In iOS 9, you need to use the *plist* file to define the URLs that you want to be able to open or to check whether URLs can be opened. If you define too many APIs or unrelated APIs, your app might get rejected. If you try to open a URL that you have not defined in the *plist*, you will get a failure. You can use `canOpenUrl(_:)` to check whether you can access a URL before trying to open it: the method returns `true` if you have indicated that you can open that kind of URL, and `false` otherwise.

Let's check out an example. I'll try to find first whether I can open the Instagram app on the user's device:

```
guard let url = NSURL(string: "instagram://app") where
  UIApplication.sharedApplication().canOpenURL(url) else{
  return
}
```

Now that I know I can open the URL, I'll proceed to do so:

```
guard UIApplication.sharedApplication().openURL(url) else{
  print("Could not open Instagram")
  return
}

print("Successfully opened Instagram")
```

I'll then go into the `plist` file and tell iOS that I want to open URL schemes starting with "instagram":

```
<plist version="1.0">
<array>
        <string>instagram</string>
</array>
</plist>
```

11.4 Authenticating the User with Touch ID and Timeout

Problem

You want to ask the user for permission to read secure content in the keychain. This includes setting a timeout after which you will no longer have access.

Solution

Follow these steps:

1. Create your access control flags with `SecAccessControlCreateWithFlags`, as you saw in Recipe 11.2.
2. Instantiate a context object of type `LAContext`.
3. Set the `touchIDAuthenticationAllowableReuseDuration` property of your context to `LATouchIDAuthenticationMaximumAllowableReuseDuration`, so your context will lock out only after the maximum allowed number of seconds.
4. Call the `evaluateAccessControl(_:operation:localizedReason:)` method on your context to get access to the access control.
5. If you gain access, create your keychain request dictionary and include the `kSecUseAuthenticationContext` key. The value of this key will be your context object.
6. Use the `SecItemCopyMatching` function with your dictionary to read a secure object with the given access controls.

Discussion

Whenever you write an item to the keychain, you can do so with the access controls as we saw in Recipe 11.2. So assume that your item requires Touch ID. If you want to read that item now, you need to request permission to do so. Let's define our context and the reason why want to read the item:

```
let context = LAContext()
let reason = "To unlock previously stored security phrase"
```

Then define your access controls as before:

```
guard let flags =
  SecAccessControlCreateWithFlags(kCFAllocatorDefault,
    kSecAttrAccessibleWhenPasscodeSetThisDeviceOnly,
    SecAccessControlCreateFlags.TouchIDAny, nil) else{
      print("Could not create the access control flags")
      return
}
```

Also specify how long you can get access. After this time passes, the user will be forced to use Touch ID again to unlock the context:

```
context.touchIDAuthenticationAllowableReuseDuration =
LATouchIDAuthenticationMaximumAllowableReuseDuration
```

Last but not least, gain access to the given access controls and read the item if possible:

```
context.evaluateAccessControl(flags,
  operation: LAAccessControlOperation.UseItem,
  localizedReason: reason) {[unowned context] succ, err in
```

```
guard succ && err == nil else {
  print("Could not evaluate the access control")
  if let e = err {
    print("Error = \(e)")
  }
  return
}

print("Successfully evaluated the access control")

let service = "onlinePasswords"

let attrs = [
  kSecClass.str() : kSecClassGenericPassword.str(),
  kSecAttrService.str() : service,
  kSecUseAuthenticationUI.str() : kSecUseAuthenticationUIAllow.str(),
  kSecAttrAccessControl.str() : flags,
  kSecReturnData.str() : kCFBooleanTrue,
  kSecUseAuthenticationContext.str() : context,
]

//now attempt to use the attrs with SecItemCopyMatching

print(attrs)

}
```

The operation argument of the evaluateAccessControl(_:operation:localize
dReason:) method takes in a value of type LAAccessControlOperation that indicates
the type of operation you want to perform. Some of the values that you can use are
UseItem, CreateItem, CreateKey, and UseKeySign.

See Also

Recipe 11.2

CHAPTER 12

Multimedia

The current version of iOS brings some changes to multimedia playback and functionality, especially the AVFoundation framework. In this chapter, we will have a look at those additions and some of the changes.

 Make sure that you have imported the AVFoundation framework in your app before running the code in this chapter.

12.1 Reading Out Text with the Default Siri Alex Voice

Problem

You want to use the default Siri Alex voice on a device to speak some text.

Solution

Instantiate AVSpeechSynthesisVoice with the identifier initializer and pass the value of AVSpeechSynthesisVoiceIdentifierAlex to it.

Discussion

Let's create an example out of this. Create your UI so that it looks like Figure 12-1. Place a text view on the screen and a bar button item in your navigation bar. When the button is pressed, you will ask Siri to speak out the text inside the text view.

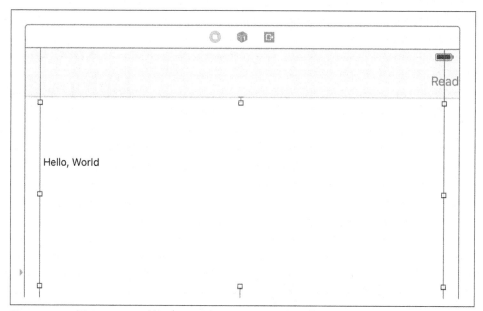

Figure 12-1. Text view and button in the UI

I've linked the text view to a property in my view controller called `textView`:

```
@IBOutlet var textView: UITextView!
```

When the Read button is pressed, check first whether Alex is available:

```
guard let voice = AVSpeechSynthesisVoice(identifier:
    AVSpeechSynthesisVoiceIdentifierAlex) else{
    print("Alex is not available")
    return
}
```

Instances of `AVSpeechSynthesisVoice` have properties such as `identifier`, `quality`, and `name`. The identifier can be used later to reconstruct another speech object. If all you know is the identifier, then you can re-create the speech object using that. The `quality` property is of type `AVSpeechSynthesisVoiceQuality` and can be equal to values such as `Default` or `Enhanced`. Let's print these values to the console:

```
print("id = \(voice.identifier)")
print("quality = \(voice.quality)")
print("name = \(voice.name)")
```

Then create the voice object (of type `AVSpeechUtterance`) with your text view's text:

```
let toSay = AVSpeechUtterance(string: textView.text)
toSay.voice = voice
```

Last but not least, instantiate the voice synthesizer of type `AVSpeechSynthesizer` and ask it to speak out the voice object:

```
let alex = AVSpeechSynthesizer()
alex.delegate = self
alex.speakUtterance(toSay)
```

See Also

Recipe 3.4 and Recipe 3.7

12.2 Downloading and Preparing Remote Media for Playback

Problem

You have some remote assets such as sound files and would like to download them, even if in the background. Along the way, you want to provide real-time feedback of the download process.

Solution

Follow these steps:

1. Create an instance of `AVURLAsset` with the URL to your asset.
2. Use the `backgroundSessionConfigurationWithIdentifier(_:)` class method on `NSURLSessionConfiguration` to create a background session configuration.
3. Create a session of type `AVAssetDownloadURLSession` and pass your configuration to it.
4. Construct the URL where your asset has to be downloaded onto the disk.
5. Use the `assetDownloadTaskWithURLAsset(_:destinationURL:options)` method of your session to create a download task of type `AVAssetDownloadTask`.
6. Call the `resume()` method on your task to start the task.
7. Conform to the `AVAssetDownloadDelegate` protocol to get events from your task.

All the classes I discussed whose names start with "AV" are in the AVFoundation framework, so make sure to import it.

Discussion

Let's imagine that you have an *.mp4* file that you want to download and play back in your app. First set up your vc:

```
import UIKit
import AVFoundation

class ViewController: UIViewController, AVAssetDownloadDelegate {

    let url = NSURL(string: "http://localhost:8888/video.mp4")!
    let sessionId = "com.mycompany.background"
    let queue = NSOperationQueue()
    var task: AVAssetDownloadTask?
    var session: AVAssetDownloadURLSession?

    ...
```

 I am using MAMP to start a local server on my machine and host the file *video.mp4* on my own computer; hence the URL that you are seeing. You can and probably should change this URL to a valid media file that AVFoundation can handle, like *mov* or *mp4*.

Now define some of the delegate methods defined in AVAssetDownloadDelegate and NSURLSessionTaskDelegate:

```
func URLSession(session: NSURLSession, task: NSURLSessionTask,
    didCompleteWithError error: NSError?) {
    //code this
}

func URLSession(session: NSURLSession,
    assetDownloadTask: AVAssetDownloadTask,
    didLoadTimeRange timeRange: CMTimeRange,
    totalTimeRangesLoaded loadedTimeRanges: [NSValue],
    timeRangeExpectedToLoad: CMTimeRange) {
    //code this
}

func URLSession(session: NSURLSession,
    assetDownloadTask: AVAssetDownloadTask,
    didResolveMediaSelection resolvedMediaSelection: AVMediaSelection) {

}
```

Next, create an asset by its URL. At the same time, tell the system that you don't want cross-site references to be resolved using a dictionary with a key equal to AVURLAsse tReferenceRestrictionsKey and value of AVAssetReferenceRestrictions.Forbid CrossSiteReference:

```
let options = [AVURLAssetReferenceRestrictionsKey :
    AVAssetReferenceRestrictions.ForbidCrossSiteReference.rawValue]

let asset = AVURLAsset(URL: url, options: options)
```

Now it's time to create the configuration object of type NSURLSessionConfiguration:

```
let config = NSURLSessionConfiguration
    .backgroundSessionConfigurationWithIdentifier(sessionId)
```

Create the session of type AVAssetDownloadURLSession:

```
let session = AVAssetDownloadURLSession(configuration: config,
    assetDownloadDelegate: self, delegateQueue: queue)
self.session = session
```

 You must have noticed that I keep a reference to the session and the task that we are going to create soon. This is so we can refer to them later and cancel or reuse them if necessary.

Now construct the URL where you want the video to be downloaded on disk, using NSFileManager:

```
let fm = NSFileManager()
let destinationUrl = try! fm.URLForDirectory(.CachesDirectory,
    inDomain: .UserDomainMask, appropriateForURL: url, create: true)
    .URLByAppendingPathComponent("file.mp4")
```

And last but not least, construct the task and start it:

```
guard let task = session.assetDownloadTaskWithURLAsset(asset,
    destinationURL: destinationUrl, options: nil) else {
    print("Could not create the task")
    return
}

self.task = task

task.resume()
```

12.3 Enabling Spoken Audio Sessions

Problem

You have an eBook reading app (or similar app) and would like to enable a specific audio session that allows your app's audio to be paused—but another app is playing back voice on top of yours (such as an app that provides navigation information with voice).

Solution

Follow these steps:

1. Go through the available audio session categories inside the `availableCatego ries` property of your audio session and find `AVAudioSessionCategoryPlay back`.
2. Go through values inside the `availableModes` property of your audio session (of type `AVAudioSession`). If you cannot find `AVAudioSessionModeSpokenAudio`, exit gracefully.
3. After you find the `AVAudioSessionModeSpokenAudio` mode, set your audio category to `AVAudioSessionCategoryPlayback` using the `setCategory(_:withOp tions:)` method of the audio session.
4. Activate your session with the `setActive(_:withOptions:)` method of your audio session.

Discussion

Suppose you are developing an eBook app and have a "Read" button in the UI that the user presses to ask the app to read the contents of the book out loud. For this you can use the `AVAudioSessionModeSpokenAudio` audio session mode, but you have to check first whether that mode exists. Use the `availableModes` property of your audio session to find this information out.

Let's work on an example. Let's find the `AVAudioSessionCategoryPlayback` category and the `AVAudioSessionModeSpokenAudio` mode:

```
let session = AVAudioSession.sharedInstance()

guard session.availableCategories.filter(
  {$0 == AVAudioSessionCategoryPlayback}).count == 1 &&
  session.availableModes.filter(
    {$0 == AVAudioSessionModeSpokenAudio}).count == 1 else{
  print("Could not find the category or the mode")
  return
}
```

After you confirm that the category and mode are available, set the category and mode and then activate your audio session:

```
do{
  try session.setCategory(AVAudioSessionCategoryPlayback,
    withOptions:
    AVAudioSessionCategoryOptions.InterruptSpokenAudioAndMixWithOthers)

  try session.setMode(AVAudioSessionModeSpokenAudio)
```

```
    try session.setActive(true, withOptions:
        AVAudioSessionSetActiveOptions.NotifyOthersOnDeactivation)

} catch let err{
    print("Error = \(err)")
}
```

See Also

Recipe 12.1

CHAPTER 13

UI Dynamics

UI Dynamics allow you to create very nice effects on your UI components, such as gravity and collision detection. Let's say that you have two buttons on the screen that the user can move around. You could create opposing gravity fields on them so that they repel each other and cannot be dragged into each other. Or, for instance, you could provide a more live UI by creating a turbulence field under all your UI components so that they move around automatically ever so slightly (or through a noise field, as described in Recipe 13.4) even when the user is not interacting with them. All of this is possible with the tools that Apple has given you in UIKit. You don't have to use any other framework to dig into UI Dynamics.

One of the basic concepts in UI Dynamics is an *animator*. Animator objects, which are of type `UIDynamicAnimator`, hold every other effect together and orchestrate all the effects. For instance, if you have collision detection and gravity effects, the animator decides how the pull on an object through gravity will work hand in hand with the collision detection around the edges of your reference view.

Reference views are like canvases where all your animations happen. Effects are added to views and then added to an animator, which itself is placed on a reference view. In other words, the reference view is the canvas and the views on your UI (like buttons, lables, etc.) will have effects.

13.1 Adding a Radial Gravity Field to Your UI

Problem

You want to add a radial gravity field to your UI, with animations.

Solution

Use the `radialGravityFieldWithPosition(_:)` class method of `UIFieldBehavior` and add this behavior to a dynamic animator of type `UIDynamicAnimator`.

Discussion

A typical gravity behavior pulls items in a direction. A radial gravity field has a center and a region in which everything is drawn to the center, just like gravity on earth, whereby everything is pulled toward the core of this sphere.

For this recipe, I designed a UI like Figure 13-1. The gravity is at the center of the main view and the orange view is affected by it.

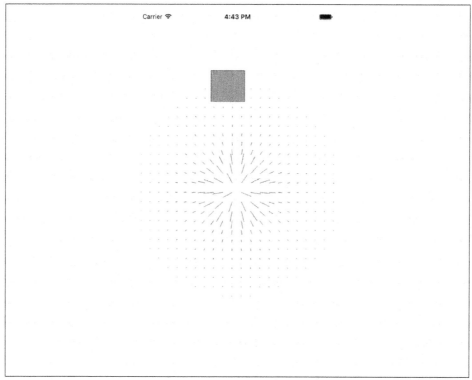

Figure 13-1. A main view and another view that is an orange square

The gravity field here is not linear. I would also like this gravity field to repel the orange view, instead of pulling it toward the core of gravity. Then I'd like the user to be able to pan this orange view around the screen and release it to see how the gravity affects the view at that point in time (think about pan gesture recognizers).

Let's have a single-view app that has no navigation bar and then go into IB and add a simple colorful view to your main view. I've created mine, colored it orange(ish), and have linked it to my view controller under the name orangeView (see Figure 13-2).

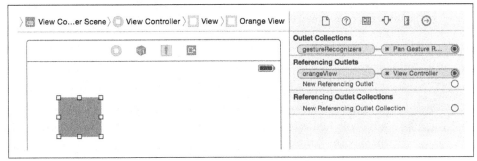

Figure 13-2. My view is added on top of the view controller's view and hooked to the view controller's code

Then from the object library, find a pan gesture recognizer (see Figure 13-3) and drop it onto your orange view so that it gets associated with that view. Find the pan gesture recognizer by typing its name into the object library's search field.

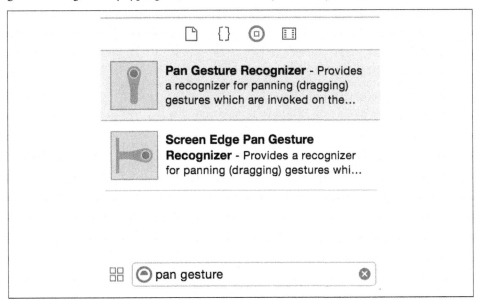

Figure 13-3. Getting the pan gesture recognizer

Then associate the pan gesture recognizer's code to a method in your code called pan ning(_:). So now your view controller's header should look like this:

```
import UIKit
import SharedCode

class ViewController: UIViewController {

  @IBOutlet var orangeView: UIView!

  ...
```

 Whenever I write a piece of code that I want to share between various projects, I put it inside a framework that I've written called SharedCode. You can find this framework in the GitHub repo of this book. In this example, I've extended CGSize so that I can find the CGPoint at the center of CGSize like so:

```
import Foundation

extension CGSize{

  public var center: CGPoint{
    return CGPoint(x: self.width / 2.0, y: self.height / 2.0)
  }

}
```

Then in the vc, create your animator, specifying this view as the reference view:

```
lazy var animator: UIDynamicAnimator = {
  let animator = UIDynamicAnimator(referenceView: self.view)
  animator.debugEnabled = true
  return animator
}()
```

If you are writing this code, you'll notice that you'll get a compiler error saying that the debugEnabled property is not available on an object of type UIDynamicAnimator. That is absolutely right. This is a *debug only* method that Apple has provided to us and which we should only use when debugging our apps. Because this property isn't actually available in the header file of UIDynamicAnimator, we need to create a bridging header (with some small Objective-C code) to enable this property. Create your bridging header and then extend UIDynamicAnimator:

```
@import UIKit;

#if DEBUG

@interface UIDynamicAnimator (DebuggingOnly)
@property (nonatomic, getter=isDebugEnabled) BOOL debugEnabled;
@end

#endif
```

When the orange view is repelled by the reversed radial gravity field, it should collide with the edges of your view controller's view and stay within the bounds of the view:

```
lazy var collision: UICollisionBehavior = {
  let collision = UICollisionBehavior(items: [self.orangeView])
  collision.translatesReferenceBoundsIntoBoundary = true
  return collision
  }()
```

Then create the radial gravity of type `UIFieldBehavior`. Two properties in this class are quite important:

region

This is of type `UIRegion` and specifies the region covered by this gravity.

strength

A floating-point value that indicates (id positive) the force by which items get pulled into the gravity field. If you assign a negative value to this property, items get repelled by this gravity field.

In our example, I want the gravity field to consume an area with the radius of 200 points and I want it to repel items:

```
lazy var centerGravity: UIFieldBehavior = {
  let centerGravity =
  UIFieldBehavior.radialGravityFieldWithPosition(self.view.center)
  centerGravity.addItem(self.orangeView)
  centerGravity.region = UIRegion(radius: 200)
  centerGravity.strength = -1 //repel items
  return centerGravity
  }()
```

When the user rotates the device, recenter the gravity:

```
override func viewWillTransitionToSize(size: CGSize,
  withTransitionCoordinator
  coordinator: UIViewControllerTransitionCoordinator) {

    super.viewWillTransitionToSize(size,
      withTransitionCoordinator: coordinator)

    centerGravity.position = size.center

}
```

Remember the center property that we just added on top of CGSize?

When your view is loaded, add your behaviors to the animator:

```
override func viewDidLoad() {
  super.viewDidLoad()

  animator.addBehavior(collision)
  animator.addBehavior(centerGravity)

}
```

To handle the panning, consider a few things:

- When panning begins, you have to disable your animators so that none of the behaviors have an effect on the orange view.
- When the panning is in progress, you have to move the orange view where the user's finger is pointing.
- When the panning ends, you have to re-enable your behaviors.

All this is accomplished in the following code:

```
@IBAction func panning(sender: UIPanGestureRecognizer) {

  switch sender.state{
  case .Began:
    collision.removeItem(orangeView)
    centerGravity.removeItem(orangeView)
  case .Changed:
    orangeView.center = sender.locationInView(view)
  case .Ended, .Cancelled:
    collision.addItem(orangeView)
    centerGravity.addItem(orangeView)
  default: ()
  }

}
```

See Also

Recipe 13.2, Recipe 13.3, and Recipe 13.4

13.2 Creating a Linear Gravity Field on Your UI

Problem

You want to create gravity that follows a vector on your UI.

Solution

Use the `linearGravityFieldWithVector(_:)` class method of `UIFieldBehavior` to create your gravity. The parameter to this method is of type `CGVector`. You can provide your own x- and y-values for this vector when you construct it. This is now your gravity field and you can add it to an animator of type `UIDynamicAnimator`.

 I am basing this recipe on Recipe 13.1. There are some things, such as the bridging header to enable debugging, that I mentioned in Recipe 13.1 and won't mention again in this recipe. I might skim over them but won't go into details.

Discussion

Whereas the Recipe 13.1 has a center and a radius, a linear gravity has a direction only (up, down, right, left, etc.). In this example, we are going to have the exact same UI that we created in Recipe 13.1. So create the little orange view on your storyboard and link it to an `orangeView` outlet on your code. Add a pan gesture recognizer to it as well and add it to a method called `panning(_:)`.

Right now, your view controller's code should look like this:

```
import UIKit
import SharedCode

class ViewController: UIViewController {

  @IBOutlet var orangeView: UIView!

  lazy var animator: UIDynamicAnimator = {
    let animator = UIDynamicAnimator(referenceView: self.view)
    animator.debugEnabled = true
    return animator
    }()

  lazy var collision: UICollisionBehavior = {
    let collision = UICollisionBehavior(items: [self.orangeView])
    collision.translatesReferenceBoundsIntoBoundary = true
    return collision
    }()

  ...
```

The next step is to create your linear gravity:

```
  lazy var gravity: UIFieldBehavior = {
    let vector = CGVector(dx: 0.4, dy: 1.0)
    let gravity =
    UIFieldBehavior.linearGravityFieldWithVector(vector)
```

```
gravity.addItem(self.orangeView)
return gravity
}()
```

Last but not least, handle the panning and add the effects to the animator (see Recipe 13.1):

```
override func viewDidLoad() {
  super.viewDidLoad()

  animator.addBehavior(collision)
  animator.addBehavior(gravity)

}

@IBAction func panning(sender: UIPanGestureRecognizer) {

  switch sender.state{
  case .Began:
    collision.removeItem(orangeView)
    gravity.removeItem(orangeView)
  case .Changed:
    orangeView.center = sender.locationInView(view)
  case .Ended, .Cancelled:
    collision.addItem(orangeView)
    gravity.addItem(orangeView)
  default: ()
  }

}
```

If you run your app now you should see an interface similar to Figure 13-4. Our linear gravity pulls all objects down and to the right. This is because in our vector earlier I specified a positive y-delta that pulls everything down and a positive x-delta that pulls everything to the right. I suggest that you play around with the delta values of type CGVector to get a feeling for how they affect gravity.

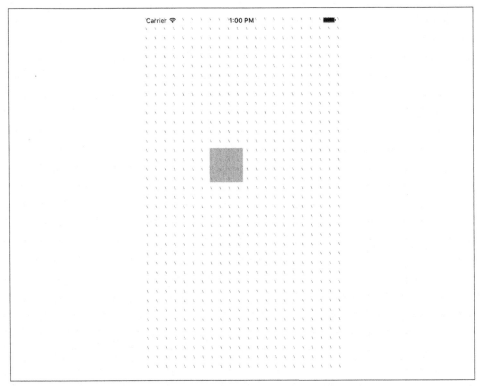

Figure 13-4. Linear gravity acting on an object

You can also go ahead and change some aspects of your gravity field. For instance, set the `strength` property of the gravity to 20 and see how much more gravity is applied to your objects. Similarly, play with the `animationSpeed` property of your gravity to set the animation speed.

See Also

Recipe 13.1, Recipe 13.3, and Recipe 13.5

13.3 Creating Turbulence Effects with Animations

Problem

You want to simulate turbulence in your animator and have your UI components flail about when they hit the turbulent region.

Solution

Instantiate your turbulence with the `turbulenceFieldWithSmoothness(_:animationSpeed:)` class method of `UIFieldBehavior`. Then do the following:

1. Set the `UIFieldBehavior` class's `strength` property according to your needs.
2. Set its region property to an instance of `UIRegion`. This defines in which region of the screen your turbulence behavior is effective.
3. Set its position property to a `CGPoint` instance in your reference view.

After you are done setting up the turbulence behavior, add it to your animator of type `UIDynamicAnimator`.

Discussion

In this recipe, I want to create an effect very similar to what we got in Recipe 13.2, but in addition add a turbulence field in the center of the screen so that, when we take our little orange view (see Figure 13-1) and drop it from the top-left corner of the screen, it will fall down (and to the right; see Figure 13-4). But on its way down, it will hit our turbulence field and its movements will be affected.

Set up your gravity exactly as we did in Recipe 13.2. I won't go through that here again. Then create a turbulence field in the center of the screen with a radius of 200 points:

```
lazy var turbulence: UIFieldBehavior = {
  let turbulence = UIFieldBehavior.turbulenceFieldWithSmoothness(0.5,
    animationSpeed: 60.0)
  turbulence.strength = 12.0
  turbulence.region = UIRegion(radius: 200.0)
  turbulence.position = self.orangeView.bounds.size.center
  turbulence.addItem(self.orangeView)
  return turbulence
}()
```

Make sure to add this field to your animator. When the user is panning with the gesture recognizer (see Recipe 13.1), disable all your behaviors, and re-enable them when the panning is finished:

```
override func viewDidLoad() {
  super.viewDidLoad()

  animator.addBehavior(collision)
  animator.addBehavior(gravity)
  animator.addBehavior(turbulence)

}

@IBAction func panning(sender: UIPanGestureRecognizer) {
```

```
switch sender.state{
case .Began:
  collision.removeItem(orangeView)
  gravity.removeItem(orangeView)
  turbulence.removeItem(orangeView)
case .Changed:
  orangeView.center = sender.locationInView(view)
case .Ended, .Cancelled:
  collision.addItem(orangeView)
  gravity.addItem(orangeView)
  turbulence.addItem(orangeView)
default: ()
}

}
```

Give it a go and see the results for yourself. Drag the orange view from the top-left corner of the screen and drop it. It will be dragged down and to the right, and when it hits the center of the screen (inside a radius of 200 points), it will wiggle around a bit because of turbulence.

See Also

Recipe 13.1 and Recipe 13.2

13.4 Adding Animated Noise Effects to Your UI

Problem

You want to add a noise field on your UI and have your UI components surf in all directions on this field.

Solution

1. Create a noise field using the `noiseFieldWithSmoothness(_:animationSpeed:)` class method of `UIFieldBehavior`.
2. Add the views you want affected by this noise to the field using its `addItem(_:)` method.
3. Add your noise field to an animator of type `UIDynamicAnimator` (see Recipe 13.1).

This recipe is based on what you learned in Recipe 13.1, so I won't be going through all the details that I have already explained.

Discussion

Noise is great for having an item constantly move around on your reference view in random directions. Have a look at the noise field in Figure 13-5. This noise field is shown graphically on our UI using a UI Dynamics debugging trick (see Figure 13-5).

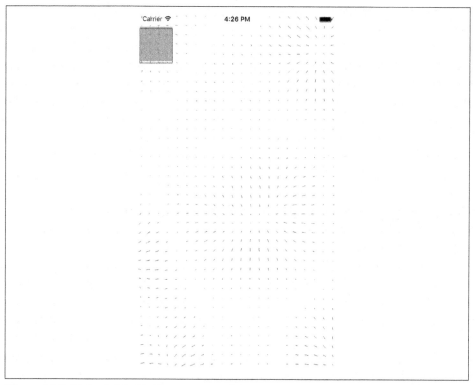

Figure 13-5. Noise field affecting a square view

The direction of the noise that you see on the fields dictates in which direction the field repels the items attached to it. In this case, I've used negative gravity (think of it that way). If you want to limit the effective region of your noise field on your reference view, simply set the `region` property of your field. This is of type `UIRegion`.

Now create your UI exactly as you did in Recipe 13.1. You should have an orange view that is accessible through the `orangeView` property of your view controller. Create a collision detector and an animator using what you learned in the aforementioned recipe. Now go ahead and create your noise field:

```
lazy var noise: UIFieldBehavior = {
  let noise = UIFieldBehavior.noiseFieldWithSmoothness(0.9,
    animationSpeed: 1)
  noise.addItem(self.orangeView)
  return noise
}()
```

Add the noise field to your animator:

```
override func viewDidLoad() {
  super.viewDidLoad()
  animator.addBehavior(collision)
  animator.addBehavior(noise)
}
```

Last but not least, handle your pan gesture recognizer's event, so that when the user starts dragging the orange view across the screen, your dynamic behaviors will shut down. And as soon as the user is done with dragging, they will come back up:

```
@IBAction func panning(sender: UIPanGestureRecognizer) {

  switch sender.state{
  case .Began:
    collision.removeItem(orangeView)
    noise.removeItem(orangeView)
  case .Changed:
    orangeView.center = sender.locationInView(view)
  case .Ended, .Cancelled:
    collision.addItem(orangeView)
    noise.addItem(orangeView)
  default: ()
  }

}
```

See Also

Recipe 13.5

13.5 Creating a Magnetic Effect Between UI Components

Problem

You want to create a magnetic field between two or more UI elements.

Solution

Follow these steps:

1. Create your animator (see Recipe 13.1).
2. Create a collision detector of type `UICollisionBehavior`.
3. Create a magnetic field of type `UIFieldBehavior` using the `magneticField()` class method of `UIFieldBehavior`.
4. Add your magnetic field and collision detector to your animator.

I am basing this recipe on what we learned in Recipe 13.4 and Recipe 13.1.

Discussion

Create a UI that looks similar to Figure 13-6.

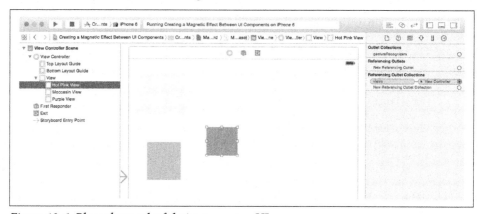

Figure 13-6. Place three colorful views on your UI

Then link all views to an outlet collection called `views` in your code:

```
class ViewController: UIViewController {

  @IBOutlet var views: [UIView]!

  ...
```

Now that you have an array of views to which you want to apply a noise field and a magnetic field, it's best to extend `UIFieldBehavior` so that you can pass it an array of UI elements instead of one element at a time:

```
extension UIFieldBehavior{
  func addItems(items: [UIDynamicItem]){
    for item in items{
      addItem(item)
```

```
      }
    }
  }
```

Also, it's best to extend `UIDynamicAnimator` so that you can add all our behaviors to your animator at once:

```
extension UIDynamicAnimator{
  func addBehaviors(behaviors: [UIDynamicBehavior]){
    for behavior in behaviors{
      addBehavior(behavior)
    }
  }
}
```

Now add a noise and collision behavior, plus your animator, using what you learned in Recipe 13.4. I won't repeat that code here. Create a magnetic field and enable it on all your views (see Figure 13-7):

```
lazy var magnet: UIFieldBehavior = {
  let magnet = UIFieldBehavior.magneticField()
  magnet.addItems(self.views)
  return magnet
}()
```

Last but not least, add your behaviors to the animator:

```
var behaviors: [UIDynamicBehavior]{
  return [collision, noise, magnet]
}

override func viewDidLoad() {
  super.viewDidLoad()
  animator.addBehaviors(behaviors)
}
```

Run the app and see the results for yourself.

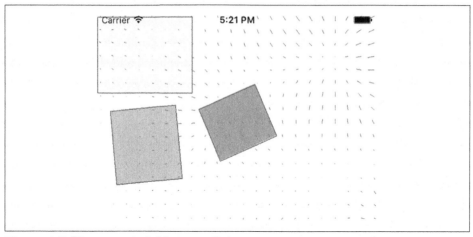

Figure 13-7. The magnetic field causes all the views to attract one another

See Also

Recipe 13.2, Recipe 13.1, and Recipe 13.4

13.6 Designing a Velocity Field on Your UI

Problem

You want to apply force, following a vector, onto your UI components.

Solution

Follow these steps:

1. Create an animator of type `UIDynamicAnimator` (see Recipe 13.1).
2. Create your collision detector of type `UICollisionBehavior`.
3. It's best to also have gravity or other forces applied to your field (see Recipe 13.1 and Recipe 13.2).
4. Create your velocity of type `UIFieldBehavior` using this class's `velocityField WithVector(_:)` method and supplying a vector of type `CGVector`.
5. Set the `position` property of your velocity field to an appropriate point on your reference view.
6. Set the `region` property of your velocity to an appropriate region (of type `UIRe gion`) of your reference view.
7. Once done, add your behaviors to your animator.

I recommend that you have a look at Recipe 13.1 where I described most of the basics of setting up a scene with gravity and an animator. I won't go into those in detail again.

In this recipe, I am also going to use a few extensions that we coded in Recipe 13.5.

Discussion

A velocity field applies a force toward a given direction to dynamic items, such as UIView instances. In this recipe, I am going to design a field that looks like our field in Recipe 13.5. On top of that, I am going to apply a slight upward and leftbound force that is positioned smack dab in the center of the screen. I am also going to position an orange view on my main storyboard and have all the forces applied to this little poor guy. I will then place the orange view on top of the reference view so that when I run the app, a few things will happen:

1. The southeast-bound gravity will pull the orange view to the bottom right of the screen.
2. The orange view will keep falling down until it hits the northwest-bound velocity field, at which point the orange view will get uncomfortable and move up and left a bit a few times, and keep falling until it gets out of the velocity field.
3. The orange view will then eventually settle at the bottom right of the view.

I now need you to set up your gravity, animator, and collision detector just as you did in Recipe 13.2 so that I don't have to repeat that code. Then set up the velocity field:

```
lazy var velocity: UIFieldBehavior = {
  let vector = CGVector(dx: -0.4, dy: -0.5)
  let velocity = UIFieldBehavior.velocityFieldWithVector(vector)
  velocity.position = self.view.center
  velocity.region = UIRegion(radius: 100.0)
  velocity.addItem(self.orangeView)
  return velocity
}()
```

Then batch up all your forces into one variable that you can give to our animator, using the extension we wrote in Recipe 13.5:

```
var behaviors: [UIDynamicBehavior]{
  return [self.collision, self.gravity, self.velocity]
}

override func viewDidLoad() {
  super.viewDidLoad()
  animator.addBehaviors(behaviors)
}
```

And when the user starts panning your orange view around, stop all the forces, then restart them when she is done dragging:

```
@IBAction func panning(sender: UIPanGestureRecognizer) {

  switch sender.state{
  case .Began:
    collision.removeItem(orangeView)
    gravity.removeItem(orangeView)
    velocity.removeItem(orangeView)
  case .Changed:
    orangeView.center = sender.locationInView(view)
  case .Ended, .Cancelled:
    collision.addItem(orangeView)
    gravity.addItem(orangeView)
    velocity.addItem(orangeView)
  default: ()
  }

}
```

See Also

Recipe 13.2, Recipe 13.3, and Recipe 13.4

13.7 Handling Nonrectangular Views

Problem

You want to create nonrectangular-shaped views in your app, and want your collision detection to work properly with these views.

Solution

Follow these steps:

1. Subclass UIView and override the collisionBoundsType variable of type UIDynamicItemCollisionBoundsType. In there, return UIDynamicItemCollisionBoundsType.Path. This makes sure that you have your own Bezier path of type UIBezierPath, and you want that to define the edges of your view, which are essentially the edges that your collision detector has to detect.
2. Override the collisionBoundingPath variable of type UIBezierPath in your view and in there, return the path that defines your view's edges.
3. In your UIBezierPath, create the shape you want for your view. The first point in this shape has to be the center of your shape. You have to draw your shape in a convex and counterclockwise manner.
4. Override the drawRect(_:) method of your view and draw your path there.

5. Add your behaviors to your new and awesome view and then create an animator of type `UIDynamicAnimator` (see Recipe 13.1).
6. Optionally, throw in a noise field as well to create some random movements between your dynamic items (see Recipe 13.4).

 I am going to draw a pentagon view in this recipe. I won't teach how that is drawn because you can find the basic rules of drawing a pentagon online and that is entirely outside the scope of this book.

Discussion

Here, we are aiming to create a dynamic field that looks like Figure 13-8. The views I have created are a square and a pentagon. We will have proper collision detection between the two views.

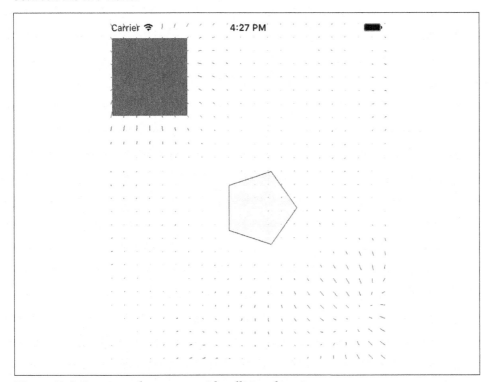

Figure 13-8. Square and pentagon with collision detection

Let's start off by creating a little extension on the `StrideThrough` structure. You'll see soon, when we code our pentagon view, that I am going to go through five points of the pentagon that are drawn on the circumference of the bounding circle, plot them on the path, and draw lines between them. I will use `stride(from:through:by:)` to create the loop. I would like to perform a function over every item in this array of numbers, hence the following extension:

```
extension StrideThrough{
  func forEach(f: (Generator.Element) -> Void){
    for item in self{
      f(item)
    }
  }
}
```

Let's move on to creating a class named `PentagonView` that subclasses `UIView`. I want this view to be constructed only by a diameter. This will be the diameter of the bounding circle within which the pentagon will reside. Therefore, we need a diameter variable, along with our constructor and perhaps a nice class method constructor for good measure:

```
class PentagonView : UIView{

  private var diameter: CGFloat = 0.0

  class func pentagonViewWithDiameter(diameter: CGFloat) -> PentagonView{
    return PentagonView(diameter: diameter)
  }

  init(diameter: CGFloat){
    self.diameter = diameter
    super.init(frame: CGRectMake(0, 0, diameter, diameter))
  }

  required init?(coder aDecoder: NSCoder) {
    super.init(coder: aDecoder)
  }

  var radius: CGFloat{
    return diameter / 2.0
  }

  ...
```

We need next to create our `UIBezierPath`. There are five slices inside a pentagon and the angle between each slice, from the center of the pentagon, is 360/5 or 72 degrees. Using this knowledge, we need to be able to, given the center of our pentagon, plot the five points onto the circumference of the bounding circle:

```
func pointFromAngle(angle: Double) -> CGPoint{

  let x = radius + (radius * cos(CGFloat(angle)))
  let y = radius + (radius * sin(CGFloat(angle)))
```

```
  return CGPoint(x: x, y: y)

}

lazy var path: UIBezierPath = {
  let path = UIBezierPath()
  path.moveToPoint(self.pointFromAngle(0))

  let oneSlice = (M_PI * 2.0) / 5.0
  let lessOneSlice = (M_PI * 2.0) - oneSlice

  oneSlice.stride(through: lessOneSlice, by: oneSlice).forEach{
    path.addLineToPoint(self.pointFromAngle($0))
  }

  path.closePath()
  return path
}()
```

That was *the* most important part of this recipe, if you are curious. Once we have the path, we can draw our view using it:

```
override func drawRect(rect: CGRect) {
  guard let context = UIGraphicsGetCurrentContext() else{
    return
  }
  UIColor.clearColor().setFill()
  CGContextFillRect(context, rect)
  UIColor.yellowColor().setFill()
  path.fill()
}
```

The next and last step in creating our pentagon view is to override the collision
BoundsType and the collisionBoundingPath variable:

```
override var collisionBoundsType: UIDynamicItemCollisionBoundsType{
  return UIDynamicItemCollisionBoundsType.Path
}

override var collisionBoundingPath: UIBezierPath{
  let path = self.path.copy() as! UIBezierPath
  path.applyTransform(CGAffineTransformMakeTranslation(-radius, -radius))
  return path
}
```

I am applying a translation transform on our Bezier path before giving it to the collision detector. The reason behind this is that the first point of our path is in the center of our shape, so we need to subtract the x and y position of the center from the path to translate our path to its actual value for the collision detector to use. Otherwise, the path will be outside the actual pentagon shape. Because the x and y position of the center of our pentagon *are* in fact the radius of the pentagon and the radius is half the diameter, we provide the radius here to the translation.

Now let's extend `UIView` so that we can add a pan gesture recognizer to it with one line of code. Both the square and our pentagon view will easily get a pan gesture recognizer:

```
extension UIView{
  func createPanGestureRecognizerOn(obj: AnyObject){
    let pgr = UIPanGestureRecognizer(target: obj, action: "panning:")
    addGestureRecognizer(pgr)
  }
}
```

Let's move on to the view controller. Add the following components to your view controller, just as we did in Recipe 13.4:

- An animator of type `UIDynamicAnimator`
- A collision detector of type `UICollisionBehavior`
- A noise field of type `UIFieldBehavior`

Let's bundle the collision detector and the noise field into an array. This lets us add them to our animator faster with the extensions that we created in Recipe 13.5:

```
var behaviors: [UIDynamicBehavior]{
  return [self.collision, self.noise]
}
```

The next step is to create our square view. This one is easy. It is just a simple view with a pan gesture recognizer:

```
lazy var squareView: UIView = {
  let view = UIView(frame: CGRect(x: 0, y: 0, width: 100, height: 100))
  view.createPanGestureRecognizerOn(self)
  view.backgroundColor = UIColor.brownColor()
  return view
  }()
```

The juicy part, now! The pentagon view. Create it with the constructor of `Pentagon View` and then place it in the center of your view:

```
lazy var pentagonView: PentagonView = {
  let view = PentagonView.pentagonViewWithDiameter(100)
```

```
view.createPanGestureRecognizerOn(self)
view.backgroundColor = UIColor.clearColor()
view.center = self.view.center
return view
}()
```

Group your views up and add them to your reference view:

```
var views: [UIView]{
  return [self.squareView, self.pentagonView]
}

override func viewDidLoad() {
  super.viewDidLoad()
  view.addSubview(squareView)
  view.addSubview(pentagonView)
  animator.addBehaviors(behaviors)
}
```

Last but not least, handle panning. As soon as the user starts to pan one of our views around, pause all the behaviors. Once the panning is finished, reenable the behaviors:

```
@IBAction func panning(sender: UIPanGestureRecognizer) {

  switch sender.state{
  case .Began:
    collision.removeItems()
    noise.removeItems()
  case .Changed:
    sender.view?.center = sender.locationInView(view)
  case .Ended, .Cancelled:
    collision.addItems(views)
    noise.addItems(views)
  default: ()
  }

}
```

Wrapping up, I want to clarify a few things. We extended UIDynamicAnimator and added the addBehaviors(_:) method to it in Recipe 13.5. In the same recipe, we added the addItems(_:) method to UIFieldBehavior. But in our current recipe, we also need removeItems(), so I think it's best to show that extension again with the new code:

```
extension UIFieldBehavior{
  public func addItems(items: [UIDynamicItem]){
    for item in items{
      addItem(item)
    }
  }
  public func removeItems(){
    for item in items{
      removeItem(item)
```

```
        }
      }
    }
```

Please extend `UICollisionBehavior` in the exact same way and add the `addItems(_:)` and `removeItems()` methods to that class as well.

Index

About the Author

Vandad Nahavandipoor currently lives in Sweden and is an iOS and OS X programmer for an international media group with over 7,000 employees in more than 29 countries. Previously he worked for Lloyds Banking Group in England to deliver their iOS apps to millions of users in the UK. He has led an international team of more than 30 iOS developers, and some of the projects he has overseen include the NatWest and RBS iOS apps running on millions of iPhones and iPads in the UK. Vandad received his B.Sc and M.Sc in Information Technology for E-Commerce from the University of Sussex in England.

Vandad's programming experience started when he first learned Basic on his father's Commodore 64. He then took this experience and applied it on his uncle's computer, running Basic on DOS. At this point, he found programming for personal computers exciting indeed and moved on to learn Object Pascal. This allowed him to learn Borland Delphi quite easily. He wrote a short 400-page book on Borland Delphi and dedicated the book to Borland. From then, he picked up x86 Assembly programming and wrote a hobby 32-bit operating system named Vandior. It wasn't until late 2007 when iOS programming became his main focus.

Colophon

The red-billed tropicbird (*Phaethon aethereus*) is also called the boatswain bird. Tropicbirds look like terns but are not genetically related to them; in fact, tropicbirds have no close living relative species, making them a bit of an evolutionary mystery. The red-billed tropicbird was featured on the Bermudan $50 bill starting in 2009, but it was subsequently replaced by the native white-tailed tropicbird, which has a higher population in Bermuda.

Red-billed tropicbirds are large, with long tails, white bodies, and the eponymous red bill that curves downward. With the tail feathers included, they are almost 40 inches long; a wingspan of one meter balances out their bodies and makes them graceful flyers. They have black markings on their flight feathers and in their eyes. Male and female birds look similar, but males can have longer tails. Red-billed tropicbirds' feet are located very far back on their bodies, so their movements on land are almost comically awkward and occur mostly on their bellies. They are not nimble swimmers either, but they move comfortably through the air over the ocean, where they hover in hopes of catching flying fish. Flying fish appear to be a favorite prey, but tropicbirds will eat other fish and even cephalopods as well.

Red-billed tropicbirds live in places like the Galápagos, the Cape Verde islands, the West Indies, and even the Persian Gulf. Despite their preference for warm, tropical waters, a particular single red-billed tropicbird keeps returning to Seal Island in coastal Maine every year. There is a large seabird population in that part of the state, but this individual is the only one of his kind to be found that far north. Some years ago, locals placed a wood decoy carving of a tropicbird out and the inexplicable visitor tried to court and mate with it. The chance of seeing this bird has meant good business for the boat charters that take birdwatchers out to see the puffins and black Guillemots that otherwise dominate the local bird scene.

Many of the animals on O'Reilly covers are endangered; all of them are important to the world. To learn more about how you can help, go to *animals.oreilly.com*.

The cover image is from the *Riverside Natural History*. The cover fonts are URW Typewriter and Guardian Sans. The text font is Adobe Minion Pro; the heading font is Adobe Myriad Condensed; and the code font is Dalton Maag's Ubuntu Mono.

Get even more for your money.

Join the O'Reilly Community, and register the O'Reilly books you own. It's free, and you'll get:

- $4.99 ebook upgrade offer
- 40% upgrade offer on O'Reilly print books
- Membership discounts on books and events
- Free lifetime updates to ebooks and videos
- Multiple ebook formats, DRM FREE
- Participation in the O'Reilly community
- Newsletters
- Account management
- 100% Satisfaction Guarantee

Signing up is easy:

1. Go to: oreilly.com/go/register
2. Create an O'Reilly login.
3. Provide your address.
4. Register your books.

Note: English-language books only

To order books online:
oreilly.com/store

For questions about products or an order:
orders@oreilly.com

To sign up to get topic-specific email announcements and/or news about upcoming books, conferences, special offers, and new technologies:
elists@oreilly.com

For technical questions about book content:
booktech@oreilly.com

To submit new book proposals to our editors:
proposals@oreilly.com

O'Reilly books are available in multiple DRM-free ebook formats. For more information:
oreilly.com/ebooks

O'REILLY®

Have it your way.

CPSIA information can be obtained at www.ICGtesting.com
Printed in the USA
BVOW10s1654201215

430201BV00001B/1/P